# GCSE
# Applied Information &
# Communication Technology
# FOR EDEXCEL

# GCSE
# Applied Information & Communication Technology
## FOR EDEXCEL

Molly Wischhusen
Janet Snell
Jenny Johnson
Andrew Scales

**www.heinemann.co.uk**
✓ Free online support
✓ Useful weblinks
✓ 24 hour online ordering

**01865 888058**

Heinemann Educational Publishers
Halley Court, Jordan Hill, Oxford OX2 8EJ
Part of Harcourt Education

Heinemann is the registered trademark of
Harcourt Education Limited

08 07 06 05 04 03
10 9 8 7 6 5 4 3 2 1

British Library Cataloguing in Publication Data is available
from the British Library on request.

ISBN 0 435 44673 8

Edited by Susan Ross
Designed by Artistix, Thame, Oxon
Typeset and illustrated by 🔺 Tek-Art, Croydon
Printed and bound by Bath Colourbooks, Ltd

**Websites**
There are links to relevant websites in this book. In order to ensure that
the links are up-to-date, that the links work, and that the sites aren't
inadvertently linked to sites that could be considered offensive, we have
made the links available on the Heinemann website at
www.heinemann.co.uk/hotlinks. When you access the site, the express
code is **6738P**.

Tel: 01865 888058  www.heinemann.co.uk

# Contents

# Photo Acknowledgements

The authors and publishers would like to thank the following individuals and organisations for permission to reproduce photographs and other copyright material:
Adaptivation Inc
Nanopac
RNIB; and:
Amstrad plc. page 183 (top)
Anthony King, Medimage pages 132 (top, left), 145 (top, left)
Brailleman page 224 (right)
British Airways page 130 (left)
Chris Honeywell page 142
Computer Cab plc. page 92
Continuing Education & Training Service (CETS) pages 85-7
Corbis pages 125, 126 (bottom), 132 (bottom, right), 140, 161, 183 (bottom, left), 194, 198, 228
Croydon Libraries page 92
Denne Construction and Horizon Housing Group page 89
Epson pages 134 (top, left), 145 (bottom left & right), 146 (bottom, left)
Haddon Davies page 192
Hemera Photo Objects page 139
J Sainsbury plc. page 177
Mini Loop Systems Ltd. page 227 (bottom)
Motion Media page 227 (top)
Pace page 185 (left)
Palmer McCarthy page 98
Pete Morris page 162
Real World Designs page 94
Reed Executive plc. page 87
Science Photo Library page 126 (top)
Sicare page 223
Siemens page 130 (top, right), 224 (left)
Smart Media page 189
Sony page 188
Techsoft page 146 (top, right)
Toshiba page 182 (right)
Trevor Clifford page 147
Trivalley Construction Ltd. page 93
Tudor Photography page 135 (left)
VisualMedia page 130 (bottom & middle, right)
Wacom page 137 (left)

Thanks to Media Logic for information on their interactive service, iSeeTV, page 211.

All screen shots have been reproduced with the permission of the Microsoft® Corporation.

Every effort has been made to contact copyright holders of material reproduced in this book. Any omissions will be rectified in subsequent printings of this book if notice is given to the publishers.

# Acknowledgements

My thanks go to Margaret Berriman and Camilla Thomas for their support throughout the production of this book. Also to Molly and Janet – it has been a pleasure to write a second book with them.

Sincere thanks also go to my sons Ian & Colin, and my daughter-in-law Helen for their proofreading and technical advice. Last but not least, deepest thanks to my husband Ray, for his encouragement and taking over the cooking!

*Jenny Johnson*

My sincere thanks once again to Margaret Berriman at Heinemann for asking me to work on another book and to Camilla Thomas for her indispensable editorial support. It has been a pleasure to work with Molly and Jenny again – thank you both for the encouragement, help and laughter! To my husband, Bob, and the rest of my family – thank you for your constant patience and understanding.

I dedicate this book to the memory of my mother who sadly died before it was completed.

*Janet Snell*

As always it is a pleasure to work with Janet and Jenny and I am very, very grateful for all their support, whilst writing this book. Much appreciation as ever, to Margaret Berriman and also to Camilla Thomas, whose cheerful, calm encouragement made it possible to keep going. Last but not least I could not have managed but for the wonderful support and practical help given by my friends and family, but special mention must go to Margaret and Roger and to my sister, Margaret, who has been truly brilliant.

*Molly Wischhusen*

# Introduction

Welcome to your Applied GCSE in Information Communication Technology. You have made a very good decision in choosing this subject since computers, as you well know, are used in every aspect of life today. Whatever studies you undertake or whatever career you pursue, it is almost certain that you will find the knowledge and skills gained on this course, will prove extremely useful, if not essential.

You will learn:

- file management and standard ways of working
- ICT Tools and Applications including word-processing, publications, spreadsheets, database, multimedia software and using the Internet
- common business documents and how to design them
- computer hardware including the main components, the design of a system and its implementation
- how ICT is used in business organisations including a number of real-life case studies which illustrate the impact of ICT
- the impact of ICT on society, including working life, personal communications, community activities and people with special needs
- legislation relating to ICT.

## What do you have to do to succeed?

The evidence you have to produce and the assessment method varies depending on which awarding body your school or college is using. You will find full details given at the end of this book.

## How to use this book

Your Applied GCSE in ICT course is divided into 3 large units. Therefore the book has been sub-divided into chapters which cover the specific topics required by the awarding body.

### Special Features

*Activity* – comprehensive worksheets designed to guide you through the practical knowledge you need to complete this course. These are all stored on the CD-ROM accompanying this book.

▷ Green arrows indicate core level activities to be attempted by everyone.

▷ Red arrows indicate extension activities to be attempted by students aiming to gain a higher grade pass.

*Find out* – are activities that encourage you to look at the real world, research various topics, and apply the theory into practise.

 *Checkpoint* – definitions of key terms.

 *Fact File* – interesting items of additional information.

 *Case Study* – case studies of real (or simulated) ICT related issues. They are aimed at enabling you to explore key issues and broaden your understanding of the subject.

 *Snapshots* – close-ups of people either working with or affected by ICT tools, applications and systems and the problems and challenges they face.

As you work through each chapter, and complete the activities, you will gain the understanding required to complete your portfolio work and pass the examination where applicable.

Throughout this book you will read about Jubilee 6th Form College and the Student's Association. You will also find that many of the activities on the CD-ROM are based round this college. We have used this fictitious college and the activities of the Students' Association to illustrate many of the topics we are introducing.

Microsoft® products have been chosen to illustrate the software applications discussed in this book. We recognise that Microsoft® is currently the market leader in both business and education. However, within a windows environment, most of the techniques discussed and used throughout this book are easily transferable for use with software applications produced by other providers.

We do hope you enjoy your Applied GCSE in ICT and wish you good luck and every success both with your studies and your future either studying a more advanced programme next year, or in obtaining employment.

Jenny Johnson
Janet Snell
Molly Wischhusen

# About the CD-ROM

The interactive CD-ROM, found at the back of this book, contains a library of resources and activity worksheets that will help you succeed in your **Applied GCSE ICT** course.

It has been divided into six sections:

- **How to use this CD-ROM** – detailed help files that explain how the CD-ROM is laid out and how to access the files that you want to use.
- **Preparatory Unit** – activity worksheets and files that will help you understand the need for good practice and standard ways of working.
- **Keyboard Exercises** – keying exercises that will build your confidence in using a keyboard.
- **Unit 1** – activity worksheets and files that will take you through various ICT tools and applications and how they are used by different organisations.
- **Unit 2** – activity worksheets and files guiding you through the ways in which organisations use ICT, the main components used to design an ICT system and how ICT systems are designed and implemented.
- **Unit 3** – activity worksheets and files that will help you understand how ICT systems affect everyday life.

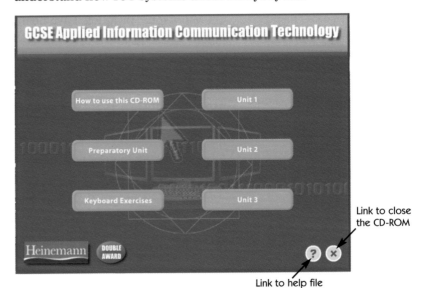

Link to close the CD-ROM

Link to help file

*Opening screen of the CD-ROM*

Throughout this book you will see activity features with this icon. All these activity worksheets are stored on the CD-ROM. Check with your tutor before you print each worksheet out – he or she may prefer to make photocopies so that you can share them with other learners.

## Running the CD-ROM

To run this CD-ROM you require Macromedia® Flash™ Player, Microsoft® Internet Explorer and software suitable for opening .jpg, .avi and .wav files to be installed on your PC. For further information please see the **readme.txt** file on the CD-ROM.

It is also assumed that the relevant software packages required to view the files on the CD-ROM are already installed on your system, files on the CD-ROM have been created in the following: Adobe® Acrobat® Reader® 4; Microsoft® Word 2000; Excel 2000; Access 2000 and PowerPoint® 2000.

For further information please see the **readme.txt** file on the CD-ROM. For help whilst using the CD-ROM please go to the **How to use this CD-ROM** section.

## Starting up

**Note:** *You may be required to restart your PC after running the CD-ROM for the first time.*

* Insert the CD into your CD-ROM drive.
* The CD-ROM should run automatically.

If your PC does not support autorun:

* Go to **My Computer** and double-click on your CD-ROM drive.
* The CD-ROM should run.

If it does not run, but instead displays a list of the files on the CD-ROM then:

* Double click on the file: **start.exe**

Again, for further information please see the **readme.txt** on the CD-ROM.

# Preparatory unit: File management and standard ways of working

This preparatory unit applies to all the other units, so it is a good idea to read this unit first. You will not remember all that it contains first-time round, so return to it from time to time to refresh your memory.

This unit is about understanding the need for good practice and standard ways of working in information and communication technology (ICT), both in your studies and in your future work. It is important to remember that the techniques you learn in this unit must be applied to *all* your Vocational GCSE work.

Most organisations have guidelines and rules that help people to work efficiently and to avoid problems. Your school or college, for example, probably has a rule against consuming food and drink in the computer labs, to avoid damaging the equipment. These rules are especially important for people working in ICT to avoid problems which might unfavourably affect the business.

Here are some typical problems that can occur in ICT environments:

- Data files may be lost, corrupted by a virus or damaged in other ways. For example, files downloaded from the World Wide Web may contain viruses. If the computer that has the downloaded virus is part of a local area network (LAN) – and they usually are – the virus can infect the ICT systems of the whole organisation.

- Computers may be damaged so that data stored in them cannot be recovered. For example, sectors of hard drives occasionally become damaged. Files in those sectors can sometimes be retrieved, but only by a slow, painstaking process.

- Unauthorised people may gain access to confidential information. This is a serious problem that you must constantly guard against. For example, it is easy in the office environment to be distracted from your work by the phone or a colleague and to forget to close a file before you leave your desk. If that file was confidential, it isn't anymore – it is there on your screen for any passer-by to read!

- People may copy original work and present it as their own. Using ICT systems and especially the Internet, it is very easy to copy any kind of data. This is called plagiarism and because it breaks copyright law (see Unit 3, Chapter 13) is a serious offence.

- Inaccurate or poorly written information may confuse or annoy readers. Standards of information presentation have greatly improved because of technology. One of the most basic requirements in website design, for example, is a presentation that makes it easy and clear for users to find what they want to know. Word processors have increasingly sophisticated spell checkers, and as a result, readers are less tolerant of any mistakes.

- Information presented professionally is often believed, even though it may be inaccurate. In some ways technology has made it harder to judge the quality of information. A beautifully laid out document containing inaccurate information may also be believed because it looks right. It gives the impression that the person or company that produced it knows what they are talking about. Advertisers are aware of this; a professionally presented product may sell much better than a poorly presented product, even if the quality is poorer.

- Poorly laid-out workplaces may cause physical stress or be hazardous to ICT operators. If you are going to be sitting in front of a computer for any length of time, you need a chair that can be adjusted for your shape and posture. Sitting on an ordinary chair will soon give you backache.

The wires and cables that connect the different parts of computers must be tidied away to prevent any possibility of catching your feet on them.

There are many reasons for having standard ways of working in ICT. The most important is that information in ICT systems can be easily lost or misused, and that having standard ways of working can help you to overcome these problems.

After studying this unit you should be able to:

- keep information secure
- protect confidentiality
- respect copyright
- save work regularly and use different filenames
- keep dated back-up copies of files in another location
- manage your work effectively
- work safely
- take account of relevant legislation and codes of practice.

## Keeping information secure

When studying or working in the computer industry you are dealing with highly valuable equipment and data. Therefore, it is essential to be aware of and *use* security techniques that protect ICT systems from accidental or intentional damage. This damage includes theft of hardware and software, fire, the loss of data and viruses.

The risk of theft depends on the environment of the system. In public places basic anti-theft procedures include building hardware into casing, bolting it to desks and locking up equipment. Doors may be fitted with keypads that need a code to open. Computer labs will probably have an individual alarm system, in addition to the alarms for the whole building. Surveillance cameras may be used to 'watch' sensitive areas either outside or inside the building. Make a point of finding out about the organisational security procedures wherever you are, and follow them carefully.

In many ways protecting data is more important than protecting hardware because it is easier, if expensive, to replace the actual hardware. It can be very difficult, or even impossible to replace data. The data held in the computer system is the life-blood of an

*Figure 1 Methods of protecting data*

organisation and its loss might result in the organisation losing valuable business or even becoming bankrupt. To prevent damage from the risk of fire or flood both data and software disks are usually kept in disaster-proof safes. Less valuable data or software disks may be kept in locked filing cabinets (see Figure 1).

## Virus checking

A computer virus is a program, developed by someone either for general mischief or to attack a particular organisation. The virus copies itself without the user intending it to, or even being aware of it happening until problems occur. Sometimes, in an attempt to prevent virus detection, the program will mutate (change) slightly each time it is copied. Problems can include clearing screens, deleting data and, in the worst-case scenario, making the whole system unusable.

Viruses can affect both floppy and hard disks and are usually transferred from one computer to another via Internet downloads or floppy disks. If disks are used only on one system, then the risk of 'catching' a virus is much lower. The more often disks are used in different computers, the greater the risk of 'catching' a virus. In fact, some organisations do not allow floppy disks to be taken from work to home or vice versa for this reason.

If a floppy disk is to be loaded into a computer just to show or demonstrate the contents, then write-protecting the disk will prevent any viruses on that computer being transferred on to the disk. Software such as Microsoft® Office is provided on a read-only CD-ROM so there is no risk of a virus infecting the software. However, some software still comes on a floppy disk. It is a good idea to write-protect disks containing software programs before putting them into the disk drive to ensure that they are not accidentally infected. You may need to re-load the program at a future date and it would be very annoying to find the disks damaged.

Computer viruses have become a serious problem, but anti-virus software, such as Mcafee VirusScan V6 or Norton AntiVirus 2002, is available. The software scans files and detects and removes any known viruses. You may find anti-virus software installed on your college network, which automatically checks every disk as it is accessed, and prevents loading of files from an 'infected' disk. Sometimes the check is not automatic, so the best precaution is to check every disk before use. It is annoying to find one of your disks has a virus, but if you do find out, at least you can stop using it and thereby prevent the virus being passed on. It is crucial to install and *regularly update* anti-virus software on a network or any computer linked to the Internet.

### Fact file

February is usually a hot month for viruses. The promise of a virtual Valentine's Day card often proves too much for unwary end users who suddenly find themselves on the end of a rather different gift.

'Somebody loves you' and 'Are you my valentine?' were just a couple of deceitful subject lines used by Valentine's Day worms.

(*Computer Active*, 7 March 2002)

## Protect confidentiality

Individuals or organisations may wish to keep information confidential. Organisations have always been at risk from dishonest staff, but the main difference is that it is so much easier to obtain the information – you do not even need to be in the room or the building. Inevitably, there has to be trust in and reliance on the users of ICT, especially in a business environment and, in fact, most people are honest and have no intention of defrauding their employer or disclosing confidential information. It is, however, essential to take security issues seriously, so that you do not *unintentionally* give access to uncensored or private materials to someone else. Also, if you *accidentally* discover uncensored or private materials, you must not take advantage of the opportunity, and it may be appropriate to report that a breach of security has occurred.

Naturally, we all chat about our jobs, but it is important to know which information should be kept to ourselves and when it is all right to talk about something to a friend or relative. If in doubt, then keep quiet. Access to medical or criminal records, for example, is controlled by privacy laws.

## Snapshot

### Lucy, medical receptionist

Lucy is a receptionist at a local doctor's surgery. She knows some of the patients personally and is, inevitably, aware of the confidential medical history of those patients.

Lucy learns from surgery records that James is having tests for cancer. She doesn't know James that well, but she knows a mutual friend, Mark.

With the best of intentions, she tells Mark about James's tests because she thinks Mark may be supportive to James while he is waiting for results. What she doesn't know is that James is in the process of buying a house and Mark works for the insurance company that is going to give life insurance to cover the mortgage (the money borrowed to buy the house). When Mark realises that James may have a serious illness he feels unable to issue the insurance policy. As a result, James cannot get the mortgage and loses the house.

In fact, the tests prove negative, but James has already spent a lot of money trying to buy the house, which he cannot get back. He's also very hurt by Mark's actions and no longer wants to have anything to do with him. All this happened because Lucy did not respect confidentiality and passed on information she should not have, although it was with *the best of intentions*. If James discovers that Lucy revealed confidential information, she could be prosecuted under the Data Protection Act (see Unit 3, Chapter 13).

In business, information can be priceless. Although you may not be dealing with priceless or highly sensitive information when you start out in your career, any information is potentially valuable to an organisation's competitors. It is essential that employees follow security and confidentiality procedures properly to prevent unauthorised access to the company's systems such as its databases.

Figure 2 *Information access must be controlled*

Different computer systems allow different confidentiality procedures. Among the most common are passwords and time-restricted access. Passwords should be changed regularly, either monthly, weekly or even daily, depending on the sensitivity of the data. Time-restricted access systems limit the time that you have to find the information you want – if you do not know the procedures, you are unlikely to retrieve the information you want within the given period.

If you use a network system in your college, you will almost certainly use a unique identity (ID) number to gain access to the system, followed by a password that you personally choose. When selecting a password, you should choose one which is:

- easy to remember
- not obvious (not your own name).

Don't forget – keep the password confidential and change it frequently to make it more difficult for the password to be discovered.

You will notice that when you enter the password, the characters are not displayed on screen, but appear in a coded form, frequently as a series of asterisks (******). This is to mask the characters and is designed to prevent someone casually observing your password as it is shown on the screen.

In addition to passwords to access the system, modern software programs also allow the use of passwords when saving files. To set a password when saving a file in Word, select Tools and General Options (see Figure 3).

*Figure 3  Password dialogue box*

A password entered in the Password to open dialogue box prevents anyone opening the file unless he or she knows the password. A password entered in the Write Preservation Password dialogue box, allows access to *read* the file but prevents anyone saving changes to the file unless he or she knows the password. Passwords entered into these boxes will again appear as a series of asterisks. A tick in the Read-Only Recommended box indicates that it is advisable to read but *not* to amend the file (see Figure 4). If the user wishes to write to the file, then it should be saved under a new name, so that the original version is retained.

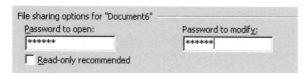

*Figure 4  Part of a dialogue box which enables passwords to limit access to the file from Word 2000*

Many organisations rank data files according to their level of confidentiality. Giving staff different privileges or security levels which limit access to only *some files* or *some fields* within a file is a common method of protecting data and maintaining confidentiality. The most senior staff would have:

- greater privileges
- a high security level
- access to all or most of the data

whereas more junior staff would have:

- fewer privileges
- low security
- access only to less important data.

## Fact file

You probably use login IDs and passwords to access your school or college computer system and a PIN number for your cash card if you have one, but have you ever forgotten your password or PIN number? In business, staff have more and more passwords or PIN numbers to remember, which are highly confidential. Biometric technology has a solution to this problem – using your fingerprint. Fingerprints are unique and have the advantage of always being with you and never forgotten!

Very small sensors, which look like a pushbutton can be built into a keyboard. You simply touch the sensor – and the sensor reads your fingerprint. This gives you, and only you, access to your accounts, websites, phone lists and e-mail.

## Naming files

A filename is the set of letters, numbers or symbols that you assign (give) to a file to distinguish it from all other files in a directory. Some programs such as MS-DOS or the older Windows versions (up to 3.11) restrict you to eight characters long, but more modern operating systems such as Windows 98 or 2000 allow many more characters, so it is easy to give your files names that remind you of the contents.

Program files and data files have sets of characters added to a filename that are called **extensions**. When you save a file the file extension is automatically added to the name you have given the file. Extensions further define the type or purpose of the file. In Windows, for example, filenames are followed by a stop (.) and then an extension of up to three letters. The extension tells the computer which program will open the file. For example, a Microsoft® Word document will be followed by .doc, an Excel file by .xls, a bitmap graphic by .bmp. The extension .exe means an executable program, one that will load and run an application. However, if you rename a file, you sometimes have to add the appropriate file extension to the new name. Below is a list of the most common file extensions:

| Extension | File type |
| --- | --- |
| .doc | Microsoft® Word document |
| .xls | Microsoft® Excel spreadsheet |
| .mdb | Microsoft® Access database |
| .tmp | temporary file |
| .exe | executable program (a file that will load and run an application) |
| .htm | hypertext document |

Have you ever lost or mislaid a file, then tried searching through the different directories? On a typical stand-alone computer there are hundreds, even thousands of files. If you happen to remember the exact filename, you can use the Find file function to search through the whole system to locate the file (see Figure 5). You can also search using a significant word or phrase, which you know was used in the file.

However, good work management would avoid the problem in the first place by creating folders or directories clearly named, and using *sensible* filenames which remind you of the

contents. This is the key to saving, then finding files and is especially true in business, where a colleague may need to find the file when you are out of the office. So rather than save that letter as <let1.doc>, call it <letter to Anna 20 Feb.doc>.

Exactly the same is true when you create new folders or directories. When you choose a name, imagine how easy it would be for someone else to find that file and to know roughly what it contains. For example, if you have a folder named 'Letters' and save all letters in that folder, with a suitable filename as suggested, it will be easy to locate a particular letter when required.

If you are working on a very long document, such as a company report or this textbook, it can also be very useful to save the draft versions with different filenames. For example, this section of the book was saved as 'Standard Ways – D1' for draft one. As I went over the work and made changes, I saved the next version as 'Standard Ways – D2. You may wonder why. Well, sometimes you make changes, and then later when you read the work again, you decide that the earlier version was better. In this case, you can copy the section from the previous version, and paste it into the latest one.

## Worksheets

As you work through each unit, you will find activities that ask you to complete worksheets. The worksheets can be found on the CD-ROM and you will need to print out the relevant worksheet for each activity. You will find all the instructions you need provided on the worksheets, so the activities in this book simply tell you which worksheet you need and the topic that it covers.

Some worksheet activities have data files prepared ready for you to use and the data file names are given on the appropriate worksheet. As you print each worksheet, *file it safely for future reference*.

The worksheets are numbered, labelled and can be found in the relevant chapter folder on the CD-ROM.

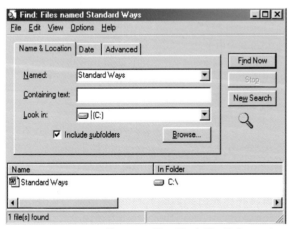

*Figure 5  The Find file dialogue box*

## Fact file

A useful work standard in many organisations
is to specify the filename and path, and the date
and time a document was produced in the
footer zone (see Figure 6). If you have a hard
copy of a document, this makes it easier to find
the file. It also helps you to know which hard
copy is the latest and most up-to-date version.
This can be especially important when a group
of people are working with the same document
and developing it throughout the day or week.
You would not want to work with a draft that
had already been updated and so contained
information that was no longer accurate.

---

Footer
© Molly Wischhusen      C:\Standard Ways.doc
Draft  Created on 09/03/02 13:36

*Figure 6  A footer showing the filename, path and
date last saved*

## Saving work regularly and making back-ups

There are always people with stories about how
they lost hours or even days of work because of a
system failure. This will not happen to you if you
save and back up your work regularly. At the
most, you will lose only a few minutes' worth.

Data is sometimes lost before it is saved,
perhaps by accidentally overloading a system's
memory and freezing it. When that happens, it
is too late to save whatever you are doing. All
you can do is to reboot the system. This is a
great shame (but not an excuse) if you are
doing your coursework. If a network fails, for
example because of a voltage overload or
spike, everyone loses unsaved work. So the
message is simple – save regularly.

## Fact file

As well as the regular saving procedure, most
industry standard software has an AutoSave
setting. This allows you to set how frequently the
computer automatically saves the file you are
working on. Although you can choose how often
the automatic save takes place, the default is
normally every ten minutes. Then, if there is a
problem, once you have sorted it out, you can
use Find file to locate a copy of the file you were
working on and recover it (see Figure 7).

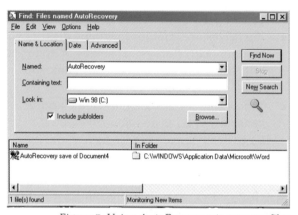

*Figure 7  Using AutoRecovery to recover files*

Saving also refers to keeping the source
documents. When valuable data, or any data
that is not easily replaced is transferred on to
disk, the source documents must be placed in a
filing cabinet or safe. Whenever you digitise
any information for someone else, always
return the hard copy when you have finished.

One of the most important ways of keeping
information secure is to have dated back-up
copies. In business, backing-up procedures are
usually carried out at the end of every day. At
the end of the week another backup is made
and stored separately from the daily back-ups.
To avoid the damage done by viruses or other
system-wide disasters, it is not enough to back
up files into a different directory in the same
computer. Files should be regularly backed up
on to other storage media. These include the
following:

● Floppy disks have been widely used for
small amounts of data, up to 1.4 Megabytes
(MB), but are becoming obsolete. This is

probably the method you would use to copy files you have created at school or college, either as a back-up or because you want to continue working on the file at home, or vice versa. They are gradually being replaced with USB memory sticks (see page 187).

- CD-R (write) or CD-RW (re-write) can store approximately 700 MB. In October 2002 Sanyo developed a new technique which doubled that capacity to 1.4 Gigabytes (GB). Most modern home PCs are now fitted with CD-RW drives which makes this a convenient and inexpensive method of backing up large amounts of data. For example, this book was backed up regularly on to CD-RW.
- Zip drives are another magnetic disk medium with storage capacities of up to 250 MB. These are also suitable for domestic or small business use.
- Tape streamer is a magnetic tape and generally used as an offline back-up for large businesses, as these have capacities of up to 40 GB.

The advantage of making back-up copies on disk is that files can be accessed directly and quickly, whereas a magnetic tape has to be read starting from the beginning until you reach the file you want, just like a tape for music. However, because of its greater capacity, tape is an ideal medium for storing large volumes of data in a business context.

In this fast moving world of digital technology, the size of hard disks is increasing all the time, which means that back-up media will have to match these changes by developing greater capacity.

## Managing your work effectively

One of the most important qualities for a student or employee (including the boss) is the ability to manage his or her work. You have probably noticed that some students progress quickly and successfully even though they do not seem to do any more work than anyone else. This is because they are good at managing

their work. In the workplace people who become good at managing their own work often step up to supervise or manage other people's work too.

## Logging ICT problems

We have already looked at naming files, using folders/directories and backing up, all of which are very important. It is also common practice in an ICT environment for staff working on a help desk, or the network manager, to keep a reference log of problems or faults that they have come across with the computer system and how the fault was resolved. Many faults are minor with an obvious cause, but some faults are difficult to identify and sort out. If a record of the solution has been kept, it will be much quicker to resolve next time. If the same fault keeps recurring, then it may be necessary to look more closely for the cause.

## Setting and meeting deadlines

Good ICT management skills include the ability to meet deadlines and evaluate your own work. Indeed, these skills are invaluable wherever you work and also in your studies. 'When will it be ready?' 'Oh, any time now, I'll get to it as soon as I can.' In an efficient and professional working environment, this is not an acceptable answer. Giving a date and time – a deadline – by when the work will be done is like a milestone. It helps you to plan your workday and week, and in the same way it helps your colleagues or customers plan theirs. For example, a secretary may be having problems with a monitor. If you can say that it will be fixed by 3 pm tomorrow, the secretary can plan to work on something different, knowing that the computer-based work will start again at the deadline you have given.

In school or college, you will be given assignments to complete over a period of two or three weeks and it is all too easy to leave the work to the last minute. Perhaps you also work part time as well as studying. Sometimes a supervisor will give you deadlines, and if he or she does not, then it is a good idea to set your own. Many people have trouble in setting deadlines because they underestimate how long a task will take. Inevitably, they end up rushing to get everything done at once.

A simple rule is to decide how quickly you could get a job done, then double it. If you take this approach to completing the assignments and plan a list of tasks you should complete and by when, you will be able to work at a comfortable pace and enjoy a sense of achievement as you pass each milestone. You may even find you complete your work *early*, in which case you can evaluate what you have done by checking it carefully to make sure nothing has been missed or identify tasks which could be improved.

## Using the spell checker and grammar checker

Even though you may be rushing to complete an assignment, do take time to use the software application's spell checker and/or grammar check. Spelling errors spoil your work and as a result you will lose marks. So always use spell checkers to spot words spelt incorrectly and repeated words (for example 'and and'). Spell checkers are not only available in word processors, but in most other applications such as spreadsheets and e-mail as well. Spell checkers check the words you have written against a list in the computer's dictionary, then any words not matching are queried and possible alternatives are suggested.

But beware! Although the spell checker is an excellent tool, it does not understand what you are trying to say and so it can be wrong. This means that *it is still important for the operator to have a reasonable level of spelling!* The words 'a lot' meaning 'many' are frequently mistyped as 'alot'. The spell checker will suggest 'allot' which means 'to give a share', but even though the sense is wrong this alternative is usually accepted. It will also not correct 'whether' for 'weather' or 'to' for 'too', and sometimes a spell checker will suggest that a word is incorrect when you know it is correct. This often happens with proper names, for example 'GNVQ' or 'Patel', although you may be able to add these words to a computer's

dictionary to fix the problem.

Figure 8 shows the spell checker checking the sentence '*Alot* of people go *two* clubs *too* meet *there* friends'. The words in italics are wrong, but the computer picked up only the first error in the sentence and ignored the words 'two' and 'too', both of which should have been 'to' in this example. Neither did the check show that the word 'there' should have been 'their'. Think of your spell checker as an assistant and remember that the final decision on whether a piece of work is accurate or not, is yours.

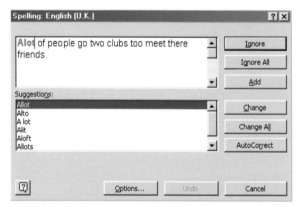

*Figure 8 Using the spell checker. 'A lot', which is the correct spelling in this instance, is the third option in the list*

### Fact file

In Microsoft® Word you will notice that a word spelt incorrectly is underlined with a wavy red line. If you highlight the word and right click the mouse, alternative suggestions are listed (see Figure 9).

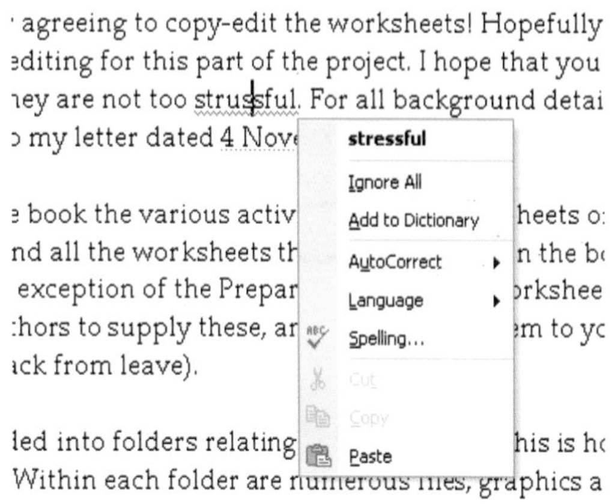

*Figure 9 Quick access to the spell checker*

Sophisticated word-processing applications also include a grammar check feature. If the spell checker and grammar checker are used on the same sentence, then the computer does identify the word 'there' as wrong (see Figure 10). In this case, the grammar check was useful, but grammar checkers tend to be rather less popular than spell checkers because the suggestions they make are sometimes not so easy to understand, even for English teachers! Meanwhile and as a starting point, the best way to use a basic grammar checker on default settings is to draw your attention to possible mistakes.

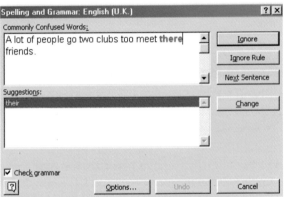

*Figure 10 Checking the same sentence with spelling and grammar checks*

With both spelling and grammar checks, if an error is suggested, it is *probable*, but *not definite*, that you have made a mistake. You need to look at the suggestions given, and try to decide the correct version.

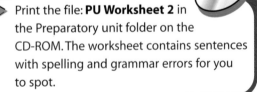

## Activity

▷ Print the file: **PU Worksheet 2** in the Preparatory unit folder on the CD-ROM. The worksheet contains sentences with spelling and grammar errors for you to spot.

## Proof-reading your work

You must proof-read your documents for errors, first on screen and then on the printed copy. Once data has been entered into the computer, none of us is keen to have to read it all again, especially if it is a long report, but there is no other way to ensure that the data makes sense. Often our thoughts and ideas run faster than our fingers can type, so words are omitted or repeated, or the sense is muddled and can be improved with some minor changes. Proof-reading numerical data is especially important as this is the only way to check for errors.

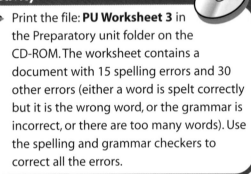

## Activity

▷ Print the file: **PU Worksheet 3** in the Preparatory unit folder on the CD-ROM. The worksheet contains a document with 15 spelling errors and 30 other errors (either a word is spelt correctly but it is the wrong word, or the grammar is incorrect, or there are too many words). Use the spelling and grammar checkers to correct all the errors.

# Relevant legislation and codes of practice

## Respect copyright

You are probably familiar with copyright warnings at the beginning of rental videos where it says something along the lines of 'All rights reserved. No part of this publication may be reproduced or transmitted, in any form or by any means, without the prior permission of the publisher'. This is the same for most computer programs, published text, pictures and graphic images.

Check for the symbol © followed by a date and sometimes a name, as shown at the beginning of this book. This indicates that a work is copyright. You must understand what copyright means and respect copyright law. This will be explained in more detail in Unit 3, Chapter 13.

## Work safely

Most ICT working environments are relatively safe. Nonetheless, you should take a responsible attitude, be aware of potential hazards and if possible remove the danger yourself or report it to an appropriate person if you cannot deal with the problem. You should also be aware of the main laws governing safety at work, which will be covered more fully in Unit 3, Chapter 13.

Apart from the law relating to copyright and health and safety, you also need to understand the law relating to:

● data protection
● computer misuse
● investigatory powers.

These will also be explained in Chapter 13.

## Ethical use of ICT systems

When you are among any group of people you expect a certain standard of behaviour to be common practice. You know instinctively whether a person's behaviour is 'good' or 'bad' or 'right' or 'wrong'. As children, you learned what was acceptable behaviour from your parents, guardians, school teachers, and so on, and you put together your own moral values based on their examples.

Just as we expect certain standards in our everyday lives, most professions have a code of **ethics** (morals) or standards that set out acceptable professional behaviour. This is true of the computer industry and the British Computer Society has a code of conduct that sets out basic standards that can be expected of users of ICT systems.

If you find yourself in a situation where you are not sure what course of action to take, as a general rule your own conscience will help you to decide the best way forward. If you ask yourself 'How would I feel if that was done to me?' or think about the effect your action might have on someone else you will generally come to the right decision.

### Checkpoint

Computer ethics are the rules or standards that IT professionals follow when carrying out their work.

As you continue with your studies for your Applied GCSE in Information and Communication Technology, please ensure that you follow good practice and standard ways of working. Return to this preparatory unit as often as you need to.

# Unit 1 — ICT tools and applications

This unit looks at ICT tools and applications and how they are used by different organisations. It investigates how local businesses use ICT tools and applications.

You will find out how to use a range of ICT applications, including:

- word processing
- publications and presentation software
- spreadsheets
- databases
- multimedia
- web browsers and e-mail.

You will also find out how to use ICT tools and applications to:

- develop documents for different purposes
- find, store and manipulate (handle) data.

## What you will learn

1. Presentation of information using word processing, publications and presentation software
2. Organisation and analysis of numerical information using spreadsheet software
3. Organisation and analysis of structured information using database software
4. Organisation and presentation of information using multimedia software
5. Communication, searching and selection of information using the Internet
6. Investigating how ICT is used in organisations
7. Developing business documents

# Presentation of information using word processing, publications and presentation software

This chapter introduces you to word processing, publications and presentation software. You will learn:

- to enter and edit text
- effective use of:
  - ➤ text alignment
  - ➤ font formatting
  - ➤ paragraph formatting
  - ➤ tables
  - ➤ bullets
  - ➤ graphical images
  - ➤ desk top publishing features
- to use headers and footers
- to create mail merge.

## Checkpoint

The term **word processing** describes the process of entering, storing and manipulating (handling) text.

## What you will learn

Enter, cut, copy, paste and move text
Format text
Document formatting features
Tables
Incorporate clip art and graphic images
Mail merge
Desktop publishing features in word processing

## Overview: Word processing

About 85 per cent of all the mail generated in the UK each year is produced by businesses and industry. A large part of this mail will have been produced on a word processor very similar to the ones you use either at school or college or at home. In addition, the production and creation of newspapers, magazines, books, posters, examination papers, menus, and so on, are

also very likely to have made use of word processing skills.

As well as being an essential skill in the business world, word processing will be invaluable to you throughout your student and adult life, so it is important that you learn how to use the word processor in the most effective and efficient way. This chapter, and the activities on the CD-ROM that accompany this book, will show you how to make the word processor work for you.

When you load your word processing software a screen will appear ready to accept the text you enter. A page of printed text will look similar to the one in Figure 1.1.

This layout is called the **default** layout and will be the same every time you switch on your computer. You will learn how to change the default settings as you work through this chapter.

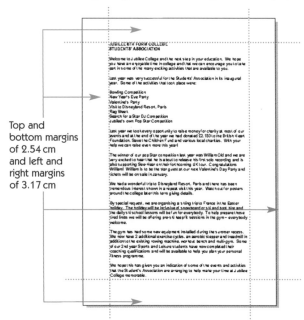

Top and bottom margins of 2.54 cm and left and right margins of 3.17 cm

Text presented in single line spacing, aligned to the left-hand margin and with a ragged (or uneven) right-hand margin. The font will usually be Times New Roman 10 pt or 12 pt

*Figure 1.1 A word processed page using the default layout*

# Enter, cut, copy, paste and move text

## Entering text

Text is usually entered through a keyboard (see Unit 2, Chapter 9 to learn more about keyboards). Figure 1.2 shows a typical computer keyboard layout where the keys you are most likely to use have been identified.

### Golden rules

As you enter text, here are a few things to remember:

- Do not press the return (or enter) key at the end of a line. The computer will do this automatically by a process known as word wrap. This means the text will run from one line to the next when you are writing a paragraph. If you then insert an extra word or two in a paragraph, the computer

will make space for it. Similarly, if you later decide to delete or remove some text, the computer will close the gap.

- Use the return (or enter) key after a heading or when you wish to start a new paragraph. Press it twice in order to leave a clear line space.
- Leave two spaces after a full stop, question mark or exclamation mark. This will help to separate the sentences and makes your work easier to read.
- Leave one space after all other punctuation.
- Use the Backspace key to delete a character to the left and the Delete key to delete a character to the right. If you are trying to insert text and characters seem to be disappearing, you have probably depressed the Insert key by mistake. This puts the computer in overtype (OVR) mode. Press it again to release it or double click the overtype button at the bottom of your screen.

**Escape** – use this to clear menus, dialogue boxes or highlighting

**Tab Key** – used to line text in columns

**Caps Lock** – used for a string of capital letters

**Function Keys** – each key has a different use.

**Backspace delete** – takes out the previous character

**Delete** – removes the following character

**Insert Key** – changes from inserting text to overtyping

**Return/ Enter** – used to move onto a new line

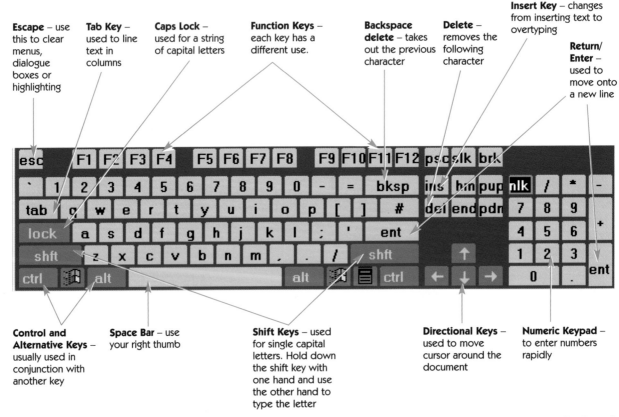

**Control and Alternative Keys** – usually used in conjunction with another key

**Space Bar** – use your right thumb

**Shift Keys** – used for single capital letters. Hold down the shift key with one hand and use the other hand to type the letter

**Directional Keys** – used to move cursor around the document

**Numeric Keypad** – to enter numbers rapidly

*Figure 1.2 A typical computer keyboard*

## Cut, copy, paste and move text

When the word processor was first introduced, it gave the user the opportunity to make changes to documents which were not possible with the traditional typewriter. To move text around a typewritten document without retyping it, the typist had to cut up the document with scissors and then stick it on to a new sheet of paper in a different order before photocopying it. This gave rise to the terms **cut**, **copy** and **paste** which are used when editing word processed documents. The word processor put an end to scissors and glue, and users were able to change the layout and content of their documents without having to retype them.

Most word processing applications offer several ways to cut, copy and paste, for example through drop down menus or icons. Some experienced users prefer to use keystrokes so they do not have to take their hands from the keyboard to operate the mouse. Figure 1.3 shows the keystrokes identified alongside the words and icons.

| ✂ Cut | Ctrl+X |
| ▣ Copy | Ctrl+C |
| ▣ Paste | Ctrl+V |

*Figure 1.3 The drop down menu shows the same icons that appear on the Formatting toolbar together with the keystrokes that can be used in place of clicking on the icons*

## Checkpoint

**Cut** means to take selected text out of the document. If you use the cut feature in your word processing software, the text is held in the computer's memory (clipboard). If you use the Delete key to remove text, it is lost forever (unless you use the Undo key to restore it).

## Checkpoint

**Copy** means to make a copy of selected text and retain (store) the copy in the computer's memory. (The block of text that you copied remains in its original position.) You can then place the same text elsewhere in the document.

## Fact file

The Clipboard in Microsoft® Office 2000 can retain the last 12 blocks of text that you have cut or copied.

## Checkpoint

**Move** means to cut selected text from one place and immediately place that text elsewhere in the document.

## Checkpoint

**Paste** describes the process of inserting text from the Clipboard elsewhere in the document. This means text that has been cut or copied and retained in the computer's memory is then placed somewhere else in the document.

## Selecting text

To change text already on the screen, first select or highlight the text. This identifies the selection as the block of text that is to be modified (altered) or reformatted.

There are several ways to select text. The most common is by clicking and dragging the mouse across the text. You will find some short cuts to selecting text in WP Worksheet 2.

## Document formatting features

### Changing font

The term font describes the style of typeface
you are using. Two popular styles are Times
New Roman and Arial.

This is an example of Times New Roman.
Times New Roman is referred to as a **serif**
font because of the 'little feet' at the end of
each line of the letter.

This is an example of Arial. Arial is
referred to as a **sans serif** font because
it does not have the little feet.

Compare the letters below. Which is the serif
font?

k k

The default font on your computer is usually
Times New Roman and the size is likely to be
12 point (or 10 point if you are working in
Microsoft® Word 97). Point refers to the size of
the character and the higher the number, the
larger the font. A point size of 72 would give
you a letter approximately 2.54 cm (1 inch) tall.

It is important that you choose a style and
size of font to suit the task you are doing.
You can also add emphasis to text by applying
**bold**, *italic* or underline.

To try these out, first select the text you
wish to change and choose from the options
offered by the Format, Font drop down menu or
the Formatting toolbar.

### Text alignment

Look again at the notice about the forthcoming
skiing trip for the Students' Association that you
produced for WP Worksheet 1. You will see that
the text automatically lines up against the left-
hand margin and the right-hand margin is ragged
or uneven. This is because the default style of
paragraph or text alignment is **left aligned**.

The text in this box is left aligned and the right-hand
margin is uneven or ragged. This is the usual default
setting. The spaces between the words are always
equal.

In this example the alignment is **justified** and both
the left- and right-hand margins are straight. The
computer automatically adjusts the space
between each word in order to distribute the text
evenly between the margins.

This shows text that is centred between the
margins. It is generally used for presentation and
display rather than letters or notes.

Can you see **how** difficult *some styles* are to read?

For example it would not be sensible to write a letter in a font like this.

WHEREAS A FONT LIKE THIS MIGHT SUIT A POSTER.

The easiest way to change the alignment of text is to select it and choose from the options on the Formatting toolbar, although you can also change the alignment through the Paragraph dialogue box.

## Paragraph indentation

Indenting a paragraph is a way of making a paragraph stand out from other paragraphs and is usually applied through the Paragraph dialogue box.

> This example shows text with a first line indent. The first line in the paragraph is set in from the margin and subsequent lines wrap back to the margin.
>
> The following paragraph also starts with a first line indent.

> This example shows text with a hanging indent. This style is used with numbered or bulleted lists.
> It is also sometimes used to display information in a CV or resumé.

> You can indent from both the left and right margins.
>
> This paragraph is an example of text with a left and right indent.
>
> Do you think indentation makes the paragraph stand out?

You can also use the Increase Indent button on the Formatting toolbar.

(You will be able to experiment with paragraph indenting on WP worksheet 4.)

## Line spacing

The distance between each line of text in a paragraph is known as the line spacing. The default setting on your computer will produce text in single line spacing. However, sometimes you may wish to leave a wider space between the lines, for instance if you want to make a section of text stand out or to leave room between lines to make handwritten notes.

> This example of text has been produced in **single line spacing**. This is the most commonly used setting.

> This example shows text in **one and a half line spacing**. It is used to make things stand out and easier to read.

> This example of text has been produced in **double line spacing**. This is particularly effective if you wish to make manuscript notes between the lines.

### Activity

▷ Print the file: **WP Worksheet 4** from the Chapter 1 folder on the CD-ROM. This worksheet will help you to become familiar with the features of the Paragraph dialogue box. You will be able to change the paragraph alignment and line spacing of the notice about the skiing trip and will also practise paragraph indenting.

## Margins

The margin is the area round the edge of the page where generally there is no text – see Figure 1.4. The default margins leave approximately 2.54 cm (1 inch) at the top and bottom of the page and 3.17 cm (1.25 inches) on the left and right sides. For most word

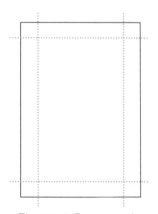

*Figure 1.4 Page margins*

processing you will not need to change the default margins.

Sometimes, however, you may need to change one or more of the margin settings, for example if you are producing a document that is to be bound, where a wider left-hand margin would be required.

Margins are usually changed through File, Page Setup.

## Page orientation

Most text documents are produced using the default page orientation of portrait style – where the narrower edge of the paper appears at the top. Sometimes you may need to display the document with the wider edge of the page at the top, for example if working in columns or producing tables of data. In this case, you will need to change the page orientation from portrait to landscape – see Figure 1.5.

Portrait

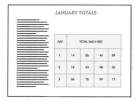
Landscape

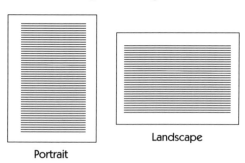

JANUARY TOTALS

Landscape can be very effective if you are working in columns or producing tables of data

*Figure 1.5 Page orientation*

**Activity**

Print the file: **WP Worksheet 5** from the Chapter 1 folder on the CD-ROM. Use the activity in this worksheet to investigate File, Page Setup and see how to change the margins and page orientation.

## Tabulation

If you look closely at the ruler in Figure 1.6, you will see very faint marks along the bottom edge. These marks represent the default tabulation settings, or tab settings, and are positioned at 1.27 cm or $\frac{1}{2}$ inch intervals. The purpose of the tab settings is to help you line up text across the page.

*Figure 1.6 Default tabulation settings*

Look at the example in Figure 1.7. The student shop wanted a stock list produced. Can you see how the text has lined up across the page in line with the default tab settings?

| Product Ref | Description | Price |
|---|---|---|
| HA 269 | Pencil, HB | £0.65 |
| GC 457 | Felt tip pen, Blue | £1.05 |
| WM 129 | Adhesive labels | £1.75 |

*Figure 1.7 Text lined up with the default tab settings*

**Activity**

Print the file: **WP Worksheet 6** from the Chapter 1 folder on the CD-ROM. This worksheet looks at tabs in some detail and shows you how they can be used to line up text in different ways. It will also show you how to set and change tabs directly on the ruler.

## Columns

Most documents look fine if they are prepared within the default settings, but sometimes a little extra effort to modify (alter) the layout can make a big difference to the final presentation. This is particularly important if you want to make something eye catching.

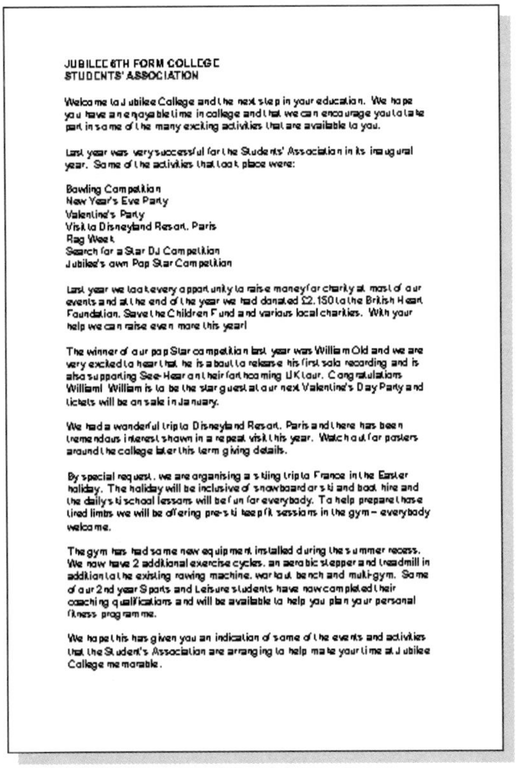

Figure 1.8 A document prepared using the default settings and the same document reformatted into columns with some extra changes to the presentation

The Students' Association at Jubilee 6th Form College is proud of its fund raising activities. It decides to publicise these and the events it has planned for the coming year. It has produced a document to hand out to students giving details of past and future events. The same document has been reformatted into columns. The documents are shown in Figure 1.8. Which do you think looks the more attractive?

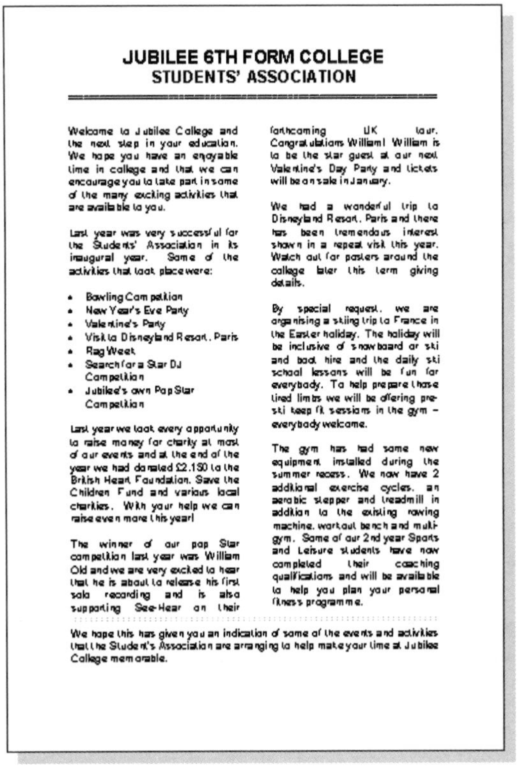

## Bullet points and numbering

Look at Figure 1.8 and you will see that bullet points were added to the list in the right-hand document to make the items stand out. Sometimes, it is better to number a list. Both bullet points and numbering can be applied using the icons on the Formatting toolbar or the Format, Bullets and Numbering dialogue box, as shown in the following examples.

---

**Freshers Fair**
**28 September 2002**

Find out about:

- Sports activities
- New Year's Eve Party
- Skiing trip to France
- Bowling evening
- Spotlight Nightclub
- Charity events

---

**Freshers Fair**
**28 September 2002**

Find out about:

☐ Sports activities
☐ New Year's Eve Party
☐ Skiing trip to France
☐ Bowling evening
☐ Spotlight Nightclub
☐ Charity events

---

**Freshers Fair**
**28 September 2002**

Find out about:

1. Sports activities
2. New Year's Eve Party
3. Skiing trip to France
4. Bowling evening
5. Spotlight Nightclub
6. Charity events

---

**Activity**

▷ Print the file: **WP Worksheet 7** from the Chapter 1 folder on the CD-ROM. Use the data file on the CD-ROM to reformat the college handout in the same way as the example above.

## Symbols

Did you notice that the word resumé in the paragraph describing hanging paragraph indents on page 17 has a French accent above the letter é? Accents, such as those common to the French language, are not available through the UK keyboard. However these, and other symbols that are quite widely used, can be accessed through the Insert, Symbol dialogue box.

For example:

ç ¾ % ✂ € ☒ ☑ ❶ ⬆ ⬇ ☺ ☹ 🕸 ✉ © 🌐 ✈

How many of these do you recognise?

### Fact file

Did you know that the symbol for the euro is on the keyboard alongside the number 4 key? You can insert it by holding down the key to the right of the spacebar with the letters Alt Gr and pressing 4 or by holding down Ctrl + Alt and pressing 4.

### Activity

▷ Print the file: **WP Worksheet 8** from the Chapter 1 folder on the CD-ROM. The venue for the French skiing trip must be changed from Tignes to Megève. Use this worksheet to learn how to insert the è symbol and also how to automatically find one word and replace it with another (Find and Replace).

## Headers and footers

The document header is the space in the top margin above the first line of text on a page. The header is used to show information that is to be repeated on every page such as a company logo or page number. When you produce work at school or college you will need to include your name on every page. By using the header you can ensure the information appears on every page.

The document footer is the space at the bottom of the page after the last line of text. Anything you insert in the page footer will appear on every page.

### Fact file

The Insert AutoText option in the Header and Footer dialogue box inserts the file path and file name of your document into the header or footer. This will help you to find the document at a later date. You can also insert the date which is useful if you need to check that you are looking at the most recent print of a document.

### Activity

▷ Print the file: **WP Worksheet 9** from the Chapter 1 folder on the CD-ROM. Learn how to insert your name in the document header, how to use page numbers and how to insert the date together with the file name and path.

## Tables

Tables are used to organise and present information and to align numbers in columns – see Figure 1.9. A table is a grid of rows and columns broken down into cells – rather like a spreadsheet. You can enter text, images or even more tables in the cells. You can enhance (add to) the appearance by adding borders and shading, merging cells, changing the text alignment and you can insert a formula to add up a column of figures.

| JUBILEE COLLEGE STUDENTS' ASSOCIATION CHARITY DONATIONS 2002 | | |
|---|---|---|
| | Charity | Donation £ |
| Bowling Competition | British Heart Foundation | 300 |
| Rag Week | Various local charities | 1500 |
| Search for a Pop Star | Save the Children Fund | 350 |
| | **Total Raised** | **2150** |

*Figure 1.9 Tables are used to present information clearly in columns*

| JUBILEE COLLEGE STUDENTS' ASSOCIATION CHARITY DONATIONS 2002 | | |
|---|---|---|
| | Charity | Donation £ |
| Bowling Competition | British Heart Foundation | 300 |
| Rag Week | Various local charities | 1500 |
| Search for a Pop Star | Save the Children Fund | 350 |
| | Total Raised | 2150 |

*Figure 1.10  This table uses the style 3D effects 3*

You can also choose from a variety of table presentation styles using AutoFormat. Look at Figure 1.10. It is the same table as the one in Figure 1.9, but the style **3D effects 3** has been applied to it using AutoFormat.

## Activity

▷ Print the file: **WP Worksheet 10** from the Chapter 1 folder on the CD-ROM. This worksheet will help you to create and reformat tables. You will also learn how borders and shading can improve the presentation of your work.

# Clip art and graphic images

As you look through this book, you will see many graphic images – some are screen prints of the computer, some are photographs and some are drawings; some are in black and white and some are in colour. They are intended to make the book more interesting to read and help you understand what you are reading about.

At some time you will want to include graphic images in your work and you are most likely to use clip art or perhaps create your own image.

Look at the images in Figure 1.11. The one on the left is from clip art and the Jubilee 6th Form College logo is an image that has been created using graphics software.

*Figure 1.11  A clip art image, on the left, and one created using graphics software*

# Wrapping text around images or objects

You can control the relationship between the image and surrounding text by applying different formatting techniques. Look at the examples below.

In this example the image is formatted to sit square with the text. You can see the text is in a straight line at the sides of the image.

In this example    the image is formatted        so that the text              clings tightly to            the shape of the image,        creating a totally different      effect.

This shows how an image can be formatted to sit in front of text. However, as you can see,  this makes it difficult to read the text.

This example shows the same image formatted as a watermark which has been placed behind the text.

# The Drawing toolbar

The Drawing toolbar can be used to create graphic effects by combining shapes, AutoShapes and Text Boxes to create a layered image. In Figure 1.12 some simple shapes and the addition of colour and texture have been used to create the image.

## Activity

▷ Print the file: **WP Worksheet 11** from the Chapter 1 folder on the CD-ROM. This worksheet will teach you all you need to know about working with graphic images. You can try to recreate your house and also the logo for Jubilee 6th Form College. You will learn how to create and add a watermark and images to the information sheet about the skiing trip.

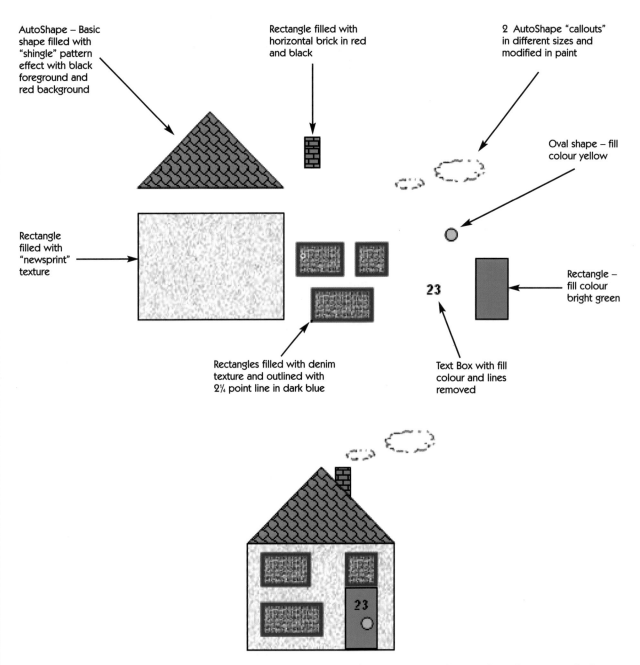

AutoShape – Basic shape filled with "shingle" pattern effect with black foreground and red background

Rectangle filled with horizontal brick in red and black

2 AutoShape "callouts" in different sizes and modified in paint

Oval shape – fill colour yellow

Rectangle filled with "newsprint" texture

Rectangle – fill colour bright green

Rectangles filled with denim texture and outlined with 2¼ point line in dark blue

Text Box with fill colour and lines removed

23

*Figure 1.12  Simple shapes, colour and texture are used to produce the image of a house*

## Mail merge

Ask at home if you can look at some of the mail your family receives each week. Many of the letters your parents or carers receive will be addressed to them personally and will start with 'Dear Mr ...', 'Dear Mrs ...' or 'Dear Ms ...'. Some of the letters will have been produced by someone sitting at a keyboard and typing them

word for word – much as you do when you produce work on the word processor.

However, much of your family's post is likely to be produced automatically using a process known as mail merge. For example, if a bank decided to write to all its customers with accounts at a particular branch to advise them of a change in opening hours, it would produce a standard letter and then personalise it by inserting the customer's name and address using a mail-merge facility. To produce such letters individually would be time consuming and costly.

To carry out the mail merge, the bank would need a data file or data source which contains data (information( about its customers (for example, names and addresses) and a standard letter where the variable information (for example, names and addresses) will be inserted.

Jubilee 6th Form College Students' Association has produced a standard letter to be sent to all students going on the skiing trip. It will use mail merge to insert the students' names and addresses on the letter. The data source will be set up in a file similar to this:

| Title | First Name | Last Name | Address1 | Town | Postcode |
|-------|-----------|-----------|----------|------|----------|
| Miss | Eleanor | Harris | 2 Lodge Road | Wayfield | ER6 4KN |
| Miss | Megan | Gosforth | 7 Wayfield Road | Wayfield | ER2 7CL |
| Miss | Hannah | Douglas | 90 The Crescent | Wayfield | ER4 4GT |
| Miss | Grace | Parker | 8 Lodge Road | Wayfield | ER6 4KN |
| Mr | Michael | Gates | 12 Green Lane | Wayfield | ER3 7JB |

The file might be within a database, spreadsheet or word processing application.

The standard letter would look similar to the one in Figure 1.13. Notice that the column headings from the table above have been incorporated into the letter.

The column headings are the same as 'field names' in a database. When the letter and data source are merged, the individual names and addresses will replace the field names

«Title» «FirstName» «LastName»
«Address1»
«Town»
«Postcode»

Dear «FirstName»

I am pleased to confirm that a place has been reserved for you on the forthcoming skiing trip to Megève. Please would you let me have your deposit before the end of the month.

*Figure 1.13 Standard letter in a mail merge showing "field names"*

When the standard letter and data source are merged, the first few letters would look like those in Figure 1.14.

Miss Eleanor Harris
2 Lodge Road
Wayfield
ER6 4KN

Dear Eleanor

I am pleased to confirm that a place has been reserved for you on the forthcoming skiing trip to Megève. Please would you let me have your deposit before the end of the month.

Miss Hannah Douglas
90 The Crescent
Wayfield
ER4 4GT

Dear Hannah

I am pleased to confirm that a place has been reserved for you on the forthcoming skiing trip to Megève. Please would you let me have your deposit before the end of the month.

Miss Megan Gosforth
7 Wayfield Road
Wayfield
ER2 7CL

Dear Megan

I am pleased to confirm that a place has been reserved for you on the forthcoming skiing trip to Megève. Please would you let me have your deposit before the end of the month.

**Activity**

Print the file: **WP Worksheet 12** from the Chapter 1 folder on the CD-ROM. In this you will practise a mail merge exercise using a data source that you created in WP Worksheet 10.

*Figure 1.14 Letters produced by mail merge*

## Desktop publishing

Until quite recently organisations would use a specialist print company to produce their letter headings, leaflets, newsletters, business cards and so on. Nowadays many organisations are able to do this work for themselves in-house by using desktop publishing software. If you have access to desktop publishing software you will find a variety of templates available for producing business documents. However, word processing software has become more sophisticated, it is possible to reproduce many desktop publishing effects that were once only available in specialised desktop publishing software. For example, you have already practised formatting text into columns and seen how to incorporate graphic images. Those images have been edited by using the cropping tool and you have looked at various ways of wrapping text around them.

If you have access to desktop publishing software you will find a variety of templates to help produce leaflets, newsletters, business cards etc.

## Kerning

One feature of desktop publishing is **kerning**, the process of reducing the spacing between certain pairs of letters to improve the appearance of the text. A feature similar to this can be carried out in word processing by expanding or condensing be carried out in word processing by expanding or condensing the character spacing. Look at the three text boxes in Figure 1.15. They each contain exactly the same characters, but the effects are different.

**Jubilee College**

Normal spacing

**Jubilee College**

Expanded by 1.7 pts

**Jubilee College**

Condensed by 0.8 pt

*Figure 1.15 The effects of different character spacing*

For the creation of documents such as newsletters, the word processor is more than adequate. However, documents requiring more complex formatting, such as magazine layouts and this book, would generally be prepared using desktop publishing software. Text produced using a word processor can be imported into desktop publishing software. Documents produced in a desktop publishing application are usually put together using a system of frames – text frames and picture frames. Think of a frame as similar to a text box. The user can move the frames around to fit the space available.

The Students' Association shop in Jubilee 6th Form College had some special offers for students and used some desktop publishing features to produce the flyer in Figure 1.16.

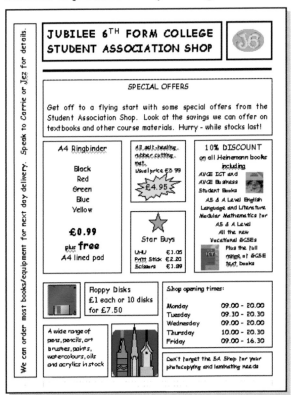

*Figure 1.16 Flyer produced using the desktop publishing features in a word processing application*

**Activity**

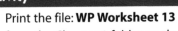

▷ Print the file: **WP Worksheet 13** from the Chapter 1 folder on the CD-ROM. Produce your own flyer using desktop publishing software or use the desktop publishing tools in your word processing software.

# Chapter 2

# Organisation and analysis of numerical information using spreadsheet software

This chapter introduces you to spreadsheets. You will find out how to:

- enter a range of data, e.g. text, numbers
- format cells to match data types
- enter formulae
- print spreadsheets, including printing selected areas
- cut, copy, paste and move data between cells, rows and columns
- use relative and absolute cell references and replicate (copy) formulae
- use simple functions, e.g. SUM, AVERAGE, IF
- create macros
- produce charts with labels, e.g. axes titles, legends.

### What you will learn

Enter data

Format cells

Formulae

Print the spreadsheet

Cut, copy, paste and move data

Insert and delete rows and columns

Relative cell reference

Absolute cell reference

Simple spreadsheet functions

Linking worksheets

Macros

Graphs and charts

## Overview: Spreadsheets

### What is a spreadsheet?

What does the term spreadsheet mean? Whereas the main purpose of a word processor is to enter, edit and manipulate, or handle, text, the main purpose of a spreadsheet is to enter, edit and manipulate numerical data, and to make calculations using this data.

You have already discovered in Chapter 1 how the word processor has made it so easy to produce letters, flyers, posters, and so on. You might think that the word processor is the most frequently used software application, but spreadsheet software is just as vital to the modern business.

### What are spreadsheet programs used for?

Spreadsheet programs make financial tasks such as calculating staff wages, profit made on goods sold, VAT (value added tax) returns and bank accounts much easier. A spreadsheet programme is an invaluable tool for all kinds of

organisations – from small ones such as a local baker's shop, to your own school or college, to huge companies such as Next, Virgin Megastores, Lloyds TSB or government departments such as the Inland Revenue. On a personal level, people might use a spreadsheet to keep track of how much income they receive, what expenses they have and how much is left to save. Calculators can also be used for these purposes, but the spreadsheet allows you to save the files containing all this data, which can then be retrieved and updated as necessary.

### Workbooks and worksheets

Spreadsheet files are known as **workbooks** and may include several **worksheets** all related to the main purpose of that file, rather like chapters in a book. Sophisticated programs can link worksheets or workbooks, so that when you change the numbers on one sheet, the numbers in linked worksheets or files are updated automatically.

## Enter data

A spreadsheet is divided into rows and columns, creating a grid of cells. Each row and column in a spreadsheet is given a unique number or letter, so each cell can be identified rather like a map reference – A1, B6, C12, and so on. The data text or number is entered into the cell. Figure 2.1 shows a very basic spreadsheet layout before formulae have been entered.

### Activity

▷ Print the file: **SS Worksheet 1** from the Chapter 2 folder on the CD-ROM. In this worksheet you will find instructions to create the spreadsheet shown in Figure 2.1.

## Format cells

A typical spreadsheet will have row and column headings, as well as text and numerical data. Since most of the data in a spreadsheet is numerical, it is essential that the spreadsheet is set out in a way that is easy to read. Look again at the spreadsheet in Figure 2.1. Can you see that the text in column A is hidden by data in column B, and text in column C is overlapping into column D? The presentation can be improved by formatting the cells. Just as in word processing software, you can enhance the text in a spreadsheet by:

● using bold, italics or underline
● changing the font size for main or subheadings
● using different font styles.

You can also improve the appearance of the spreadsheet by:

● displaying a heading at an angle or vertically within cells – see Figure 2.2
● centring a heading horizontally across cells or across two or more columns
● centring a heading vertically within cells, that is, centred from top to bottom
● wrapping text within a cell to avoid having a very wide column
● aligning text to the right to avoid overlapping the next cell
● adjusting the cell width or row height
● placing borders around or using colour for significant (important) cells, e.g. cells showing totals
● using shading or colour for the background of significant cells.

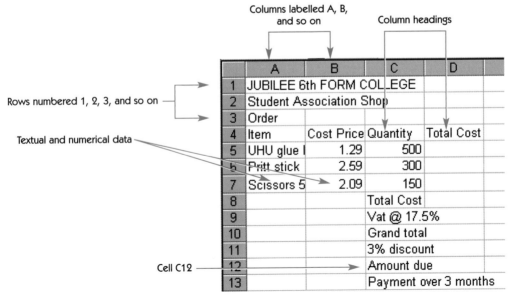

*Figure 2.1 A basic spreadsheet*

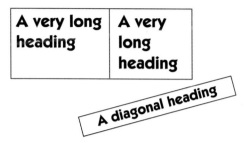

Figure 2.2 Some heading styles

When designing your spreadsheet you need to think about the following points when formatting your data:

- Is the data type numeric or text?
- In what format do you wish to display dates?
- Should numeric data be displayed as an integer (whole number e.g. 500)? If not, how many decimal places do you need?
- Do you wish to show the currency symbol? If yes, is it too cluttered to show the £ sign everywhere, or might it be better to use it just for the totals?
- Do you wish to show negative numbers in red? This can be set automatically.
- Do you need to format the data as a percentage?

Look at the spreadsheet in Figure 2.3. It includes some of the formatting features described above.

## Formulae

### What is a formula?

A formula (plural: formulae) is used to make calculations such as adding (+), subtracting (-), multiplying (*), dividing (/), finding the average or a percentage.

A formula is a sequence of values (numbers), cell references (for example D5), or operators (for example addition or multiplication symbols) that produces a *new* value from *existing* values.

The important point to remember is that in Microsoft® Excel **a formula always starts with an equal sign (=)**. This tells the spreadsheet that a calculation is to be carried out. The spreadsheet can do everything a calculator can do – *but so much more.*

### Checkpoint

A **formula** is used to make a calculation in the spreadsheet and in Excel always starts with an = sign.

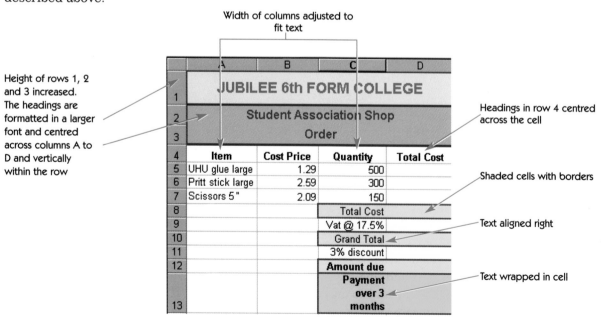

Width of columns adjusted to fit text

Height of rows 1, 2 and 3 increased. The headings are formatted in a larger font and centred across columns A to D and vertically within the row

Headings in row 4 centred across the cell

Shaded cells with borders

Text aligned right

Text wrapped in cell

Figure 2.3 The basic spreadsheet has been formatted to improve the layout

Formulae enable the spreadsheet application to make a wide range of automatic calculations that take place instantaneously. The spreadsheet will calculate a very simple formula, such as:

|  | Formula | Result |
|---|---|---|
| Formula using values: | =1.29*500 | 645 |

but usually cell references are used in formulae. For example, in Figure 2.4, in cell D5 the formula =B5 * C5 would be used to calculate the cost of UHU glue.

|  | Formula | Result |
|---|---|---|
| Formula using cell references: | =B5*C5 | 645 |

The advantage of using formulae is that the spreadsheet will automatically recalculate if any changes are made to the data. For example, if the price of UHU glue increases to £1.35 each, when the new price is entered in cell B5, the total cost will be recalculated automatically.

| Formula | Result |  |
|---|---|---|
| =B5*C5 | 675 | Price increase entered into cell B5, new cost automatically updated in cell D5. |

Although formulae range from the easy to the very complicated, the basic formula types are used over and over again. It is worth getting to know some of these. As long as you write the formula correctly, the results are never wrong. However, first you have to decide what you need to do *manually* and then find the most suitable formula.

## Arithmetic operators

Formulae use **arithmetic operators** and **comparison operators**. (For more about comparison operators, see page 33).

Arithmetic operators perform basic mathematical operations such as addition, subtraction, multiplication, division, and so on. Look at Figures 2.4 and 2.5. Figure 2.5 shows where the following formulae have been added:

| To: | add | Cell D10 | =D8+D9 |
|---|---|---|---|
|  | subtract | Cell D12 | =D10-D11 |
|  | divide | Cell D12 | =D12/3 |
|  | multiply | Cell D5 | =B5*C5 |
|  |  | Cell D6 | =B6*C6 |
|  |  | Cell D7 | =B7*C7 |
|  | percentage | Cell D9 | =D8*17.5% |
|  |  | Cell D11 | =D10*3% |
|  | sum (total) | Cell D8 | =SUM(D5:D7) – this means add all cells in the range D5 to D7 (see note below) |

*Note:* It is quite quick to enter =D5+D6+D7, but using =SUM followed by the range of cells is much easier and quicker if you have to total 20 or 30 rows.

| | A | B | C | D |
|---|---|---|---|---|
| 1 | JUBILEE 6th FORM COLLEGE | | | |
| 2 | Student Association Shop | | | |
| 3 | Order | | | |
| 4 | Item | Cost Price | Quantity | Total Cost |
| 5 | UHU glue large | 1.29 | 500 | 645.00 |
| 6 | Pritt stick large | 2.59 | 300 | 777.00 |
| 7 | Scissors 5" | 2.09 | 150 | 313.50 |
| 8 | | | Total Cost £ | 1,735.50 |
| 9 | | | Vat @ 17.5% £ | 303.71 |
| 10 | | | Grand total £ | 2,039.21 |
| 11 | | | 3% discount £ | 61.18 |
| 12 | | | Amount due £ | 1,978.04 |
| 13 | | | Payment over 3 months £ | 659.35 |

Figure 2.4 *The data view showing the results after the formulae have been entered*

| | A | B | C | D |
|---|---|---|---|---|
| 1 | JUBILEE 6th FORM COLLEGE | | | |
| 2 | Student Association Shop | | | |
| 3 | Order | | | |
| 4 | Item | Cost Price | Quantity | Total Cost |
| 5 | UHU glue large | 1.29 | 500 | =B5*C5 |
| 6 | Pritt stick large | 2.59 | 300 | =B6*C6 |
| 7 | Scissors 5" | 2.09 | 150 | =B7*C7 |
| 8 | | | Total Cost | =SUM(D5:D7) |
| 9 | | | Vat @ 17.5% | =D8*17.5% |
| 10 | | | Grand total | =D8+D9 |
| 11 | | | 3% discount | =D10*3% |
| 12 | | | Amount due | =D10-D11 |
| 13 | | | Payment over 3 months | =D12/3 |

Figure 2.5 *The formula view*

## Testing the spreadsheet

It is easy to assume that because the computer has worked something out for you it must be right! However, the computer is only as accurate as the data and formulae that have been entered. Therefore, it is important to check that the result of a formula is correct. When you design a spreadsheet, check the calculations using a calculator. If the results do not match, then you know you need to find out where the problem lies. Is the spreadsheet wrong or did you make a mistake using the calculator? If all is well, you can feel confident that any future calculations will be accurate.

For example, it may be that when entering a formula, the user makes a simple typing error, pressing the + key instead of * to multiply. A result will appear in the cell, but it will be inaccurate. Look at the spreadsheets on page 28 showing the data view and the formula view. The formula to multiply the quantity by the unit price in cell D5 is =B5*C5. If an error had been made and the formula entered was =B5+C5, this would have been the result:

| Data to enter in: | | Expected result | Actual result | Formula correct? |
|---|---|---|---|---|
| **Cell B5** | **\*Cell C5** | | | |
| 1.29 | 500 | 645.00 | 645.00 | Yes ✓ |
| **Cell B5** | **+Cell C5** | | | |
| 1.29 | 500 | 645.00 | 501.29 | No ✗ |

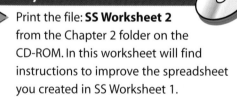

### Activity

▷ Print the file: **SS Worksheet 2** from the Chapter 2 folder on the CD-ROM. In this worksheet will find instructions to improve the spreadsheet you created in SS Worksheet 1.

## Print the spreadsheet

To print from Microsoft® Excel, click on the Print 🖶 icon or select File, Print and OK. It is a good idea to check Print Preview before sending the file to print, to make sure the printout will look as you want it. As with word processing, you can:

- change the margins
- print portrait or landscape
- include a header or footer.

The spreadsheet can also be printed:

- with or without gridlines
- with or without row and column headings
- showing the values or the formulae.

In business, row and column headings are often left out, but your teacher may want them included, especially if he or she is checking a formula printout. Spreadsheets used in business are often very large. One worksheet in Microsoft® Excel allows you to use hundreds of columns and more than *10,000* rows! It is very unlikely that you will need to produce such a large spreadsheet, but you may want to print out just a part of a spreadsheet file. The software allows you to select a range of cells and print the selection.

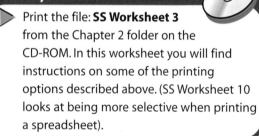

### Activity

▷ Print the file: **SS Worksheet 3** from the Chapter 2 folder on the CD-ROM. In this worksheet you will find instructions on some of the printing options described above. (SS Worksheet 10 looks at being more selective when printing a spreadsheet).

## Cut, copy, paste and move data

Once you have set up your spreadsheet, you may want or need to make changes. This may be because you have identified some improvements that could be made or because you have learned more about spreadsheet facilities. In business, changes are often made as the needs of the business alter.

You can cut, copy, paste and move data between cells, rows and columns using the same icons as you used in Word.

# Insert and delete rows and columns

You may also want to insert or delete rows or columns. Once again, spreadsheet software allows you to make such changes easily.

## Activity

▶ Print the file: **SS Worksheet 4** from the Chapter 2 folder on the CD-ROM. This worksheet introduces you to some of the above facilities. Others will be practised in later worksheets.

# Relative cell reference

One of the advantages of using a spreadsheet is the facility to replicate, or copy, formulae across columns or down rows. It is very convenient to be able to replicate the formula, rather than having to keep entering it again and again. If you need to have totals down several rows or across several columns, you can enter the formula into the first cell and then replicate the formula across to the last column or down to the last row. The spreadsheet will automatically change the formula to give the correct cell reference.

Figure 2.6 shows the formula view for the Jubilee 6th Form College's Art & Design Department's quiz scores in an inter-departmental competition. Notice the formulae in cell F4, which calculates Tim's total score. The formula = SUM(B4:E4) was entered in cell F4 and then copied down the column. As the formula was copied, the spreadsheet automatically changed the cell references to = SUM(B5:E5) to = SUM(B6:E6) and so on.

There is a similar change when formulae are copied across columns. The formula =SUM(B4:B7) to calculate the total scores for each round in the quiz was entered in cell B8. As the formula was copied across the columns, the cell reference automatically changed to =SUM(C4:C7), to =SUM(D4:D7), and so on. The spreadsheet assumes that as the formula is copied from cell to cell, the formula should be **relative** to, not the same as, the previous cell.

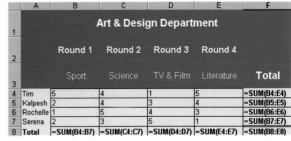

*Figure 2.6 Notice how the formula references change as they are copied down column F and across row 8*

# Absolute cell reference

Sometimes you may wish to refer to a particular cell many times, so when you replicate the formula, the cell address needs to remain the same. This is known as an **absolute cell reference.** For example, a shopkeeper's spreadsheet has one cell containing the rate for VAT (the government's value added tax on items we buy). When people purchase goods, they are not interested in how much of that money has to be given to the government, but it is essential for the shopkeeper to know this.

Figure 2.7 illustrates this point. The Students' Association shop has to calculate the amount of VAT payable on each item and also gives a discount of 3 per cent to students. A spreadsheet has been set up which automatically calculates the prices:

- The rate for VAT is 17.5 per cent and is entered into cell **C4**.
- The discount is entered in cell **F4**.
- The trade price of the item is entered in column **C**.
- The amount of VAT to be paid is calculated in column **D**.
- The price including VAT is calculated in column **E** by adding the trade price and the VAT.
- The discount is calculated in column **F**.
- The price the students have to pay is calculated in column **G** by deducting the discount from the price including VAT.

You will notice that the formulae in column **D** and in column **F** show $ signs before the **C** and **4** and before the **F** and the **4** in the cell reference (Figure 2.8). These signs are used in Microsoft® Excel to show that when replicating the formula, this cell reference must *not* be changed, that is, it is an absolute cell reference. Although in the example shown, it would be very quick to key in the formula on each new line, in a business spreadsheet, the formula might need to be replicated down hundreds of rows. The other benefit is that if either the rate of VAT or the discount is changed, it is a simple matter to enter the new rate in cell **C4** or **F4**, and all cells depending on those formulae will change automatically.

Notice that the formula reference for VAT in cell **C4** does *not* change as it is copied down the rows in column **D** because the $ signs before the C and the 4 indicate that this reference should remain fixed or *absolute*.

However, the cell reference for the Total Price C6, does change to C7, C8 etc.

The same applies to the formulae for discount in column **F**. The cell reference **F4** remains *absolute* as it is copied down the rows because of the dollar ($), but the cell reference to E6 changes to E7 etc.

## Activity

▷ Print the file: **SS Worksheet 5** from the Chapter 2 folder on the CD-ROM. This worksheet gives you further formatting practice and also introduces replicating formulae.

| | A | B | C | D | E | F | G |
|---|---|---|---|---|---|---|---|
| 1 | JUBILEE 6th FORM COLLEGE | | | | | | |
| 2 | Student Association Shop | | | | | | |
| 3 | Price List | | | | | | |
| 4 | | | VAT | 17.5% | | Student Discount | 3% | |
| 5 | Catalogue Reference | Item | Trade Price Excluding VAT | VAT | Price Including VAT | Discount | Selling Price |
| 6 | 232 201 | Eraser | 0.30 | 0.05 | 0.35 | 0.01 | 0.34 |
| 7 | 401 601 | File - A4 Ringbinder | 0.66 | 0.12 | 0.78 | 0.02 | 0.75 |
| 8 | 401 602 | File - Lever Arch | 0.87 | 0.15 | 1.02 | 0.03 | 0.99 |
| 9 | 300 780 | Highlighters - jumbo size - 6 pack - assorted colours | 2.19 | 0.38 | 2.57 | 0.08 | 2.50 |
| 10 | 300 781 | Highlighters - pocket size - 6 pack - assorted colours | 1.94 | 0.34 | 2.28 | 0.07 | 2.21 |
| 11 | 351 341 | Notebook - spiral bound | 0.43 | 0.08 | 0.51 | 0.02 | 0.49 |
| 12 | 351 340 | Notepad - A4 Ruled - 80 sheets | 0.87 | 0.15 | 1.02 | 0.03 | 0.99 |
| 13 | 297 141 | Pencil | 0.31 | 0.05 | 0.36 | 0.01 | 0.35 |
| 14 | 297 145 | Pencil sharpener | 0.66 | 0.12 | 0.78 | 0.02 | 0.75 |

*Figure 2.7 Part of a price list spreadsheet showing value*

| | A | B | C | D | E | F | G |
|---|---|---|---|---|---|---|---|
| 1 | JUBILEE 6th FORM COLLEGE | | | | | | |
| 2 | Student Association Shop | | | | | | |
| 3 | Price List | | | | | | |
| 4 | | | VAT | 17.5% | | Student Discount | 3% | |
| 5 | Catalogue Reference | Item | Trade Price Excluding VAT | VAT | Price Including VAT | Discount | Selling Price |
| 6 | 232 201 | Eraser | 0.30 | =C6*$C$4 | =C6+D6 | =E6*$F$4 | =E6-F6 |
| 7 | 401 601 | File - A4 Ringbinder | 0.66 | =C7*$C$4 | =C7+D7 | =E7*$F$4 | =E7-F7 |
| 8 | 401 602 | File - Lever Arch | 0.87 | =C8*$C$4 | =C8+D8 | =E8*$F$4 | =E8-F8 |
| 9 | 300 780 | Highlighters - jumbo size - 6 pack - assorted colours | 2.19 | =C9*$C$4 | =C9+D9 | =E9*$F$4 | =E9-F9 |
| 10 | 300 781 | Highlighters -pocket size - 6 pack - assorted colours | 1.94 | =C10*$C$4 | =C10+D10 | =E10*$F$4 | =E10-F10 |
| 11 | 351 341 | Notebook - spiral bound | 0.43 | =C11*$C$4 | =C11+D11 | =E11*$F$4 | =E11-F11 |
| 12 | 351 340 | Notepad - A4 Ruled - 80 sheets | 0.87 | =C12*$C$4 | =C12+D12 | =E12*$F$4 | =E12-F12 |
| 13 | 297 141 | Pencil | 0.31 | =C13*$C$4 | =C13+D13 | =E13*$F$4 | =E13-F13 |
| 14 | 297 145 | Pencil sharpener | 0.66 | =C14*$C$4 | =C14+D14 | =E14*$F$4 | =E14-F14 |

*Figure 2.8 Part of a price list spreadsheet showing the formulae*

## Simple spreadsheet functions

Spreadsheet functions are simply formulae pre-written into the software, which can be used either on their own, or as part of a more complex formula. The three you are going to use are **SUM**, **AVERAGE**, and **IF**.

### SUM

If you are using Microsoft® Excel at your school or college, you will find the AutoSum **Σ** icon on the toolbar. To find the total of a column or row of figures, select the cell at the bottom of the column or to the right of the row, click on the icon and the formula will be written for you. Be careful when using the AutoSum. It is important to check that Excel has selected the range of cells you require. AutoSum was used to calculate the Total No Sold in Figure 2.9, but the range selected was not quite right.

### Activity

▶ Print the file: **SS Worksheet 6** from the Chapter 2 folder on the CD-ROM. This worksheet gives you further formatting practice and also introduces AutoSum and setting the print area.

### Fact file

Quite often students enter =SUM as part of a formula when it is not necessary. Look back at the price list spreadsheet (Figure 2.8) showing the formulae. The formula in cell **E6** is **=C6+D6**, but some students will enter **=SUM(C6+D6)**. This will work, but it is not required in this case. The only time it is necessary to include the word **SUM** in a formula is when you are adding a range of cells.

### AVERAGE

When calculating an average, you are not trying to work out the correct number but what is typical of a group or situation. To calculate an average, add up all the relevant totals, and divide by the number of totals. For example, to find out the average number of goals scored per match by your favourite football team during the season, add up the scores and divide by the number of matches played. Look at Wayfield United's average weekly score in Figure 2.10. Clearly, it is not possible to score three-quarters (0.75) of a goal, but on *average* Wayfield United scored nearly two goals each week.

The formula for calculating the average is shown in the status line in the spreadsheet. If

Status line showing the formula selected by the AutoSum – notice the error

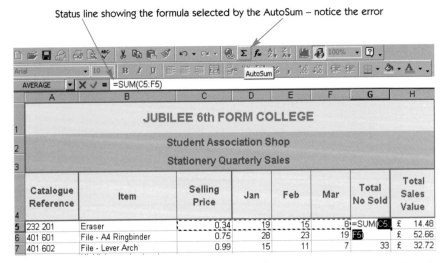

*Figure 2.9  The AutoSum function has been used in cell **G5**, but it has selected the range **C5:F5**, which includes the price of the item. The range **D5:F5** only is necessary to obtain the total number sold. To correct the error, either enter **=SUM(D5:F5)** or scroll across cells D5 to F5 by dragging with the mouse.*

you were working out the average goals scored by Wayfield United yourself, you would need to add up the total of goals scored – 7, check how many games have been played – 4, and then divide the total by the number of games played to get the result – 1.8. The advantage of using the Average function available in the spreadsheet is that these various stages are all worked out automatically for you.

The Students' Association shop wants to find out its average quarterly sales over the year. To do this, it adds up the sales for each quarter and divides by the number of quarters (Figure 2.10). In this case, there is no actual quarterly sales figure of £2,400.14 – this was the *average* or typical sales per quarter.

The formula in Cell **B8** calculates the average score

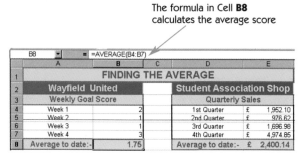

Figure 2.10 Finding out an average

## Activity

Print the file: **SS Worksheet 7** from the Chapter 2 folder on the CD-ROM. This worksheet provides further practice in entering data and formatting and introduces the average function.

## IF

## Comparison operators – IF, THEN, ELSE

Comparison operators compare two values to find out whether something is true or false. You will be looking for a number greater than, less than or equal to, or combinations of these possibilities. Comparison operators include:

> greater than
< less than

= equal to
>= greater than or equal to
<= less than or equal to
<> not equal to.

In a spreadsheet, comparison operators are usually used with the **IF** function.

In the statement '*If* the weather is fine, *then* we'll have a barbecue', the implication, or unsaid meaning, is that if it is not fine, we will do something *else*. In other words, the statement is a condition – only if one thing happens will a particular action take place. The words 'If the weather is not fine, we won't have a barbecue' are not actually said, but the listener would understand the meaning.

| The condition | True or false | Action |
|---|---|---|
| The weather is fine | True | We'll have a barbecue |
| The weather is fine | False – it is not fine | We won't have a barbecue |

*Two conditions*

Spreadsheets offer this same facility, so that you can ask the spreadsheet to provide answers depending on a certain condition. If that condition is *true*, then the spreadsheet performs a particular action; if the condition is *false*, then the spreadsheet performs a different action. For example, manufacturers frequently offer discounts to customers who order goods over a certain value. When sales managers are deciding how much discount they can afford to offer, the spreadsheet IF function is a valuable tool in making these calculations.

Jubilee 6th Form College's Purchasing Department obtains its stationery supplies from several different wholesalers (companies which sell to shops rather than individuals), depending on which one offers the best price for the particular item required. One of these companies, Select Stationery Ltd, is trying to encourage customers to buy all their supplies from it by offering a 1.5 per cent discount for orders over £400. Look at Figure 2.12 – cell **B5** shows the amount that the college has spent; cell **B3** shows the discount.

The status line shows the formula for the discount:

=IF(B5>399,B5*$B$3,0)

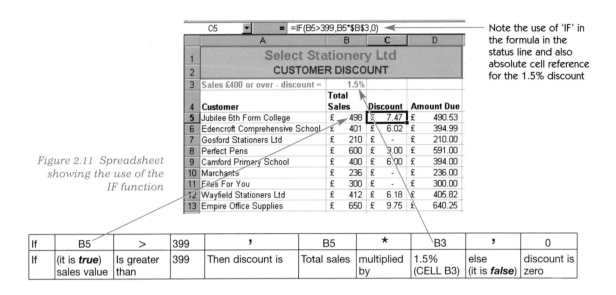

Note the use of 'IF' in the formula in the status line and also absolute cell reference for the 1.5% discount

C5 = =IF(B5>399,B5*$B$3,0)

**Select Stationery Ltd**
**CUSTOMER DISCOUNT**

| | A | B | C | D |
|---|---|---|---|---|
| 3 | Sales £400 or over - discount = | 1.5% | | |
| 4 | Customer | Total Sales | Discount | Amount Due |
| 5 | Jubilee 6th Form College | £ 498 | £ 7.47 | £ 490.53 |
| 6 | Edencroft Comprehensive School | £ 401 | £ 6.02 | £ 394.99 |
| 7 | Gosford Stationers Ltd | £ 210 | £ - | £ 210.00 |
| 8 | Perfect Pens | £ 600 | £ 9.00 | £ 591.00 |
| 9 | Camford Primary School | £ 400 | £ 6.00 | £ 394.00 |
| 10 | Marchants | £ 236 | £ - | £ 236.00 |
| 11 | Files For You | £ 300 | £ - | £ 300.00 |
| 12 | Wayfield Stationers Ltd | £ 412 | £ 6.18 | £ 405.82 |
| 13 | Empire Office Supplies | £ 650 | £ 9.75 | £ 640.25 |

*Figure 2.11 Spreadsheet showing the use of the IF function*

| If | B5 | > | 399 | , | B5 | * | B3 | , | 0 |
|---|---|---|---|---|---|---|---|---|---|
| If | (it is **true**) sales value | Is greater than | 399 | Then discount is | Total sales | multiplied by | 1.5% (CELL B3) | else (it is **false**) | discount is zero |

C5 = =IF(B5>399,B5*$B$3,0)

Notice that the formula has stayed the same, but the values in the Discount and Amount Due columns have changed

**Select Stationery Ltd**
**CUSTOMER DISCOUNT**

| | A | B | C | D |
|---|---|---|---|---|
| 3 | Sales £400 or over - discount = | 1.5% | | |
| 4 | Customer | Total Sales | Discount | Amount Due |
| 5 | Jubilee 6th Form College | £ 350 | £ - | £ 350.00 |
| 6 | Edencroft Comprehensive School | £ 520 | £ 7.80 | £ 512.20 |
| 7 | Gosford Stationers Ltd | £ 490 | £ 7.35 | £ 482.65 |
| 8 | Perfect Pens | £ 815 | £ 12.23 | £ 802.78 |
| 9 | Camford Primary School | £ 400 | £ 6.00 | £ 394.00 |
| 10 | Marchants | £ 380 | £ - | £ 380.00 |
| 11 | Files For You | £ 420 | £ 6.30 | £ 413.70 |
| 12 | Wayfield Stationers Ltd | £ 550 | £ 8.25 | £ 541.75 |
| 13 | Empire Office Supplies | £ 795 | £ 11.93 | £ 783.08 |

*Figure 2.12 Spreadsheet showing changes to the discount when the total sales have changed*

In other words, *if* it is *true* that the value in cell B5 is more than 399, *then* multiply the value in Cell B5 (£498) by Cell B3 (1.5 per cent) to calculate the discount payable. *If* it is *false*, that is, £399 or less (*else* or otherwise), enter '0' in the cells. In column **E** the discount is deducted from the sales to give the amount due. Notice what happens if the sales figures are changed – see Figure 2.12.

The managing director of Select Stationery Ltd is so pleased with the increase in business since introducing the discount for orders over £399, she has decided to introduce a second level of discount – 3 per cent for orders over £799. This can be done by 'nesting' two IF formulae.

It is important to give the larger discount first. If Excel is 'asked' to search for sales over £399 first, it will include all sales over this amount and apply the 1.5 per cent discount to them. It will not then look for amounts over

£799. If amounts over £799 are searched for first, the spreadsheet will find those amounts, and apply the discount, and then search again for the second IF function, that is, amounts over £399, and apply the 1.5 per cent discount to those values. Everything else will show zero discount. Figure 2.13 shows 'nesting' formulae.

C6 = =IF(B6>799,B6*$B$4,IF(B6>399,B6*$B$3,0))

**Select Stationery Ltd**
**CUSTOMER DISCOUNT**

| | A | B | C | D |
|---|---|---|---|---|
| 3 | Sales £400 or over - discount = | 1.5% | | |
| 4 | Sales £800 or over - discount = | 3% | | |
| 5 | Customer | Total Sales | Discount | Amount Due |
| 6 | Jubilee 6th Form College | £ 498 | £ 7.47 | £ 490.53 |
| 7 | Edencroft Comprehensive School | £ 401 | £ 6.02 | £ 394.99 |
| 8 | Gosford Stationers Ltd | £ 210 | £ - | £ 210.00 |
| 9 | Perfect Pens | £ 815 | £ 24.45 | £ 790.55 |
| 10 | Camford Primary School | £ 400 | £ 6.00 | £ 394.00 |
| 11 | Marchants | £ 236 | £ - | £ 236.00 |
| 12 | Files For You | £ 300 | £ - | £ 300.00 |
| 13 | Empire Office Supplies | £ 412 | £ 6.18 | £ 405.82 |
| 14 | Emprie Office Supplies | £ 795 | £ 11.93 | £ 783.08 |

*Figure 2.13 Two IF formulae. Up to seven IF functions can be nested in Microsoft® Excel 97 or 2000*

# Using the IF function to display text

The IF function can also be used to display text rather than to make a calculation. To make sure that Jubilee 6th Form College did not lose out on the discount by ordering goods worth just under £400, the purchase order clerk added an IF statement to the college purchase order form. If the net value of the order (that is, excluding VAT) is under £400 a message appears as shown in Figure 2.14.

In this case, the formula is:

=IF(E23<400,"REMEMBER DISCOUNT ORDERS £400 +","")

This time the formula in A24 is saying that if the total of the order in cell **E23** is less than **£400,** the words "REMEMBER DISCOUNT OVER £399" will appear on the screen to remind the clerk it may be worth adding in another item. If the order is £400 or more, then nothing appears on the screen.

## Activity

▷ Print the file: **SS Worksheet 8** from the Chapter 2 folder on the CD-ROM. This worksheet will enable you to create spreadsheets using 'IF' functions and gives further practice in using relative and absolute cell references.

| Formula | IF | E23 | < | 400 | , | "REMEMBER DISCOUNT ORDERS £400 +" | , | "" |
|---|---|---|---|---|---|---|---|---|
| Stands for | IF | (it is *true*) the Sub Total | is less than | 400 | then | Print the words between the inverted commas | else (it is *false*) | print nothing – because no text appears between the second set of inverted commas. If you wanted a different message to appear, you could include it within the second set |

Order excluding VAT is just below £400, so a prompt appears in the screen indicating that a discount is available for orders over £400

*Figure 2.14 Jubilee 6th Form College's purchase order contains an IF statement which brings a message on screen*

## Linking worksheets

It is common to link worksheets so that a value on one sheet is carried forward to another.

### Activity

> Print the file: **SS Worksheet 9** from the Chapter 2 folder on the CD-ROM. This worksheet will help you discover how spreadsheet worksheets can be linked in a spreadsheet workbook.

### Fact file

If you want to make the same change to matching cells on several worksheets, you can do this all at once by grouping the worksheets together. You can also use this method if you wish to create the same layout on several worksheets.

### Activity

> Print the files: **SS Worksheet 10, SS Worksheet 11** and **SS Worksheet 12** from the Chapter 2 folder on the CD-ROM. SS Worksheet 10 explains a quick method of editing linked worksheets in a spreadsheet file by grouping them, as well as how to print a selection of the worksheet. SS Worksheets 11 and 12 provide further practice in editing – cut, copy, paste and move techniques – as well as printing linked worksheets.

### Activity

> Print the file: **SS Worksheet 13** from the Chapter 2 folder on the CD-ROM. In this worksheet you will find out how to create linked worksheets.

## Macros

### What is a macro?

Have you ever used a cassette recorder to record a favourite song from the radio or a video recorder to record a football match or film? The purpose of recording it was so that you could play it back whenever you wanted to.

A macro is very similar – only this time you are recording a series of key strokes or mouse clicks that you regularly perform using the computer so you can 'play them back' automatically. It is a sequence of commands that is activated by a special key combination, selecting an icon or through the drop down menus.

For example, every time you click on the Print  icon you are activating a macro which automatically goes through the process of selecting File, Print, OK – one click instead of three. Clicking the icon is usually quicker than using the menus, but sometimes there are advantages to using the 'longer route', such as when you wish to print part of a document, or more than one copy.

### Checkpoint

A **macro** is a series of actions you perform regularly, which can be activated or operated by a special key combination or clicking on an icon.

### Purpose of macros

The general purpose of macros is to make the use of software applications convenient, easier and more effective. They do this:

- by reducing input errors
- by speeding up processing
- by standardising routine procedures.

All three save time by replacing often-used, sometimes lengthy series of keystrokes with shorter versions. This eliminates frequent retyping, and reduces the risk of typing errors. It also enables users who are unfamiliar with a program to replay sets of instructions pre-recorded by someone who is more familiar with the application.

There are many macros pre-prepared in the software. You probably already use them without realising it, for example, the icon on the toolbar ⟦ABC⟧ that starts the spell checker or the icon ⟦✏⟧ that activates the Drawing toolbar. Whenever you click the AutoSum button **Σ** to add up a column of numbers in a spreadsheet, you are using a calculation macro.

When you use the Chart ⟦📊⟧ icon to create a chart you are using a macro called a wizard. Wizards take you step by step through a sequence of actions and help you to carry out automated routines. Macros are also available in word processing and database applications.

You can also design your own personal macros for tasks that you need to repeat often. For example, it is useful to include a footer in your documents giving your name, the name of the file and the date it was created. This takes about 20–25 keystrokes depending on the length of your name. By creating a macro, the text could be inserted with only one keystroke each time it is needed.

All these examples show how the use of macros can save time and make everyday tasks easier. Creating macros in most applications software is easy. Although the way macros are recorded varies in different applications, the general procedure is the same. You start the macro recorder, record a sequence of actions and stop the recording. You can then run (play back) the macro whenever you need to perform that same sequence.

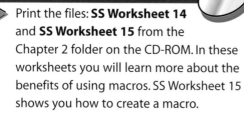

## Activity

▷ Print the files: **SS Worksheet 14** and **SS Worksheet 15** from the Chapter 2 folder on the CD-ROM. In these worksheets you will learn more about the benefits of using macros. SS Worksheet 15 shows you how to create a macro.

## Fact file

Macros can help organisations to deal with enquiries efficiently and collect information by standardising enquiry procedures. For example, a person wanting a quote for car insurance might telephone the insurance company and talk to an operator in the call centre. The operator will ask the customer a series of questions. He or she will be following screen prompts to request information, which will then be entered into a form on the screen. This is to ensure that all relevant information is gathered. When all the data has been entered, a macro will automatically calculate an insurance premium based on the information the customer has given. At the same time, the company can collect useful information to help it monitor its service and again macros can be used to total the number of times specific requests have been made.

## Graphs and charts

A textbook such as this will almost certainly include photos, drawings and diagrams, which help to clarify the information given in the text. Graphs or charts are often used to illustrate numerical information or data, and spreadsheet programs provide easy-to-use facilities to create them. However, it is important to choose the right type of graph/chart to display the data, and it must be clearly labelled. The 'reader' must be able to understand the graph/chart easily and find it useful to have the information presented in this way.

The most frequently used examples of graphs and charts are:

- bar graphs
- pie charts
- column charts
- line graphs.

A well-presented graph or chart might include:

- a main title
- axes titles
- axes scale labels
- data or series labels
- a legend (key).

The graphs created in spreadsheet files for Jubilee 6th Form College's inter-departmental quiz are shown below.

The bar graph showing the individual results for Jubilee Quiz 3 is shown in Figure 2.15. It includes a main title, axes titles and data labels. There is no legend as there is just one set of data for each competitor.

The graph is simple. It illustrates the data very clearly, shows at a glance how well each competitor did in the quiz and identifies their individual scores on the data labels.

To see how the same data would look on a pie chart – see Figure 2.16.

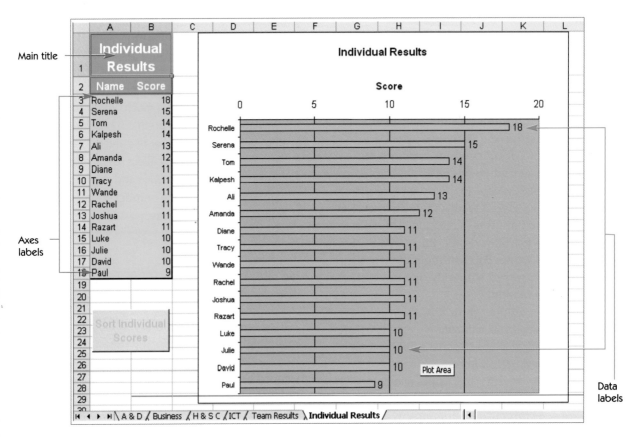

Figure 2.15 Bar graph showing individual results in the Jubilee Quiz competition

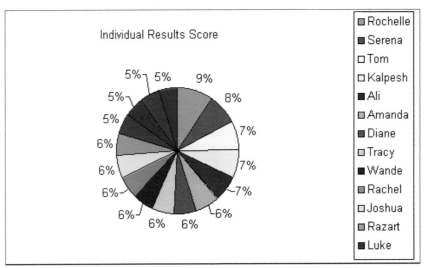

Figure 2.16 Individual scores in the Jubilee Quiz displayed as a pie chart

Charts or graphs should make the data easier to understand. Clearly, the pie charts on page 38 were not the right choice for these data. There are far too many segments (slices) in the pie to make any sense of the data.

Let's now consider the chart showing the team results by round – see Figure 2.17. This time a column chart was chosen, data labels, main and axes titles included, and also a legend. The legend is useful because the different colours represent the scores for different teams.

In this case, the data values have been included. You may feel they are helpful, or that they make the chart too cluttered.

Now, look at the same data displayed as a line graph – see Figure 2.18. Which do you prefer – the column chart or the line graph? Which represents the data most clearly?

Finally, the totals scored by the four teams in the Jubilee Quiz are shown both as a bar chart and a pie chart – see Figure 2.19. The bar chart is very clear, but even though the pie

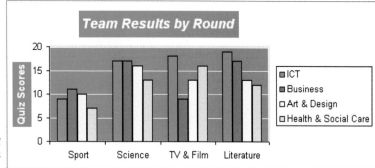

*Figure 2.17 Column chart showing results by round in the Jubilee Quiz*

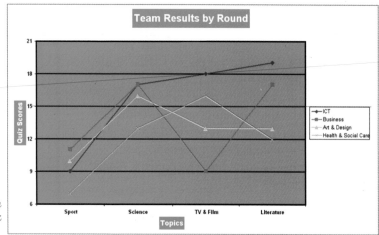

*Figure 2.18 Line graph showing team results by round in the Jubilee Quiz*

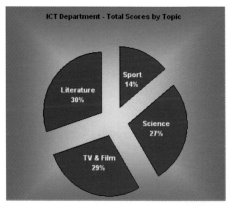

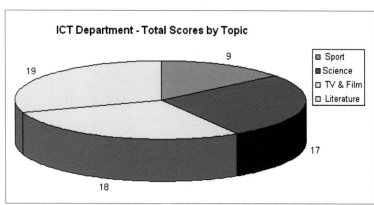

*Figure 2.19 Two different pie charts showing the final totals for the teams in the Jubilee Quiz*

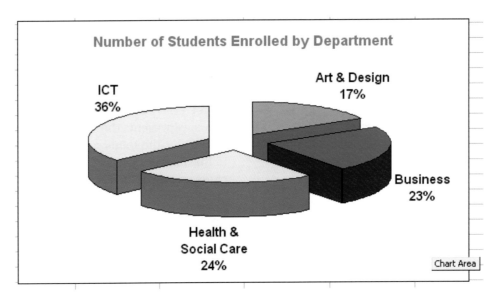

**Number of Students Enrolled by Department**

ICT
36%

Art & Design
17%

Business
23%

Health &
Social Care
24%

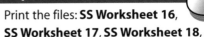
Chart Area

*Figure 2.20 Pie chart showing the percentage of students in each department at Jubilee 6th Form College*

chart has only four segments, the data is poorly presented. Pie charts are most suitable when there is a total value and each of the segments shows part of that total. The maximum marks possible for each team were 80 and the bar chart shows each team's score out of 80. The pie chart gives the score but doesn't show that it was out of 80.

Compare this with the pie chart shown in Figure 2.20. The pie segments show the number of students enrolled in each department at Jubilee 6th Form College as a percentage of the total number of students. The chart is clear and meaningful.

When creating graphs or charts, it is essential to be clear about what data you wish to illustrate as a graph or chart. Then when you have completed the graph or chart, check whether you made the right choice.

**Activity**

▷ Print the files: **SS Worksheet 16,**
▷ **SS Worksheet 17, SS Worksheet 18,**
**SS Worksheet 19** and **SS Worksheet 20**
from the Chapter 2 folder on the CD-ROM.
In SS Worksheet 16 you will learn how to create a column chart.
SS Worksheets 17–20 provide further practice in creating a variety of chart types and also how to customise the colour scheme and font.

# Organisation and analysis of structured information using database software

**Chapter 3**

This chapter introduces you to databases. You will find out how to:

- prepare a database structure and set up validation rules for different types of data
- set up a relationship between fields in two tables
- enter data, including the use of data entry forms
- search and sort, including the use of related tables

- produce reports showing the results of searches and sorts.

### What you will learn

Database structure
Checking for accuracy
Testing the database
Using the database
The user interface

## Overview: Databases

### What is a database?

You may think that a database is only to be found in computers, but a database is any organised collection of data or information. For example, your personal address or telephone book is a database. The more phone numbers or other information you add to your database, the more space you need and the harder it is to find the exact piece of information you want.

Every business, large or small, needs to store and access databases of information. For example, the company that publishes this book will have information on its authors, its customers, such as your own school or college, staff who work for the company, printers who produce the textbooks, and so on. A computer-based system can store vast amounts of data, organised for easy, quick access.

Nowadays, information about us is held on a wide range of databases because it is so much easier to store and transfer data held on a computer than it was when all databases were hand-written. Have you ever done any of the following:

- subscribed to a magazine
- opened a bank or building society account
- obtained a young person's identity card
- applied to a college
- joined a club or society?

If you have said 'yes' to any of the above, then details about you will be stored in a database file.

The important point to remember is that a database is a store of **related** data. Your school or college will have a database of student records, and each record will contain the same **items** of data such as:

- last name
- first name
- address
- telephone number
- date of birth.

So what are the benefits of storing data in a computerised database compared with using a paper-based system, such as an address book or a ring binder containing each student's application form filed in alphabetical order of surname?

| Computerised databases – advantages | Paper-based databases – disadvantages |
|---|---|
| A vast amount of **data** can be stored on one disk | A large number of files would be needed to store the same quantity of data |
| Records are entered once, but can be searched in all kinds of ways, e.g. alphabetically, numerically, selectively, by date. | Student details would be stored alphabetically. To search the files for information such as date of birth would be time consuming. To store them in order of date of birth would require the forms to be photocopied and filed in date order. There would then be the problem that both sets of files would need to be kept up-to-date |
| Searching for **information** is fast, even in a huge database | Searching for information can be very slow |
| Data can be lost but can usually be retrieved (found) if back-ups are kept | When a paper form is removed from the file, it can be easily mislaid, filed in the wrong place, lost or damaged |
| Easy to update details, e.g. a change of address | Easy to write a new address in an address book, but eventually the book wears out and all the data has to be written in a new book |
| Can perform calculations, e.g. the database can be searched to check the dates of birth of all students and provide a list of those aged over 18. The report will be produced almost immediately | To search the system, each form must be checked and then the relevant names copied onto a separate sheet. If the school or college has hundreds or even thousands of students this would be very slow and boring |

*The advantages of computer databases and the disadvantages of paper-based systems*

## Data and information

The table above uses the terms **data** and **information**. What is the difference?

- Data is the small, individual details such as the students' names and dates of birth.
- Information is what can be discovered from the data.

The table explained that by checking students' birth dates – the data – a list of those aged over 18 could be obtained – the information.

To give another example, if the Students' Association shop at Jubilee 6th Form College wanted to find out how much profit was being made from various items, the difference between cost price and selling price – two items of data – would be the profit – the information. The percentage profit could also be calculated, to provide further information on the most profitable lines – see the table below. Notice that there is not much difference between the selling price of the two items, but there is a 16 per cent difference in the profit. This kind of information is invaluable to businesses and very quick to obtain from a computerised system.

### Fact file

The fact that it is so easy to store and search vast amounts of data in a computerised database has its drawbacks. In June 2002 the Labour government was planning to extend the Regulation of Investigatory Powers Act (2000) to allow various government departments 'to have access to details of all our personal phone calls and e-mails'. The government originally said that the Bill would be aimed only at increasing the powers of the police, Customs, the intelligence services and the Inland Revenue. But it later became clear that seven government departments, every local authority, health bodies and 11 other organisations were to be included.

There was such an outcry in the press, by civil liberty campaigners, members of Parliament and the House of Lords that the government abandoned its plan.

| Data | | | Information | |
|---|---|---|---|---|
| Item | Cost price | Selling price | Profit | Percentage profit |
| Pritt Stick (large) | £2.59 | £3.00 | £0.41 | 14% |
| Scissors 5" | £1.83 | £3.00 | £0.91 | 30% |

*Data and information*

## Database structure

A database consists of a **file**, containing many **records**. Each record will include the **fields**, into which will be entered the **data**. Each record will contain the same fields, but sometimes a field is left blank in a particular record, for example if there is no e-mail address, the field for e-mail will be left blank.

Figure 3.1 shows a paper-based database – an address book – the file. An address book will usually include an A–Z index, and on each page the layout will be the same. Usually, there will be spaces for name, address, phone number, mobile number, fax and e-mail, which are the fields. All these fields together make up one record. The data entered into each field will be different for each record.

An electronic database will contain the same records, fields and data but is much more flexible. For example, it would be quite difficult to add birthdays in the address book shown in Figure 3.1 because there isn't room. You would have to keep a separate 'file'. In an electronic database, you could add another field very easily and include the extra data in the one file.

### Activity

▶ Print the file: **DB Worksheet 1** from the Chapter 3 folder on the CD-ROM. Use this worksheet to check your understanding of a database structure.

## Tables and forms

A database is usually designed through a table. Once the table design is complete, the Form view is created. The data entry clerk will use the Form view to enter new data or look at existing data on screen. The layout on screen can be designed in a variety of styles, just as forms for different purposes are laid out differently. You may wish to view one record at a time on screen or you might want to see all records listed under the different field names. A computerised database provides great flexibility in the way you look at the data and it is easy to switch between viewing one record on screen or a list of all records.

Jubilee College's Students' Association Shop purchases most of its stationery requirements from Select Stationery Ltd, a wholesaler. Select Stationery purchases the products from several different manufacturers and keeps records of the suppliers and the stock in a database. Figure 3.2 shows the Table or Datasheet view for records of three suppliers. Figure 3.3 shows just one record.

### Activity

▶ Print the file: **DB Worksheet 2** in the Chapter 3 on the CD-ROM. This worksheet shows you how to view records in both table and form view, and also how to enter new records.

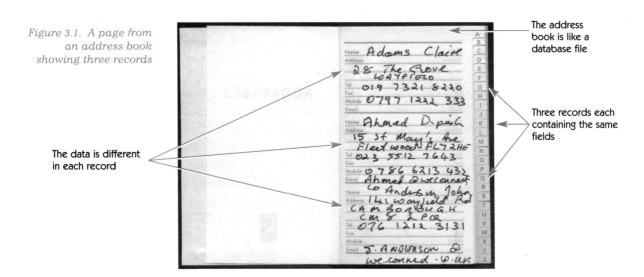

*Figure 3.1. A page from an address book showing three records*

The address book is like a database file

Three records each containing the same fields

The data is different in each record

The column headings are the field names

Each row in the table is one record

| Supplier ID | Supplier name | Address | Town | Post Code | Contact Title | First Name | Last Name | Job Title | Phone Number | Fax Number | E-mail Address |
|---|---|---|---|---|---|---|---|---|---|---|---|
| NEA005 | Neat Nibs | 125 Fleetwood Road | WAYFIELD | ER6 7TH | Mrs | Margaret | Jones | Product Manager | (019) 5233 6661 | (019) 5233 6662 | NeatNibs@ weconnect.co.uk |
| PER001 | Perfect Paper Ltd | Unit 10 The Business Park | FLEETWOOD | FL2 8HE | Mr | Martin | Wyman | Stationery Manager | (023) 4477 8813 | (023) 4477 8814 | PerfectPaper@ weconnect.co.uk |
| TOT010 | Total Office Ltd | 89 Cumberland Avenue | WAYFIELD | ER18 6RE | Mr | Ranjit | Patel | Sales Manager | (097) 6082 7934 | (019) 6082 7935 | TotalOffice@ weconnect.co.uk |

*Figure 3.2 Database records shown in Table or Datasheet View*

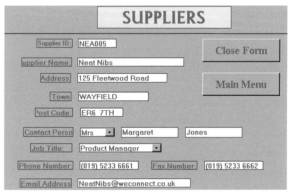

*Figure 3.3 One database record shown in Form View*

## Database design

When planning a computerised database, it is important to *think carefully* about the design *before* you start creating the fields in the database. It would be possible to create every field as text, because text allows you to enter letters, numbers and/or symbols into the field. However, if you used all text fields, you would not be able to:

- make calculations, such as finding out the VAT on the price of an item
- use a date field to search for orders placed in a specific month, or before or after a particular date
- search easily for a particular category, such as paper, pens/pencils.

To enable you to carry out these tasks, the field design for the price of the item must be numerical, the field design for the date an order is placed must be in date format and it will be much easier to find a category if the categories are specified (identified) in a list. Let's look at this in more detail.

## Setting up a computerised database

### Field names, field length, field data type

Once you have decided the purpose of your database, you then need to decide the following:

1. **The fields you need** – that is, the *names* of the fields, e.g. Supplier ID (identity), Supplier name. The name of the field indicates which data should be entered into it.

2. **The data type for each field** – you could just use text for everything, because text will accept both letters and numbers. However, as explained above, your database would be much less effective when it comes to searching, and it would not be possible to make any calculations.

3. **Encoding the data** – you might want to include a gender field to show male or female, but the field might be encoded as 'm' or 'f', keeping the field size to one digit, which reduces the space required for storage and display.

4. **The length of the fields** – how many characters are needed in each field? With fields such as names and addresses, you need to allow enough space to enter a long name or long street reference, although it is possible to increase the length of the field later if necessary.

For numerical data, you will need to decide whether the field can be an integer (whole number) or whether decimal places are required, and if so how many. You would not design a field with decimal places for the price of a house, as house prices are not quoted as £56,789.58p. However, the price of stationery items ranges from less than a £1 upwards, therefore two decimal places would be necessary. So you might fix the length of the field for a house price at seven digits, which would allow a price up to £9,999,999. For items sold by Select Stationery, you would probably fix the length at three spaces to the left and two to the right of the decimal point, which would allow prices up to £999.99.

It is good practice to have just enough space for the data you wish to enter, as unnecessary extra space can waste the memory capacity of the computer and increase the display area on screen. It is much easier to look at a record, if all or most of the details are visible in one screen page.

5 **Is the field required?** – is it essential to have data in the field or can it remain blank? For example, since not everyone has an e-mail address, it would not be sensible to make a field for e-mail required.

The table below lists some typical fields which are useful in a database (you may not find all these data types available in the database program you are using).

| Type of field | Purpose | Advantages/possible uses |
|---|---|---|
| **Text/character** – sometimes called alphanumeric | Any data – letters, numbers or symbols on the keyboard – can be entered into a text field | Names/addresses<br>Where you might include extra detail/description |
| **Numerical:**<br>Integer<br>Select the number of digits required, e.g. 3 | A whole number<br>Allows space for a maximum of three digits, e.g. 156 | Restricts data entry to whole numbers<br>Reduces the risk of errors<br>Can be sorted in numerical order<br>Can also ask for list of items above/below or equal to a specific number<br>Reduces space for storage and display |
| Decimal | A number with decimal places – you can usually decide on how many to the right and left of the decimal point, e.g. 13.67 | Suitable for money where prices include pence, e.g. 13.67<br>Measurements, e.g. 4.25 km |
| Currency | Can be set as an integer or with decimal places | Suitable for money and would show the currency specified e.g. £3.67, $287, €18 |
| Counter or AutoNumber | A numeric value – as each new record is entered, the counter automatically selects the next number in the sequence | Suitable for a member ID, student ID, account no, and so on<br>The operator does not have to enter the number, and if a number has already been used, the computer will not allow you to use it again<br>Ensures that each member ID, account number, and so on, remains unique |
| **Date** | A typical date format will be prepared, e.g. —/—/— | Restricts data entry to 1–31 for the day, and 1–12 for the month<br>Reduces the risk of errors<br>Can be used to calculate a person's age, which will automatically update once his or her birthday has passed<br>Can search for:<br>• birthdays in a given month<br>• those older or younger than a given age<br>• birthdays between particular dates<br>• orders placed before, after or on a given date |
| **Time** | A typical time format will be prepared, e.g. —:—:—<br>Data entry is limited to the selection that has been set up | Might be used where employees are paid by the hour:<br>• Hours worked can be calculated from time clocked on and off<br>• Wages can be calculated on length of time worked multiplied by the hourly rate<br>Speeds up data entry |
| **Category list:**<br>male/female<br>true/false<br>colours:<br>  red/blue/green/<br>  yellow<br>yes/no | Choice fields can also be encoded, e.g. M for male, F for female, R for red | Can search for specific entries, such as 'male', 'true', 'green' or 'yes'<br>Reduces space for storage and display |

*Fields used in databases*

## Relationships

When a database is designed, it is usually divided into two or more sections known as tables, which are **related** or connected to each other, rather than having many separate files or one huge file. Most businesses would probably have several related tables in their databases, but let's look at just two related tables in the Select Stationery database – Suppliers and Stock.

The Suppliers table includes the fields:

- Supplier ID (a unique reference)
- Supplier Name
- Address
- Town
- Post Code
- Contact Person – Title
- First Name
- Last Name
- Telephone No
- Fax
- E-mail.

The Stock table includes the fields:

- Catalogue Reference (each item would have a unique reference)
- Description
- Trade Price
- Category
- Supplier ID.

To connect the tables it is essential that one unique field is repeated in each of the linked tables. In the Suppliers and Stock tables above, the fields for Supplier ID link the tables. Figure 3.4 also illustrates this point.

When tables are linked in this way, it is possible to search each table separately or to search using data in both tables. From the *data* in the databases above, it would be possible to find out *information*, such as:

1  the contact person for a given supplier
2  which items are available in a particular product category
3  which supplier to contact to restock a particular item.

Notice that the first 2 queries search for data in one table only but the third query searches for data from both tables.

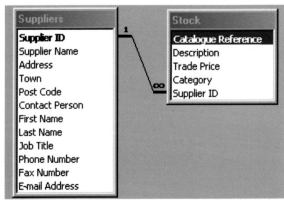

Figure 3.4  *The relationship between two tables in the Select Stationery database*

## Key fields – primary and foreign

You have already seen that each record in a database usually has one unique field, which identifies that record as different from every other record in the file, or in table format identifies each row from every other row. This field is the **primary key**. When you enrolled at school or college you were probably given a student ID number, which is different from every other student in the school or college. It is essential that the primary key is unique, otherwise the computer will not be able to identify the record required if two students have the same name. Records are automatically sorted in order of the primary key. Did you notice the order in which the records in Select Stationery were stored changed when you entered the new records?

When this unique field is used in another table, it is known as a **foreign key**. In the Select Stationery database the primary and foreign keys are shown in the table below.

| Table | Primary key | Foreign key |
| --- | --- | --- |
| Suppliers | Supplier ID | |
| Stock | Catalogue Reference | Supplier ID |

*Select Stationery database*

## Wizards

Designing a database is a complex procedure. To help you, modern database programs include **wizards** to make it easier to design the table. A wizard takes you step-by-step through the process, giving you choices at each stage. For example, if you are setting up a new database file, the Table Wizard has samples already designed. Wizards are available for many stages of database design (for example creating a form from the table or designing a query or report).

Figure 3.5 shows a wizard where a form is being created from the Suppliers table. You can select which fields you want to use by highlighting the relevant one and clicking on the > box. If you click on the >> box, all fields will be selected. Even if you use the wizard, you can still customise the table to suit your particular purpose – you can rename fields,

alter the format or you can add additional fields, which are not already included in the sample.

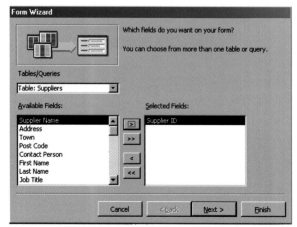

*Figure 3. 5 Form Wizard dialogue box*

## Combo boxes and check boxes

Combo boxes and check boxes help make data entry easier and more accurate.

### Combo boxes

Combo *boxes* are used where the data is limited to a particular selection. For example:

- male/female
- child/adult
- red/blue/yellow/green
- part time/full time
- Mr, Mrs, Miss, Ms.

Figure 3.6 shows examples of combo boxes from the Select Stationery database. The data entry clerk does not have to key in the words. He or she simply clicks on the correct choice, which speeds up data entry and reduces the risk of error.

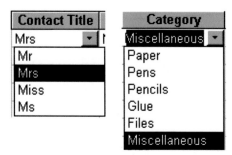

*Figure 3.6 Combo boxes from the Select Stationery database showing drop down lists*

## Check boxes

Check boxes are used where there is a yes/no option. The data entry clerk clicks in the box to indicate 'yes' and a ☑ appears, or leaves the box blank to indicate 'no' – see Figure 3.7.

**Delivery Required**

| |
|---|
| ☑ |
| ☐ |
| ☑ |
| ☐ |
| ☐ |
| ☐ |

*Figure 3.7 A check box*

## Checking for accuracy

The most sophisticated data handling system in the world will be useless if the data entered into the system is not accurate. A common phrase used to describe this is 'Garbage in, garbage out'.

Manual systems rely on the operator to proof read for accuracy, whereas a computerised system can build in accuracy checks to *reduce* the risk of errors.

## Validation rules

The word valid means suitable. If you wish to watch a film, you might hire it from a video library. Films are recorded on video tape or on DVD. If you have a DVD player, and the film is only on tape, you won't be able to watch it because the DVD player is not suitable or valid for watching video tape. Two very important **validation** checks used in computerised data-bases are **type** and **range checks**. If invalid data is entered, the computer will indicate an error.

## Type check

The table below shows the various data types that may be used in a database. If a field has been designed for numbers, the computer will not accept letters in that field. If a field has been designed to accept a choice of titles – Mr, Mrs, Miss, Ms – it should not accept any other title in that field. Clearly, it is still possible for the data entry clerk to make errors, but some errors will be obvious immediately, often by a bleep and an error message on screen. Figure 3.8 shows an example of an error message.

| Data to be entered | Data actually entered | Data correct |
|---|---|---|
| 25 | 25 | ✓ |
| 25 | 52 | ✗ – but it is accepted because it is of the correct *type* |
| 25 | q5 | ✗ – because 'q' is not a number, that is, the *wrong* type |
| Mr | Mr | ✓ |
| Mr | Mrs | ✗ – but it is accepted because Mrs is one of the options, that is, the correct *type* |
| Mr | Doctor | ✗ – because Doctor is not one of the titles listed in the choice, that is, the *wrong* type |

*A type check*

## Range check

A number field may include a second check as well as the type check. The field can be limited within a set *range*, by giving a minimum or maximum figure or both. For example, a date field will include an automatic range so that 13 will not be accepted as a month and 31 will not be accepted as a day for the months of February, April, June, September and November – see the table below.

**Microsoft Access**

**The value you entered isn't valid for this field.**

For example, you may have entered text in a numeric field or a number that is larger than the FieldSize setting permits.

OK

*Figure 3.8 An error message when the date entered was 31/02/56*

| Data to be entered | Data actually entered | Data correct |
|---|---|---|
| 13/04/86 | 13/04/86 | ✓ |
| 13/04/86 | 15/05/86 | ✗ – but it is accepted because it is within the correct range |
| 13/04/86 | 31/04/86 | ✗ – computer immediately signals an error, because there are only 30 days in April; 31 is outside the *range* |

*A range check*

## Activity

▷ Print the file: **DB Worksheet 3** from the Chapter 3 folder on the CD-ROM. This worksheet gives you the opportunity to learn more about designing a database.

## Verification

To verify means to check. Verification can be carried out in the following ways:

- A visual check where the operator reads the entries and checks them again against the original document.
- An oral check where a second operator reads the data out loud from the original document to the first operator, who checks on screen that the entries match. This is particularly useful for numerical data, as it is easy to make keying in errors with numbers. Numerical errors cannot easily be spotted just by proof reading, whereas spelling or grammatical errors, or words missed out or repeated, are more noticeable.
- Entering the data twice. The computer indicates any differences. An example, which you may well have used, is setting a password. Because the original entry is masked, usually displayed as asterisks, you are always asked to enter the password again, just in case you made an error the first time – see Figure 3.9.

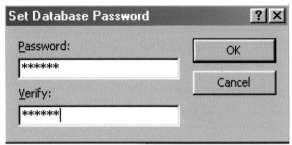

*Figure 3.9 Entering the data twice – to confirm your password*

## Fact file

Did you know that when you use the spell checker, the word is checked against a dictionary stored in the computer? If the word does not match one in the list, then it is queried. This is known as validation.

## Testing the database

Once you have created the fields and built the relationships, you should check that the database is working as you intended. You will need to consider testing the following:

- Entry of data by type, e.g. will the field accept text when it should only accept numbers?
- Entry of data out of range, e.g. there are no more than 31 days in a month – will the field accept 32 as the day in a date field?
- Is it easy to enter, add, delete or change data? If not, does the layout need changing? Is the field format unsuitable?
- Is it easy to move between different screens in the database you have set up? If not, what can you do to simplify it? Do the command buttons open the right form? (See Figure 3.17, page 55)

## Log of testing

You should make a log of testing in which you decide on data to enter into each field, the result you expect and then compare it with what actually happens. Let's look at some examples of test data, which might be used for the tables or forms in the Select Stationery database.

| Field name | Field type | Data to enter | Expected result | Actual result |
|---|---|---|---|---|
| **Suppliers table** | | | | |
| Supplier ID | Text with input mask – LLL000 | NEA005 | Accepted | Accepted |
| Supplier ID | Text with input mask – LLL000 | NE6005 | Rejected | Rejected |
| Contact Person | Combo box – Mr, Mrs, Miss, Ms | Mrs | Accepted | Accepted |
| Contact Person | Combo box – Mr, Mrs, Miss, Ms | Doctor | Rejected | Rejected – but perhaps you need to consider adding this category to the list |
| Job Title | Combo box – Product Manager, Sales Manager, Stationery Manager | Product Manager | Accepted | Accepted |
| Job Title | Combo box – Product Manager, Sales Manager, Stationery Manager | Chief Buyer | Rejected | Accepted – did you remember to select 'Yes' in the 'Limit to List' box? |
| **Stock table** | | | | |
| Trade Price | Currency | £4.99 | Accepted | Accepted |
| Trade Price | Currency | Four pounds ninety-nine pence | Rejected | Rejected |
| Trade Price | Currency | Four pounds ninety-nine pence | Rejected | Accepted – field type probably set as text and not currency |
| **Stock form – testing calculated control for the VAT field. VAT = 17.5%** | | | | |
| VAT | Currency | Automatic calculation based on Trade Price – 0.30p | 0.05p | 0.05p – correct |
| VAT | Currency | Automatic calculation based on Trade Price – £1.00 | 0.18p | £1.80 – need to check data for Trade Price is correct and check the formula for the calculation. |

*Log of testing*

It is very important **NOT** to assume the database will work as you intend. If the result of your testing is not as expected, you need to change the design. Once you have tested the database successfully, the data from your information sources can be entered.

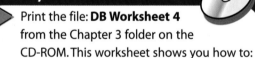

## Activity

▷ Print the file: **DB Worksheet 4** from the Chapter 3 folder on the CD-ROM. This worksheet shows you how to:
- implement the design you planned in DB Worksheet 3
- prepare a log of testing
- enter the data from the test log.

## Activity

▷ Print the file: **DB Worksheet 5** from the Chapter 3 folder on the CD-ROM. This worksheet provides further practice in database design as well as building a relationship between two tables.

## Using the database

### Data capture

You are now ready to enter the real data. This may be by keying in the data from a paper-based form, or by direct data capture. Direct data capture removes the need to key in data from source documents, which reduces the risk of error and is much faster. It is becoming a more common method of transferring data into the computer. Examples of direct data capture include:

- bar codes read by light pens or scanners – used in most shops
- magnetic ink character recognition – used on bank cheques to input the unique branch sort code, customer account number and amount
- optical mark readers (OMR) – often used for attendance registers in schools and colleges and for marking multiple choice examination papers
- optical character recognition (OCR), which identifies the *shape* of the character – often used to scan text into a word processor, which can then be edited as required

- hand-held terminals – used for gas or electric meter readings. The new reading is logged from the meter into the hand-held terminal. This data is uploaded from the terminal into the gas or electricity company's database, from which the customer's bill is calculated.

## Paper-based sources for data capture

Any kind of form can be used as a paper-based source of data capture. Examples include application forms for college or university, driving licence, car/house/health insurance, TV licence. It is also common for such data to be given over the telephone and entered directly into the computer without actually writing any details on paper. Where a paper-based source is used, it is very important that the data capture form and the computer

screen follow a similar pattern so that it is easy and quick to copy the data into the computer. If the order in which the data is presented is very different on the form to that on the screen, it is much more likely that a data entry error will occur or that the process will be much slower.

## Editing the database

Editing a computerised database is usually much easier than making changes to a manual system. From time to time, you may need to:

- add new fields or change existing ones
- edit a record – e.g. if an address changes
- add a new record – e.g. a new customer
- delete a record – e.g. a product item is discontinued.

With the small sample of records available in the Select Stationery database, it does not take long to look at each one in turn until you find a particular record. However, this would be time consuming if the database had hundreds of records. You can 'ask' the computer to search the database by selecting Edit and Find, entering suitable data into a relevant field and clicking on Find Next – see Figure 3.11. If a record contains matching data in that field, the record will be located (found).

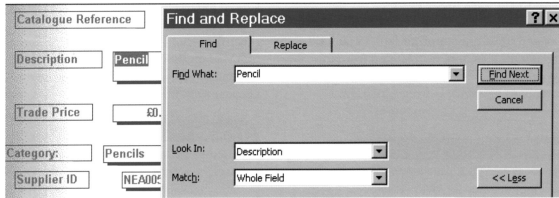

*Figure 3.11 Searching for a record*

When you add a new record to the database, it will automatically be filed in the correct order of the primary key. Any fields that have been indexed will also be updated automatically.

## Database queries

Searching the database to find specific information is known as a query. The query defines the parameters, that is, what do you need to know. The result of your search/query may be presented on screen or printed on paper. A well-designed database file, with appropriately linked tables, allows the user to search for – to *query* – information by selecting fields from *any* of the tables.

Let's imagine that the buyer at Select Stationery wants to identify in which towns the suppliers are based. It would be possible to *ask* the database to select just this information. Figure 3.12 might be result of this query, although in practice Select Stationery would probably use many more suppliers.

### Towns : Select Query

| Supplier Name | Town |
|---|---|
| Neat Nibs | WAYFIELD |
| Paper Clips | NEWTOWN |
| Perfect Paper Ltd | FLEETWOOD |
| Stunning Stationery | CAMBOROUGH |
| Total Office Ltd | WAYFIELD |
| Wayfield Office Supplies | WAYFIELD |

*Figure 3.12 The result of a query*

To find this information in a manual system you would need to:

● look at each individual card
● make a list of the company name and town.

This would be a slow process if Select Stationery had 50 or more suppliers! The chances of making a mistake when copying the information or missing out a supplier is also high. A computerised database will use the same criteria, but find the information very quickly. Remember, that if you design the database using only text fields, searching for information will be limited. Fields such as date, number, choice make it much easier to search for specific criteria, as explained in the table on page 45. Let's now look in more detail at the different ways of carrying out a database query.

### Sort by selected key field

This means presenting a query in a particular order, for example alphabetical, numerical, order of date. The order can be **ascending** (lowest to highest), that is, A–Z or 1–100, or **descending** (highest to lowest), that is, Z–A or 100–1. The results of the query shown in Figure 3.12 might have been requested *in alphabetical order of town* – the selected key field – in which case the report would have looked like Figure 3.13. You could have chosen alphabetical order when designing the query, but it is very easy to sort a query after saving it, by highlighting the field name – in this case Town – and clicking on the A–Z 🔤 icon.

## Towns : Select Query

| Supplier Name | Town |
|---|---|
| Stunning Stationery | CAMBOROUGH |
| Perfect Paper Ltd | FLEETWOOD |
| Paper Clips | NEWTOWN |
| Wayfield Office Supplies | WAYFIELD |
| Total Office Ltd | WAYFIELD |
| Neat Nibs | WAYFIELD |
|  |  |

*Figure 3.13 The query sorted in alphabetical order of town*

## Using comparison operators

If you search a database using comparison operators, you will be looking for a number **greater than**, **less than** or **equal to**:

- < – less than
- > – greater than
- = – equal to
- <> – not equal to
- <= – less than or equal to
- >= – greater than or equal to.

## Using logical operators

When you search a database using logical operators, the criteria for selection is **and**, **or**, **not**. The computer checks to see whether it is true or false that any applicants match the criteria. If a *true* match is found, then the records will be displayed.

The search shown in Figures 3.14 and 3.15 illustrate the use of comparison and logical operators. Figure 3.14 shows the Design View of the query and Figure 3.15 shows the information produced from the query. The buyer at Select Stationery wishes to find out which pens are available at under £2.00 in price and the name of the supplier. The criteria for the search were:

- Trade Price less than 2.00
- Category – Pens.

Look at the Criteria line in Figure 3.14 – the selection is limited by the criteria, which requested items priced *less than* £2.00 (the comparison operator*) and* (the logical operator) in the Pens category.

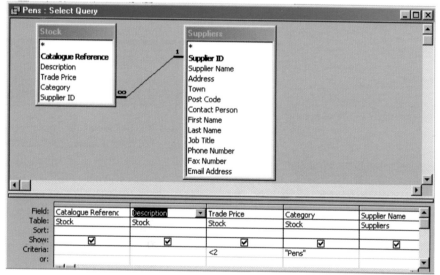

*Figure 3.14 The Design View of a query*

## Pens : Select Query

| Catalogue Reference | Description | Trade Price | Category | Supplier Name |
|---|---|---|---|---|
| 300 781 | Highlighters - pocket size - 6 pack - assorted colours | 1.94 | Pens | Neat Nibs |
| 297 146 | Pens stick - 12 pack | 1.19 | Pens | Neat Nibs |

*Figure 3.15 The result of the query shown in Figure 3.14*

## Database reports

The result of a query is presented in table format. If you wish to present the results with a specific layout, you can design a **report**. Figure 3.15 shows the query in table format, whereas Figure 3.16 shows the same query in report format. You can choose various options in the report design, and once again wizards can help you design the report layout quickly and easily.

### Pens

| | |
|---|---|
| Catalogue Reference | 300 781 |
| Description | Highlighters - pocket size - 6 pack - assorted colours |
| Trade Price | 1.94 |
| Category | Pens |
| Supplier Name | Neat Nibs |
| Catalogue Reference | 297 146 |
| Description | Pens stick - 12 pack |
| Trade Price | 1.19 |
| Category | Pens |
| Supplier Name | Neat Nibs |

*Figure 3.16 The Report view of the same query shown in Figure 3.15*

## The user interface

One of the benefits of a modern database is the ease with which user friendly screens can be developed. You need to know how to design and create effective data-entry screens, both in content and layout, and also simple methods of moving from screen to screen.

## Layout of screen

Although the Form Wizard makes it very easy to create a Form view from the Table view, the result will probably be in column format, where all fields are listed one under the other (as shown in Figure 3.16). The right-hand side of the window is wasted, and the form may not fit in the screen window. Another common ready-prepared format is tabular, where all the field names are listed across the screen with the data in rows underneath. This is not much different from Table view. It may be convenient to use the wizard so that all the fields are *transferred* from the table into the form, but you can then rearrange them into a more appropriate layout.

## Moving between screens

A complex database is likely to include several forms. It is much easier for the user to access the form required if an opening screen has been designed with command buttons to open each part of the database – see Figure 3.17. It is also possible to include command buttons on a form to switch back to the opening screen. Did you find the buttons on the opening form for Select Stationery helpful?

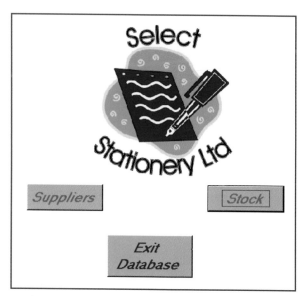

*Figure 3.17 An opening screen with buttons. If you click on the relevant button, it will take you to the form named, for example Suppliers. The button 'Exit Database' takes you out of the program. The buttons on the Suppliers form will close the form or take you back to the Main Menu*

It is easy and quick to learn how to enter data into a ready-made database, but much more complex to design an effective database yourself. However, if you have completed all the worksheets correctly, you will have learned a great deal about database design.

The most important key to success when creating a database as part of your Applied GCSE portfolio, is to *plan carefully* using the skills explained in the textbook and the worksheets, *before* you begin to create the tables and fields on the computer.

# Organisation and presentation of information using multimedia software

**Chapter 4**

This chapter looks at Microsoft® PowerPoint® which is an example of multimedia presentation software. You will learn the necessary skills to create a presentation using this software. Web authoring tools, such as Microsoft® FrontPage®, are also an example of multimedia software and you should refer to Chapter 5 to learn more about using FrontPage® to create a website.

## What you will learn

Text on slides
Using clip art
Viewing slides
Features to improve your slides
Special effects
Other useful features

## Checkpoint

A **storyboard** consists of boxes that show the slides/screens/web pages of a presentation, each box showing what will appear. A **structure diagram** is a planning tool used to show how the components (i.e. slides, screens or web pages) of a multimedia presentation link together.

## Overview: Multimedia presentations

### Producing a presentation in PowerPoint

A PowerPoint® presentation is made up of individual parts, called **slides**. You can build up a series of slides to create a presentation. Often you will see a PowerPoint® presentation displayed through a digital projector onto a screen – your teachers may do this in your lessons. Presentations can also be shown on a computer screen as an on-screen display, for example the presentation about forthcoming theatre productions mentioned above.

PowerPoint® has many features to help you make your presentation look professional. You can:

- make the text move, slide and scroll
- include clip art and graphics
- include digitised film clips

- include sound – short highlights or a complete commentary.

It is important to **plan** a presentation prior to creating it. A storyboard as shown in Figure 4.1 was used to plan the presentation you will create in the worksheets for this chapter. A storyboard was also used to plan the simple website described in Chapter 5. In both these examples, a structure diagram was created to show how the slides of the PowerPoint® presentation, and the pages of the FrontPage® web, link together. Look at page 64 for examples of structure diagrams.

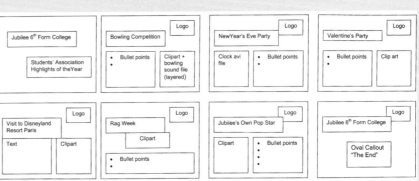

*Figure 4.1 A storyboard*

# Wizards

You may already be familiar with the wizards used in applications such as Access. In PowerPoint®, **AutoContent Wizard** will guide you step by step through the creation of a presentation – see Figure 4.2.

*Figure 4.2 The AutoContent Wizard*

# Templates

PowerPoint® provides a wide range of **design** and **presentation templates** that you can use to create a professional looking presentation – see Figure 4.3.

A design template is a file that has been designed with special backgrounds and layouts ready to use. Using a design template is a time saving feature, and can also be useful if you are not particularly artistic. One useful feature is that if you do not like the colour of the background, you can change the colour to one of your choice.

Each design template always has two slide designs – one for the title slide (the first slide in a presentation) and one for the remaining slides. This means that the title slide will have a slightly different design to the other slides in a presentation.

Presentation templates are pre-structured presentations that you can choose to suit a specific purpose. For example, a company selling computer equipment could use the Selling a Product or Service presentation template to produce a promotional presentation for customers – see Figure 4.4.

## Checkpoint

A **template** is a standard layout for text, graphics and formatting in a document. Many are supplied with software such as Microsoft® Office. You can also design and save your own.

*Figure 4.3 The Design Template window*

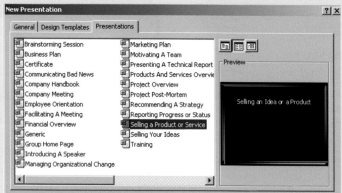

*Figure 4.4 The Presentation Template window*

One drawback of using either presentation or
design templates without making any changes to
them is that anyone who has used PowerPoint®
will be familiar with them and there is a good
chance that they will have seen them used
before. They may remember a previous
presentation and lose the point of your one!

## AutoLayouts

You may wish to design your own slides from
scratch, or to choose one of the AutoLayouts
provided by PowerPoint®. By selecting each
picture you can see a description of the slide
on the right of the dialogue box. There are 24
different layouts, including one blank slide.
There are layouts with places for charts,
pictures, bulleted lists or even movies – see
Figure 4.5.

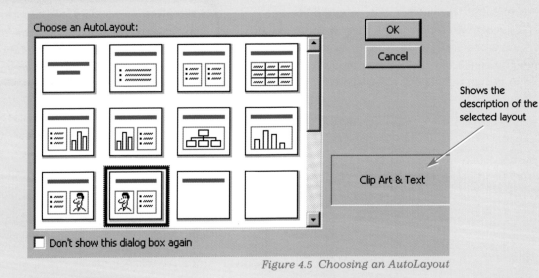

*Figure 4.5 Choosing an AutoLayout*

## Text on slides

Many of the features that you may already be
familiar with from using other packages such
as Microsoft® Word or CorelDraw can be
applied to text in PowerPoint®. You can format
text using bold, italic, underline or shadow and
align text to the left, centre, right or justify it.
The colour of text can be changed and you can
choose from a wide range of fonts and sizes.
PowerPoint® also includes a spellchecker.

Some AutoLayout designs allow for text areas
that are specifically for lists. When you start
typing in one of these, a bullet will appear
before the text. You can format the bullets to
different styles, just as you would in Word.

## Boxes/Frames

The design of each slide is broken down into areas called boxes (sometimes referred to as frames), each of which holds an object. The object can be a list, a title, a piece of clip art, a chart, and so on. Each box can be copied, moved and resized in the same way as you would a piece of clip art. Any box, irrespective of whether the object it contains is a picture, chart, text or clipart, can be layered. This means that you can put one box on top of another to create interesting slides. A box can even be rotated as shown in Figure 4.6.

A box with text which has been rotated

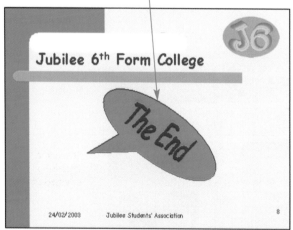

*Figure 4.6 shows a Callout AutoShape with a Text Box containing the words "The End" rotated and layered above it*

## Using clip art and pictures

Have you ever heard the expression 'A picture is worth a thousand words'? Including pictures in your presentation will help to make it more interesting, easier to understand and more memorable – see Figure 4.7. Inserting clip art or pictures into a slide is very easy.

PowerPoint® comes with a clip art gallery and, if you have an Internet connection, you can click on the Clips Online button on the Menu bar. This will connect you to Microsoft's® database of free clip art. You can also buy a CD-ROM full of pictures and clip art which you can use. Remember though to check that you are

*allowed* to use a piece of clip art. You may have to get permission from the creator. (You will learn more about this in Unit 3.)

Clip art has been used to liven up this slide

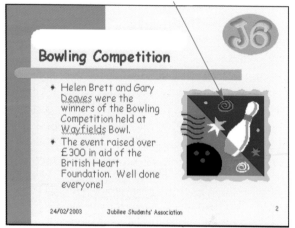

*Figure 4.7 Using clip art*

### Fact file

Clip art, unlike other pictures, is not defined as a series of dots. Clip art comprises mathematically defined lines and curves. Therefore, a clip art picture doesn't have a natural size. This means that you can adjust the clip art picture to any size you want, and the computer will draw the lines and curves to that size without losing any of its details or looking grainy.

## Viewing slides

There are five ways to view slides:

- **Normal view** displays three panes – outline, slide and note – see Figure 4.8 (overleaf). You can adjust the pane sizes by dragging the pane borders. Slides are displayed individually and you can work on the slides in this view. The notes pane allows you to enter notes that you want to make about a slide, which will help you when making a presentation.
- **Outline view** displays an outline of your presentation. This view is particularly useful for entering/editing text on the slides.
- **Slide view** displays one slide at a time. You can create or edit your slide in this view.

- **Slide Sorter view** allows you to view all the slides together in miniature – see Figure 4.9 (overleaf). Using this view, you can delete slides, change their order or insert new slides. You can also copy existing slides and paste them exactly where you want them.
- **Slide Show view** allows you to view your presentation – click on the Slide Show icon.

Figure 4.10 (below) shows the slide view icons.

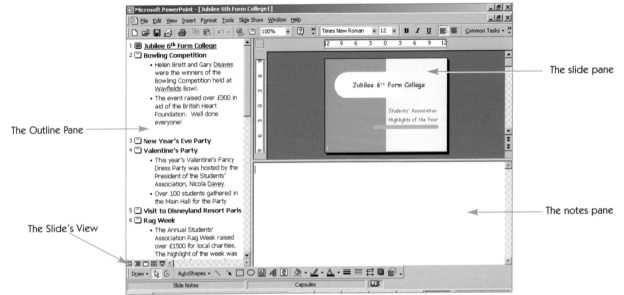

The slide pane

The Outline Pane

The notes pane

The Slide's View

Figure 4.8 The slide in Normal view

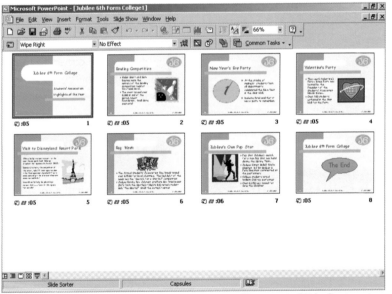

Figure 4.9 Slide Sorter view

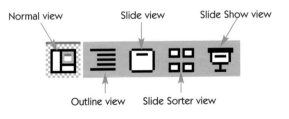

Normal view

Slide view

Slide Show view

Outline view

Slide Sorter view

Figure 4.10 The different views

**Activity**

▷ Print the file: **PP Worksheet 2** from the Chapter 4 folder on the CD-ROM. Use the exercise to add five slides to the presentation you started in PP Worksheet 1.

# Features to improve your slides

## AutoShapes

There are many ways to improve a PowerPoint® presentation. You can add lines and shapes, fill the shapes with colour, outline them and make them look three-dimensional. The **AutoShapes** button on the Drawing toolbar provides a menu of types of shape, each type having its own sub-menu, showing all the shapes available. There are 150 different shapes from which to choose!

**Callouts** are designed to hold text within the shape – see Figure 4.11. They can be simple boxes with lines pointing from them, or comic book style word and thought balloons. As with other text boxes, you can resize a callout and format the text inside it.

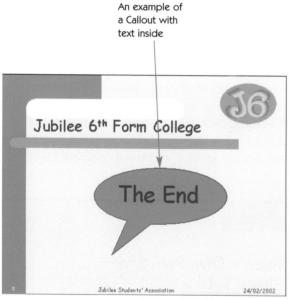

An example of a Callout with text inside

*Figure 4.11 Using a Callout*

## WordArt

As with other Microsoft® programs such as Word and Excel, you can use the WordArt tool to create a logo, or to make text more interesting – see Figure 4.12. One useful feature is that a design you make in one Microsoft® program can be used in any other Microsoft® application.

Therefore, if you created a logo using WordArt in Word, for example, you could use the same logo in a PowerPoint® presentation.

Normal text

Text created using WordArt

*Figure 4.12 Which version of 'The End' do you think looks more appealing – normal text or WordArt?*

> **Activity**
>
> ▶ Print the file: **PP Worksheet 3** from the Chapter 4 folder on the CD-ROM. Use the exercise to improve the presentation you created in PP Worksheets 1 and 2 by adding a Callout and WordArt.

## The Slide Master

PowerPoint® allows you to create a Slide Master where you can put any graphics or text that you want to appear on every slide. For example, Jubilee 6th Form College Students' Association can put the college logo on the slide master so that it will appear on every slide – see Figure 4.13.

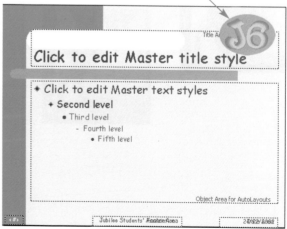

The college logo will appear on every slide of the presentation

*Figure 4.13 The Slide Master*

Remember how you learned to change **default settings** in word processing (see Chapter 1). You can also edit a slide to set the *default* text formats and styles for all slides in your presentation. The Slide Master will enable you to number each slide, include a footer and show the date a presentation was created.

# Special effects

## Animation

PowerPoint® has a feature which will allow you to make words and pictures on your slides appear and disappear when you want. This is called **Animation** – see Figure 4.14. Instead of being visible immediately when the slide appears, the object that you animate – text, a picture, or a piece of clip art, for example – comes in afterwards, appearing in a special way.

Animation controls how an object is brought onto the slide. An object can appear automatically, or wait until the user clicks the mouse button before appearing. If you have more than one animated object on a slide you can control the order they appear. The object will always end up where you put it when you were designing the slide.

## Preset Animation

The simplest way to animate your presentation is to use one of PowerPoint's® 14 Preset Animations – choose from Fly from the Top, Flying, Camera, for example. You will need to experiment to find out how these appear on the screen! Some animation styles work only with text, such as Typewriter, while others work with pictures and shapes only, such as Fly from the Top.

## Custom Animation

If you wish to be more adventurous, use the Custom Animation option, which provides more control of your animations. This offers more animation effects, and you can also pick the sound that goes with each animation, choose the order that animations take place and set the amount of time to wait between

*Figure 4.14 Animation on a slide*

animations. You can decide what happens to an object once it appears, such as making it disappear, or change colour.

## Sounds

In the same way as pictures can enhance, or add to, a presentation, so can sound if used carefully. Sound can be added in several different ways – just remember, try not to do too many at once! You can record your own sounds or play sounds off a CD to accompany your presentation. Be careful what you chose though – you may enjoy listening to 'heavy metal', but will your audience? You can add sound effects to your animations, and other special effects and if you want you can even record your own commentary. You cannot, however, use a pre-recorded commentary and another form of recorded sound at the same time. When you import a sound or video file an icon will appear on the presentation. You would use layering to hide this.

## Video files

As well as clip art, or image files, you can include video files in a PowerPoint® presentation. One problem with using video files is that a 20-second clip will take a large amount of storage space. Another is that computers with slow processors or without high quality video cards will process the video very slowly. This can mean that it either looks as if it is in slow motion or appears jerky.

## Slide Transition

You will have seen examples of **transitions** all the time, without realising it. For example, a transition happens when you are watching the television and the scene changes from one shot to another. In a PowerPoint® presentation, moving from one slide to the next is called **Slide Transition**.

When you design a PowerPoint® presentation, each slide has a transition associated with it. The transition will tell PowerPoint® how to change the display from

the last slide to the next slide. There are 12 transition styles from which to choose – cut, dissolve, wipe right, and so on – or you can select **Random Transition**. By setting the transition style to Random Transition, a different style and direction will be used each time you move onto a new slide.

### Activity

▶ Print the file: **PP Worksheet 5** from the Chapter 4 folder on the CD-ROM. Follow the worksheet to make your presentation more interesting by including animation, sounds, video files and transitions. Remember to choose any timings carefully – you must leave enough time for the slides to be read! Do not include too many different special effects. Too many special effects can be irritating and may distract from the actual content of the presentation.

## Other useful features

### Showing the presentation continuously

Jubilee 6th Form College Students' Association prepared a presentation of the events of the year to show in the reception area of the College on Open Day. The students wanted the presentation to show continuously throughout the day. PowerPoint® includes a feature that allows them to do this – the presentation will show continuously until the Esc key is pressed.

### Fact file

As with other Microsoft® packages it is possible to import files created in other packages into a PowerPoint® presentation. Text files created in Word can easily be imported into a PowerPoint® presentation by using the: **InsertFile** option from the menu. Alternatively you can create a file in 'outline view' in Word and use the **Send To** option from the file menu to import the document into your PowerPoint® slide.

## Speakers Notes

PowerPoint® has a facility called Speakers Notes which allows you to include notes to a slide. This feature gives a text display for each slide. You can add anything you want in these notes. The Students' Association could use Speakers Notes to give extra details on the events. These can be printed out to give to students and their parents – see Figure 4.15 (overleaf).

## Interactive presentations

It is possible to make a PowerPoint® presentation *interactive* and include hyperlinks or buttons to allow movement between slides. Although, in the presentation you have created using the worksheets for this chapter, movement between the slides follows a *linear* structure. This means it progresses from slide 1 to slide 2, to slide 3 etc. as shown in Figure 4.15.

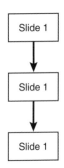

*Figure 4.15 Linear structure diagram*

You can also add interactivity. This allows the user to go, or 'jump' to a different part of the presentation, or you can even add a hyperlink to another PowerPoint® presentation or file type. You may decide to use a hierarchical structure diagram or the more complex mesh structure – see Figures 4.16 and 4.17 below.

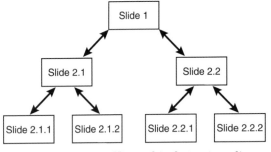

*Figure 4.16 Hierarchical structure diagram*

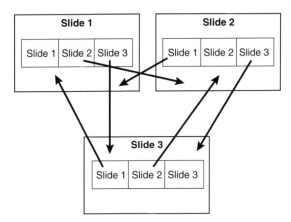

*Figure 4.17 Mesh structure diagram*

### Fact file

It is possible to blank the screen when running a presentation. This is useful if you want to catch the audience's attention. By pressing B on the keyboard, the screen will turn black, or by pressing W, the screen will turn white. You just press these keys again to return to the presentation.

### Activity

▷ Print the file: **PP Worksheet 6** from the Chapter 4 folder on the CD-ROM. Follow this worksheet to add the finishing touches to your presentation.

PowerPoint® is a very versatile package, and not all of the features have been discussed in this chapter. Once you are familiar with the basics of PowerPoint®, you may wish to experiment and learn to use even more of its features. Be warned though, it is very tempting to try to include as many different features as possible within a presentation to show off your newly acquired skills. Doing so can distract from the actual content of the presentation. You will learn more about features of a good presentation in Chapter 7.

# Chapter 5

# Communication, searching and selection of information using the Internet

This chapter looks at:

- the use of e-mail for communication between individuals and groups
- the main search principles of Internet search engines, e.g. string
- searching including multiple criteria searches
- the main features of browser software e.g. forward and back buttons, book marking and organising favourites
- purposefully navigating large web sites, e.g. locating a specific information resource in a given site.

## What you will learn

E-mail
Using the Internet to find information
How to create a web page

## Overview

E-mail was one of the first uses of the Internet and is still the most popular. This chapter looks at the different features of e-mail and how it is used for communication between individuals and groups. It also looks at how the Internet can be used to search for information, including **Internet** search engines, the main features of browser software and how to navigate large websites.

## Checkpoint

The **Internet** is the means by which different local and wide area networks are linked together to form an international network.

## E-mail

You have probably used e-mail at school or college, and increasingly more people are using e-mail at home. If you go on work experience or when you start your first job after school or college, you will almost certainly find that e-mail plays an important role in business. In fact, nowadays, few businesses would be able to function without it.

## What is e-mail?

E-mail is like an electronic letter, sent in most instances via the computer, instead of the postal service. It is a very sophisticated method of electronic transfer, where messages and documents can be sent from one computer to another using a communications link such as a modem and a telephone line.

You can receive and send the electronic equivalent of letters, pictures, sounds and if you have a **webcam** attached to your PC, you can even send a video e-mail. Documents prepared on a word processor or other software package, or a document scanned into the computer can be transferred either immediately if it is urgent, or can be stored along with the e-mail address of the receiving computer, and can be sent later. You will probably know that you can send e-mails from such devices as mobile phones and Internet televisions.

## Checkpoint

A **webcam** is a digital camera connected to a PC that enables video conferencing between people in remote locations.

## E-mail addresses

In order to send an e-mail you have to know the e-mail address of the person you wish to e-mail. This is usually a short code, often made up of the user's name followed by the **Internet Service Provider**'s **(ISP)** code, but this can vary. Look at the three e-mail addresses below.

From: PhilipDavey@globalnet.co.uk
To: RosalindDavey@aol.com
Cc: G.Davey@freeserve.co.uk

Each has a different ISP – Globalnet, AOL and Freeserve.

To send an e-mail via the Internet, you have to connect to the ISP's server. Once you are connected, you can send the e-mail. The e-mail is then sent from your ISP server to the destination ISP server.

### Checkpoint

An **Internet Service Provider (ISP)** provides access to the Internet via its services. Examples of ISPs are Btopenworld, Pipex, Freeserve and AOL. See page 180 for more about ISPs.

Many companies have internal e-mail systems via local area networks, private wide area networks or an intranet so that all their employees can communicate easily with each other. (You will learn more about the different types of networks in Unit 2).

Many people have their own web-based e-mail address through companies such as Hotmail. By logging on to the Hotmail website and entering a user name and password, you can access your e-mail wherever you are in the world.

### Fact file

When you send an e-mail two different servers at your ISP are involved. The SMTP Server – Simple Mail Transfer Protocol – handles all outgoing mail. When you receive an e-mail it is received from your ISP's POP3 Server – Post Office Protocol – the POP3 server handles all incoming mail. The SMTP server will route the e-mail to the receiving ISP POP3 server.

Unless you are sending an e-mail from a Hotmail account, or as in the example in Figure 5.1, in order to send e-mail you normally need special e-mail communications software. Examples of popular e-mail software are Microsoft® Outlook, or Microsoft® Outlook

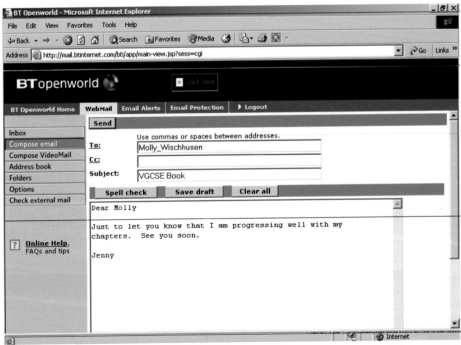

Figure 5.1 Sending an e-mail using BTopenworld.

Express, and Netscape Messenger. Many businesses also use business-orientated e-mail programs such as Lotus Notes, or Groupwise. Some ISPs such as AOL (America on Line) provide their own e-mail programs, which you must use if you have subscribed to that service.

### Find out ...

- What is your school/college's e-mail address?
- What e-mail software package does your school/college use?
- If you have a home computer, is it the same package?

You may find that the e-mail address of your school or college includes its name (possibly abbreviated) followed by .ac.uk. The 'ac' indicates that you are using an academic network that links all colleges and universities in the UK.

### Fact file

E-mails are legal documents. You can be prosecuted if you write something that is libellous.

### Sending an e-mail

The format of an e-mail depends on the system you are using. The basic features include a:

- 'From' box
- 'To' box
- 'Subject' box
- Textbox – see Figure 5.2.

E-mail systems offer many different options, and the ones that are the most useful will depend on the user's purpose:

- **Alternatives in the address line**. A business user might wish to send a copy of an e-mail to someone other than the person in the To line. The address of the person who is to receive the copy is inserted in the Cc (carbon copy) box. Some e-mail systems have the option of sending Bcc's (blind carbon copies). This allows a copy of the e-mail to be sent to someone else without the addressee – the person named in the To box – knowing.

- **Address button**. Clicking on this button will take you to your address book, which stores the names and addresses of people whom you regularly send e-mails to. This saves having to key in the full address every time you send a message. Another advantage of the address book is that it reduces the risk of making a mistake, such as a wrong spelling or putting the dot in the wrong place, which would mean your e-mail is returned unsent by the systems administrator.

- **Attachment button**. This allows you to attach (that is, to send with your e-mail) copies of file(s) stored on your computer system – text, sound, graphics, or even video files.

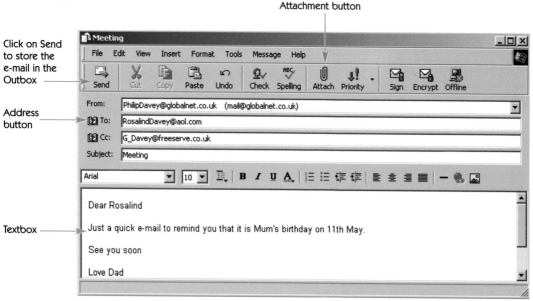

*Figure 5.2 An e-mail message ready to be sent*

**Computer viruses** are often hidden in e-mail attachments. They spread by automatically sending an e-mail to everyone in an address book. In December 2002, a 22-year-old from Wales appeared before a court in London having been charged under the Computer Misuse Act 1990 for writing and releasing computer viruses. He sent out infected e-mails to a few people which, when opened, automatically transmitted a virus known as 'Gokar' to everyone in the recipient's electronic address book. Experts estimated that over 27,000 computers in 42 countries were infected.

## Checkpoint

A **computer virus** is a program written specifically to attack computer software. It is usually disguised as something else, such as an e-mail attachment, and will often be automatically spread to other computer users.

## How to send an e-mail

To send an e-mail using software such as Outlook Express:

1 Prepare your message **offline** to save telephone charges (unless you have an ADSL connection) and click the Send button to store it in the Outbox.
2 Connect to the Internet via your ISP.
3 Click on the Send and Receive option.
4 You may have to enter a password to access your mailbox at your ISP. In Outlook Express and most other programs you can set up the program so that it automatically enters the password.
5 Your e-mail will be sent, and your mailbox at your ISP will be checked for incoming mail.

## Checkpoint

**Offline** refers to a way of working with web browsers or e-mail software without being connected to the Internet. (Online refers to a computer or other device that is connected to the Internet.)

## Activity

▷ Print the file: **EM Worksheet 1** from the Chapter 5 folder on the CD-ROM. Follow the worksheet's instructions to send an e-mail with a file attachment.

## Common features of e-mail communications software

- Work offline, save a message and send it whenever you wish.
- Create an address book of the e-mail addresses of all your friends.
- Create a distribution list – see Figure 5.3. The Jubilee 6th Form College Students' Association could divide its address box into different categories, e.g. students and suppliers, in the same way that you would organise your files on a hard disk.
- Send attachments of any file on your computer. If you want to attach a confidential file, you can add a password to the file for security.
- Send copies of a message to many people.
- Forward e-mails you have received to other users.
- Messages are automatically date and time stamped.
- Add a **Signature** – you can set up more than one, depending on the recipient (the person you are sending it to). For example, Nicola Davey, the President of the Students' Association, uses her official signature when organising trips – see Figure 5.4.

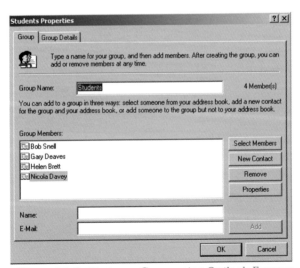

*Figure 5.3 Setting up a Group using Outlook Express*

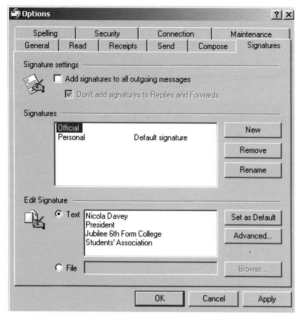

*Figure 5.4 Setting up a signature using Outlook Express*

### Fact file

In e-mail software such as Outlook Express received e-mails can be automatically stored directly into folders at the time when they are received. This means that your Inbox remains tidy and e-mails are easy to find.

### Activity

▶ Print the file: **EM Worksheet 2** from the Chapter 5 folder on the CD-ROM. In this worksheet you will learn how to create a distribution group and add your signature using Outlook Express.

## Using the Internet to find information

In this section you will learn how to *search* for information on the Internet. You will learn more about the Internet, the equipment you need to access it, the world wide web (www) and how it affects both business and home life in Unit 3.

You have probably used the term 'surf the net'. A **web browser** is the special software which lets you do this as it enables you to view web pages and to click on links – known as **hyperlinks** – to other web pages and websites. The most common web browsers are Microsoft® Internet Explorer and Netscape Navigator.

When you double click on your browser to start it up, you can access web pages only if you are connected, via your ISP, to the Internet. However, some computers are set up so that launching the browser will automatically cause the modem to dial up and connect to the Internet. When you connect to a web browser, the default web page –the **home page** – will be loaded and appear on screen. This is often the website of the company whose computer you are using, the website of your ISP, or can be any website you have chosen.

Figure 5.5 shows the toolbar and Address box in Internet Explorer.

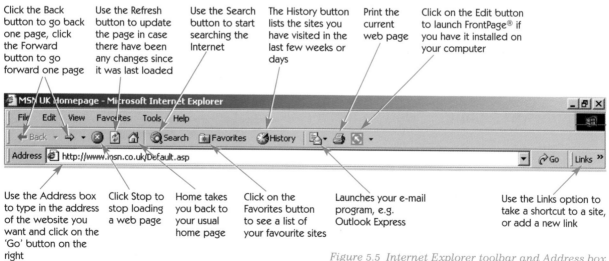

Click the Back button to go back one page, click the Forward button to go forward one page

Use the Refresh button to update the page in case there have been any changes since it was last loaded

Use the Search button to start searching the Internet

The History button lists the sites you have visited in the last few weeks or days

Print the current web page

Click on the Edit button to launch FrontPage® if you have it installed on your computer

Use the Address box to type in the address of the website you want and click on the 'Go' button on the right

Click Stop to stop loading a web page

Home takes you back to your usual home page

Click on the Favorites button to see a list of your favourite sites

Launches your e-mail program, e.g. Outlook Express

Use the Links option to take a shortcut to a site, or add a new link

*Figure 5.5 Internet Explorer toolbar and Address box*

## What is a web address?

A web page has its own unique identification or address. This is known as a **uniform resource locator (URL)** and usually starts with http:// or www. The http stands for **hypertext transmission transfer protocol**. Every address is constructed (put together) in the same way – see Figure 5.6. An example of a well-known web address is http://www.bbc.co.uk, which is the website of the BBC.

## Top level domains

The top level **domain** (TLD) in a website address (see Figure 5.6) identifies the type of site, for example:

- .ac – university, college or academic department
- .co – company
- .com – commercial organisation
- .uk.com – an alternative area for UK registrations; often used if .com or .co.uk name is not available
- .gov – government department
- .mil – military site
- .net – network related site
- .org – usually a charity or non-profit making organisation
- .sch – school
- .tv – the latest domain for television websites.

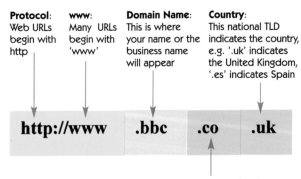

**Protocol**: Web URLs begin with http

**www**: Many URLs begin with 'www'

**Domain Name**: This is where your name or the business name will appear

**Country**: This national TLD indicates the country, e.g. '.uk' indicates the United Kingdom, '.es' indicates Spain

| http://www | .bbc | .co | .uk |

**Top Level Domain (TLD)**: The combination of letters indicates the type of site, e.g. '.ac' indicates a university, college or academic body, '.co' indicates a company

*Figure 5.6 How a web address is constructed*

## Finding a website

If you know the website's address, you can go directly to it by typing it in the Address box and clicking Go. If you are uncertain of the address of a company or organisation, try guessing. As organisations usually try to include their name in the address, it is often possible to guess correctly. There is no need to type http.

So, if you wanted to find the website of Heinemann, you could try entering www.heinemann.co.uk. You have probably guessed that its domain name will be heinemann, that it would use .co. as its TLD and that, as it is in the UK, its national TLD will be .uk.

**Activity**

Print the file: **INT Worksheet 1** from the Chapter 5 folder on the CD-ROM. Follow the worksheet's instructions to:
- open Internet Explorer
- display a given web page
- change your web browser's home page.

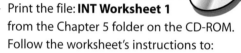
## Navigating a website

When you first visit a website, it is a good idea to familiarise yourself with how it is designed. Many organisations have very large websites with a home page and many pages about different parts of the organisation. It is easy sometimes to get lost within a large website, but a well-constructed website will always have a hyperlink to take you back to the home page (for more on hyperlinks, see below).

When you move the mouse pointer over a hyperlink, the arrow changes to a pointing hand. When you click on the hyperlink, you will be connected to the link. There will often be hyperlinks to return you back to the top of a page and to the other main areas of the site – see Figure 5.7.

Clicking here will take you directly to the BBC Sport page

**BBC SPORT**    Audio | Video
- FA Cup preview
- Kiwis consider legal action

*Figure 5.7 A hyperlink*

## Searching a site

Large organisations such as the BBC often include a search facility for their own site, so that you can quickly find the information you require – see Figure 5.8. The BBC's site even has a search help and tips page to help you find information easily. The BBC's website is a good one to bookmark in your favourites – you will find a host of useful resources to help you with your studies, both for GCSE ICT and your other subjects. You will learn about bookmarks later on in this section.

You can search the BBC's website here

*Figure 5.8 BBC home page*

## Back and Forward buttons

All the time you are online your browser is storing copies of the pages you have recently used in an area called 'cache'. If you wish to return to a page you visited before, click on the Back button until you reach the page you require. Because the computer does not have to go back to the web, but simply has to look into its internal **cache**, the page will appear quickly. You can click on the Forward button to return to the previous web page you were on. Caching pages saves time and money if you are paying for online time.

**Checkpoint**

**Cache** is the internal storage area within a browser where recently visited web pages are stored and can be reloaded quickly by using the Back and Forward buttons.

## Fact file

A good website will be updated frequently, so you should learn to visit a website regularly to see what is new. Any pages of interest can be printed just as you would in other applications.

## Viewing a site as text only

Many websites, including the BBC's, will allow you to view the site without any of the images. If this option is available, you will usually see a hyperlink which says 'Text Only'. It is also possible to set your web browser so that it will load a page without images. The advantage of doing this is that it speeds up response times as image files can be quite large.

## Fact file

You can copy and paste text from a website into another document using the same techniques as you would in Word. You can also save images from a website onto your computer. Remember to take into account copyright issues when you do this (see Unit 3).

## Activity

▷ Print the file: **INT Worksheet 2**
from the Chapter 5 folder on the CD-ROM.
Follow the worksheet's instructions to:

- navigate a large website
- search a large website
- print a web page
- display a web page without images.

## Favorites

In the same way as you put a bookmark in a book to return to a page quickly and easily, browser software allows you to 'bookmark' the sites you look at regularly in Favorites. You can create folders and file bookmarks just as as you would organise and save files on the hard drive. Rather than inputting the address of a website each time you want to access it, you simply select the name from Favorites.

If there is a particular page within a website that you are likely to return to on other occasions, you can bookmark that page, rather than the home page of the site. If you share a computer with several people, it is a good idea to create a folder for each person – see Figure 5.9. You can then keep your own Favorites separate and they will be easy to find.

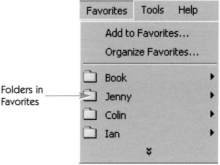

*Figure 5.9 Favorites menu*

## Activity

▷ Print the file: **INT Worksheet 3**
from the Chapter 5 folder on the CD-ROM.
Follow the worksheet's instructions to:

- create folders in which to bookmark your favourite sites
- add to Favorites in a specific folder
- organise Favorites.

### Links

You can create shortcuts – Links – to go to Favorites. This works in a similar way to bookmarking a site and adding it to Favorite3, but accesses the site in a slightly different way. It can be a faster way of going to a frequently used site.

### History

The browser stores a **history** of all the websites you have been visited over the past few days or weeks. This can be helpful if you have forgotten to bookmark a site. It is also useful if you have been surfing the net for some time, and you want to return to a page that you previously visited during the current session online. One way to go back to the page is to click the Back button, but this can be slow if you have visited quite a few pages. Another way is to use the History list to select the site – see Figure 5.10.

Selecting a site from the History list is a quick way of returning to it

*Figure 5.10 Using the History tool*

### Checkpoint

**History** refers to the records of the URLs of the websites you have visited over a period of time and which are saved in the browser in a list.

### Fact file

With your browser, you can select the text size that you view a page from Largest through to Smallest.

## Search tools

The Internet is the world's largest source of information. However, as you have probably already discovered, there are millions of websites so it is sometimes quite hard to find the information you want. If you are looking for a particular company, or piece of information, you will need to use a web search tool.

There are several different search tools. The main types are:

- search engines
- subject directories
- meta-search engines
- name directories.

### Fact file

Search tools are produced by businesses in competition with each other. Ignore the adverts and banners that appear on them, and focus on the search box and any hints or tips provided.

## Search engines

Using a **search engine**, you type in a few key words (criteria) and you will be shown a page of links to sites matching your criteria.

Search engines are indexes which work by key words and context. They use a program called a spider, robot or crawler to index huge, random collections of Internet files. Use search engines when you want to find large numbers of related documents or specific types of document such as image files, MP3 music files, or discussion lists. Popular search engines include Altavista, Ask Jeeves and Google. Go to www.heinemann.co.uk/hotlinks and click on the name of the search engine you want.

### Checkpoint

A **search engine** is a facility used to search the world wide web on specific topics. You can also use subject directories, name directories, or meta-search directories to search the web.

### Fact file

Many search engines will have their own UK version. For example, if you visit Google, you will have the opportunity to limit your search to UK websites only.

## Subject directories

Subject directories are similar to search engines, but are smaller collections of Internet files grouped by subject headings. These files are not rated for relevancy (whether they match the subject heading) by software, but by humans. Subject directories are ideal if you wish to research a general topic and you want to avoid all the irrelevant files that search engines can find. An example of a subject directory is Yahoo – see Figure 5.11. Go to www.heinemann.co.uk/hotlinks and click on Yahoo.

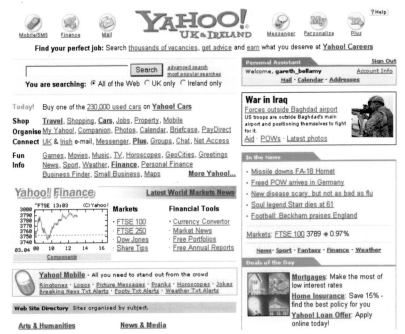

Figure 5.11 Yahoo! subject directory

## Meta-search engines

In a meta-search engine, you enter key words into a search box, and your search is sent simultaneously to several individual search engines and their databases of web pages. Within a few seconds, you get back results from all the search engines queried.

Meta-search engines do not own a database of web pages; they send your search criteria to the databases of other search engines. You can download and install a meta-search engine, such as Copernic to work alongside your browser. Go to www.heinemann.co.uk/hotlinks and click on Copernic.

Use meta-searches when you want to get an overall picture of what the web has on a topic and to check whether the web is really the best place for your search – see Figure 5.12.

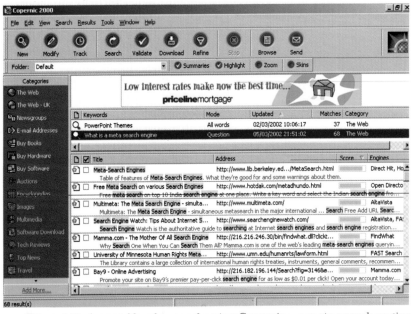

Figure 5.12 A example of a search using Copernic – a meta-search engine

*Figure 5.13  The June 2003 online version of Yellow Pages*

## Directories

Directories are used when you want to search for businesses or people by name, telephone number, e-mail address, post-code, and so on. Many cover specific places or countries, for example Yell.com provides information about businesses and services in the UK (see Figure 5.13). Go to heinemann.co.uk/hotlinks and click on Yell.

## Tips for successful searching

There is a lot of information and lots of choices available to you when it comes to searching online. Search engines index billions of documents and make information easy for you to find. Below are a few tips to help you get the best information, whether it is to help you research a project or find out the latest news on your favourite TV programme or band.

Remember that when you find information on the Internet it doesn't mean that the information is necessarily good or bad. You need to judge the quality of the source you've used – don't just take the information at face value.

Choose one search tool and just use that one for a while. If you are not sure which one to choose, ask your friends or your tutor. When you are comfortable with how it works

and what sort of results you get, then try another.

Searching can sometimes be difficult because if you do not narrow your search in some way, you can be presented with a large amount of irrelevant information. Remember that each search engine or search directory does not look for things in exactly the same way and may differ slightly in techniques you can use, so you should look at their help pages for tips.

Here are some tips to help you search successfully:

- Enter the letter T followed by a colon (:) and then the word you want to search for. By doing this, the search engine will only look for the words that are contained in the title of a document on the website.
- Enter the letter U followed by a colon (:) and then the word you want to search for. By doing this, the search engine will only look for words that are contained in the URL (the website address) of the website.
- Use lower case instead of capital letters (upper case). Searches in all capital letters will produce results that are in capitals only, whereas lower case will find results in both upper and lower case.
- Put a phrase in quotation marks. You will get more accurate information by doing this. For example, to find information about Formula One cars, type "formula one cars". This will get you information that is only about Formula One cars rather than anything to do with "formula", anything to do with "one" or anything to do with "cars".
- Some search engines, like Ask Jeeves, will allow you to type in direct questions. For example, you could type 'Where can I find information about formula one cars?'
- You can limit your search further by the use of the logical operators:
  AND, OR, NOT, +, –.
  By typing:
  "formula one cars" –models
  OR
  "formula one cars" NOTmodels

  the search will produce all sites listing Formula One cars, but exclude any reference to models.

- Use a technique called **wildcards**. Sometimes you want to make sure that you do not miss a good website by using the wrong words, so one way of searching is to use **wildcard matches**. You can use right-hand or left-hand wildcard searches. For example, by entering "biog*" will search for sites including the words biography, biographical or just biog. Entering "*biog*" would also include sites with the words autobiography or autobiographical.

## Beware inaccurate web data!

Because no single individual or organisation controls the information that is published on the web, you should not always trust the information you find. It may appear convincing and correct but, in fact, be completely wrong or at least misleading. The following are three ways to help protect yourself from inaccurate web data:

- Check whether there is a date on the site and when it was last updated.
- Is it possible to contact the site's developer? Is there an e-mail address to contact?
- Try to work out (or at least be aware of) whether the site was developed by someone or some organisation that wants to put its message across – for example, a political (sometimes, an extreme political) view.

### Activity

Print the file: **INT Worksheet 4**

from the Chapter 5 folder on the CD ROM. Follow the worksheet's instructions to use:

- Internet Explorer's search button
- a search engine
- a search directory
- more advanced search techniques, such as logical operators.

## What is a website?

From searching the Internet, you will probably have realised that most organisations and businesses will benefit from having a website.

Indeed, the Internet is a good way of advertising goods and services, and many allow customers to order goods online. (The effects of the Internet are discussed in Unit 3.)

A website is a collection of related web pages, which are electronic documents that can contain text, images, forms, graphics and other multi-media such as animation. They are viewed via web browsers such as Internet Explorer or Netscape.

## Setting up a web page in HTML

**HyperText Markup Language (HTML)** is the code used to write pages for the web. The code is in the form of **tags** (see overleaf) which surround blocks of text to indicate how the text should appear on the screen so that it looks the same when viewed through any web browser.

The author of a web page designs the page and links all the material together using HTML. When the page is viewed (either by the author or someone viewing a published web page), the web browser software interprets ('reads') the HTML language and displays the text exactly as the author intended.

HTML also enables hyperlinks to be created within the text, so that when you click on a hyperlink, you automatically jump to another part of the page or another page on the web. A hyperlink might be a word, a button or a picture.

Most word processing software today enables you to produce HTML scripts without the need to understand the coding. You can also use authoring tools, such as FrontPage® or DreamWeaver (see overleaf).

To help you understand the basic concepts of HTML, let's look at how Jubilee 6th Form College Students' Association could create a web page by coding it manually.

In order to create a web page, the Students' Association will need the following:

- A simple text editor (like Notepad) to write the HTML coding or a dedicated HTML text editor, for example Allaire's HomeSite. Instead, the Association could use dedicated authoring tools such as Microsoft® FrontPage®, Microsoft® FrontPage® Express or DreamWeaver, or standard application software such as Microsoft® Word which includes a Save as HTML option which automatically inserts HTML tags into a document and makes it ready for the web. There are also many online wizards which offer a step-by-step guide. Many ISPs offer online tools, for example. Sometimes, however, word processing applications such as Microsoft® Word are less effective for HTML than using a basic tool such as Notepad. This is because advanced word processors tend to create formatting in documents that interferes with HTML coding.

- A web browser – a dedicated software application that will enable you to browse the web and view your own web pages.
- To learn the codes (or tags) used to format and structure the text.
- Finally, and perhaps most importantly, good design and presentation skills.

## Find out ...

Use www.heinemann.co.uk/hotlinks to look at a range of websites on the Internet. Find a page that particularly interests you. Read the page to familiarise yourself with its contents.

## Viewing HTML code

You can see how a web page has been constructed with HTML code by viewing the source code through the View/Source or Document Source from the menu of your web browser. (This facility might not be available through all ISPs – if not, try clicking the right mouse button or ask your teacher.)

The source code is what the author used to enable you to see the finished page as he or she intended when it was designed. Look at the source code of a web page and see if you can pick out some of the text that appears on the actual page. The code will probably look very complicated because it was written by an expert in HTML and will include many advanced concepts.

## Tags

Did you notice words or letters inside the < and > marks in the document code you viewed?

These are known as **tags** and are the way the web browser knows how we want the document to appear. For example, they tell the web browser where to start a new paragraph or print a line of text. They usually come in pairs with the second tag of the pair beginning with a slash symbol /. As an example the <h1> and </h1> tags indicate where a main heading begins and ends.

## Checkpoint

**Tags** are code words in an HTML document that tell a browser how to display a document. All tags are written inside <angle brackets> and are mostly written in pairs at each end of the text to be formatted.

The first tag of any document is <html>, which tells the web browser that it is starting a page of information written in HTML. The closing tag </html> is put at the end of the document.

Most tags normally come in pairs, but this is not always the case. The <br> tag, used to create a line break to create larger gaps, comes on its own. Also the </p> tag (end of paragraph) is optional. The table below shows some common tags and what they mean.

| Tag (start) | Tag (finish) | What the tag does |
|---|---|---|
| <html> | </html> | Shows the beginning and the end of an HTML page |
| <head> | </head> | The head section of the web page |
| <title> | </title> | The text that will appear on the title bar |
| <body> | </body> | All the text in the document is between these tags |
| <h1> | </h1> | Inserts a heading in the largest font. Sizes go down h2, h3, h4, h5 and h6, which is the smallest |
| <b> | </b> | Displays characters in bold |
| <i> | </i> | Displays characters in italics |
| <center> | </center> | Everything between these tags is centred |
| <br> | </br> | Allows you to type words onto a new line |

*Common HTML tags*

## Comment tags

If you want to write something in your HTML page that you don't want to appear on the web page, you use a **comment** tag. The tag that turns the comment on is <!— and the tag that turns the comment off is —>. A comment is something you would use to add a note to remind you or someone else who is looking at your program about something important that needs to be remembered.

## Structure of an HTML document

There are always two parts of an HTML document – the **head** and the **body**. The first part of any document is always the head tag which is bracketed as the <head> and </head> commands.

There are several tags that can be included in the head area. The most common is the document's title, bracketed by <title> and </title>. The body of the document begins after the head: <body> </body>. The body will contain all the parts of the web page displayed in a web browser's viewing window.

### Activity

Print the file: **WB Worksheet 1** from the Chapter 5 folder on the CD-ROM. Follow the worksheet's instructions to:

- create a very simple web page using a text editor (in this exercise Notepad) and HTML
- save the web page
- view the web page using a web browser.

## Changing the colour of the background and fonts

You can include within the <body> tag different characteristics for the style of the text or the background on the web page.

There are 16 colour names to choose from:

| | | |
|---|---|---|
| Aqua | Lime | Red |
| Black | Maroon | Silver |
| Blue | Navy | Teal |
| Fuchsia | Olive | White |
| Gray | Purple | Yellow |
| Green | | |

There are also many different combinations of colours that you can achieve by entering special codes, for example the code for pale dull pink is ff99cc.

## Changing the font type and size

Apart from the headings, which come in sizes from h1 (the biggest) to h6 (the smallest), it is possible to increase the font size of standard text. The default size is 3. By using the tag <font size = 4>, the font size will be increased.

The default font type is Times New Roman, so by using the tag <font face = Arial>, the font on the web page is changed to Arial. When altering the font, do not choose unusual fonts as they may not exist on the computer of whoever is viewing your page. If they don't, the browser will choose the 'next best' view.

## Hyperlinks

All documents on the world wide web are connected by hyperlinks. When you move the mouse pointer over a hyperlink, the arrow changes to a pointing hand, and clicking on the mouse button connects you to the link. A hyperlink may be text, a button or a picture. You can create a hyperlink to one of your own documents or to a page on another website. You can also insert hyperlinks in a document that enable you to jump to a different place on the same page, for example the **Top of Page** hyperlink which is often included on a web page.

## Graphics and images

Pictures included in a web page can create more interest, add impact and help get your message across. You can use clip art or pictures downloaded from the web, pictures taken with a digital camera or draw, or scan, something yourself.

A graphic feature might be flashing text, a moving image or animated clip. Non-moving images (and moving images if they are in GIF format) can be added to web pages by using the **image tag**.

Any picture to be stored on a web page must be stored on your hard drive in a graphics file format. The two formats that can be used with a web browser are:

- GIF (pronounced 'giff') – a GIF (graphics interchange format) image is similar to a bitmap image and is made up of pixels (or dots)
- JPEG (pronounced 'jay peg') – a JPEG (joint photographic experts group) file format is ideal for displaying photographic images because it can use over 16 million colours compared to 256 for GIF images.

The size of image files will be affected by the format in which they are saved. Bitmap (BMP) files are images made up of tiny dots called pixels. They use a lot of memory and lose their quality when re-sized. A BMP file of 875 × 498 pixels will take 1.24 MB of space. The same, JPEG file will only occupy 295 KB.

### Fact file

Images files that are shrunk by dragging one of the handles on the corner of the picture retain the same file size. Use an editing package, such as Microsoft® Photo Editor or Adobe® Photoshop®, to reduce the actual image size. Images that are greatly reduced in size are called thumbnails and are often used on web pages to reduce download times.

Special software, called Shockwave, is available for producing animated graphics, videos and sound sequences. This software is designed to **download** quickly because a visitor to a web page does not want to wait a long time to see a full page. However, it is a very expensive and complex program that takes a long time to learn. At this stage, you will find it interesting just to view examples. If your system has a Shockwave **plug-in** installed you should be able to view Shockwave files.

### Checkpoint

**Download** refers to the transmission of data (a web page or a file, for example) from a server or the Internet to your computer.

### Checkpoint

A **plug-in** is a mini-program attached to your web browser that allows it to handle unusual file formats.

You can include images recorded on a webcam on a website. These can be still images that are refreshed occasionally or pre-recorded video footage. It is even possible to include a live link to a webcam. Remember that including such images can considerably slow down download times.

### Activity

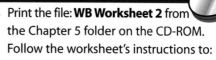

▶ Print the file: **WB Worksheet 2** from the Chapter 5 folder on the CD-ROM. Follow the worksheet's instructions to:
- open an existing html file for editing
- change the font type and size
- change the background colour of the page
- change the font colour.

## Creating a web page using dedicated authoring tools

As already mentioned, there are other ways to create a web page, which avoid you having to be an expert in HTML. You can use a word processor such as Word or a dedicated authoring tool such as FrontPage® Express, FrontPage® or DreamWeaver. When you create a web page using one of these, the software automatically inserts the HTML tags into the document. This makes developing a web page much easier and faster. These packages are often referred to as WYSIWYG (what you see is what you get) tools. This is because as you build the web page, what you see on the screen is the same as it will actually appear in a browser.

To create a web page that includes more advanced features such as tables or forms, you can easily do so using an authoring tool without having to learn more complicated aspects. FrontPage® Express comes free with Microsoft® Internet Explorer 5.0 and is a useful starting point. It is integrated with the browser, but it does not come with all the features of the full version of FrontPage®. However, as with other options, it offers templates and user friendly commands for inserting graphics and links, and for formatting text. Using FrontPage® Express or FrontPage®, for example, you could create a basic page quite quickly.

As you become more familiar with HTML, you will be able to view the code produced by an **authoring tool** and make alterations to improve the page directly into the code.

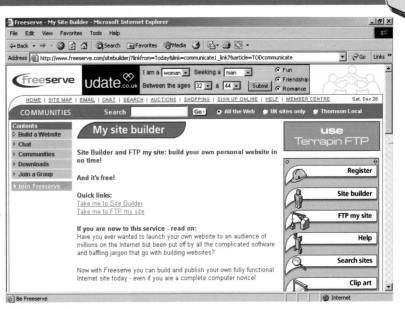

*Figure 5.14  Freeserve's website building tool*

## Checkpoint

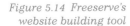

An **authoring tool** is a dedicated software package for creating websites, for example FrontPage® or DreamWeaver.

### Wizards

Before starting to create your website, you should plan on paper how you want it to appear. It is also advisable to put all your web pages and graphics into a single folder. Most authoring tools include wizards to make designing a website or page an easier process. Certainly, a beginner can create a professional looking site by following one of the wizards provided.

A wizard will take you step by step through the process, giving you options from which to chose at each stage. For example, Figure 5.15 shows that the New Website wizard in FrontPage® provides eight different designs. You can also create the folder in which to save the web at the same time. Remember that one of the benefits of using a full version authoring tool such as FrontPage® is that it provides more features.

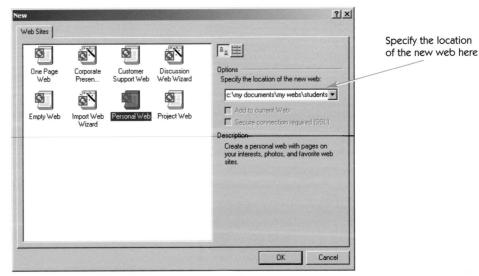

*Figure 5.15  The FrontPage® New Website Wizard*

Once you have worked through a wizard, you should select the Navigation button to see the structure of the website so far – see Figure 5.16.

It will not necessarily be the same as your paper design, but you will be able to make changes very easily.

Your next step will be to build each web page in turn. However, unlike when you are coding in HTML, you will see screen prompts on how to continue – see Figure 5.17. From this, you will see that there are three views, Normal, HTML and Preview. You use Normal view to edit the page, but you also have the option of viewing and editing the HTML code.

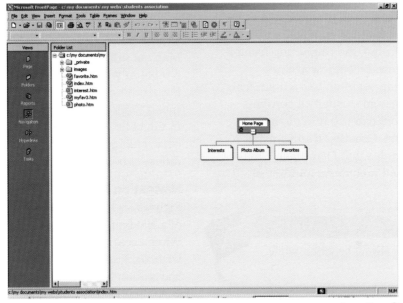

*Figure 5.16  The Navigation view in FrontPage®*

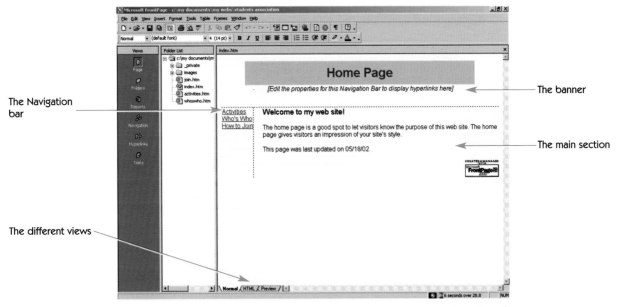

The Navigation bar

The different views

The banner

The main section

*Figure 5.17  A home page template created using FrontPage®*

The text and graphics that go across the top of each page is called a Page Banner. It would be quite a complex task to code using HTML alone, but by using FrontPage®, the process is simple.

Once you have keyed in your chosen text, changing the font type, size and colour is far easier than in HTML. Simply select the text and change the font type, size and colour to options you prefer, just like you would do in Word.

## Frames

Frames are used to break up the browser window into sections, each of which has a separate page displayed in it. When a new page is displayed in a frame, the remaining frames showing in the browser window are not changed. The frame set often has a main frame which does not change – usually a contents page so that visitors can use it to navigate around the website. Creating frames using HTML can be complex, but FrontPage® makes it a simple task and includes a number of frame templates.

### Fact file

Some frames will always be visible while others change.

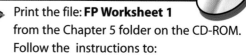

### Activity

▶ Print the file: **FP Worksheet 1** from the Chapter 5 folder on the CD-ROM. Follow the instructions to:

- use a wizard to create a basic web (in FrontPage® a web does not become a website until it has been published)
- rename pages
- delete files
- rename files
- add a banner to the home page.

## Tables

Many of the skills you have gained for creating a table in Word can be used in FrontPage®. First, create a basic structure by using the Insert Table tool and then add text or graphics in the cells – see Figure 5.18. You can merge cells, change their height and width and apply different borders just as you would in Word.

## Navigation bars

Figures 5.17 and 5.18 show different examples of a Navigation bar created by FrontPage®. When creating a web page using certain wizards, FrontPage® automatically creates a Navigation bar which has hyperlinks to the

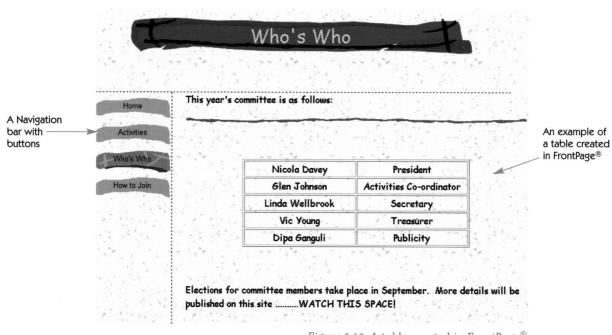

*Figure 5.18 A table created in FrontPage®*

other pages on the website. Navigation bars allow visitors to the site to move to a different page when the appropriate link is clicked. In Figure 5.17 the Navigation bar shows text hyperlinks, whereas the hyperlinks shown in Figure 5.18 are user friendly buttons. FrontPage® allows you to change the display from text to buttons very easily.

### Marquees

Marquees are scrolling text areas that scroll across the screen repeatedly. They are useful for getting across a message. For example, Jubilee 6th Form College Students' Association might include a marquee in the banner area of their website saying 'Jubilee 6th Form College Students' Association – Have You Joined?'. This would then appear on every page.

### Themes

Another benefit of using an authoring tool such as FrontPage® is that templates or themes are included, rather like the Design templates supplied with PowerPoint®. You can choose the theme for the entire web or for individual pages. It is advisable to have a uniform theme, as using a variety of themes may give the overall appearance of the site a muddled look.

> ### Activity
>
> Print the file: **FP Worksheet 2** from the Chapter 5 folder on the CD-ROM. Follow the worksheet's instructions to:
> - open an existing web using in FrontPage®
> - move between pages of a web being constructed
> - add a table
> - edit the Navigation bar
> - add a marquee
> - change the theme of a web.

## Publishing the web

In FrontPage®, a web does not become a website until it has been published and can be viewed by other people. A web host is the name given to the company that provides space on a web server for you to publish your site.

Your own ISP may offer limited space to publish your site. If you wish to publish your web created in FrontPage®, you need to find out if your ISP supports FrontPage® Server Extensions. The steps to **upload** a site can vary from one ISP to another, but it is normally quite a simple process.

Many companies will offer to publish websites free of charge on condition that they put some advertising banners on each page.

Alternatively, your school or college may have its own web server onto which you can publish your site.

If you want your site to be found easily, you should buy a domain name. In the UK, Nominet is the domain naming authority. It maintains a central database of all domains ending with .uk. If you want to find out if a particular domain name is available you can use one of the many specialised search sites. Just go to www.heinemann.co.uk/hotlinks and click on Simply. As more and more companies and individuals are purchasing domain names, different top level domains are being introduced. For example, .gb.com could be purchased if .uk or .com is unavailable.

> ### Fact file
> Banners will appear across the top of each page of a website and are often used to advertise products or services.

> ### Checkpoint
> **Upload** – the opposite to download – is the transmission of data (a web page or a file, for example) from your computer to a server on the Internet.

> ### Activity
>
> Print the file: **FP Worksheet 3** from the Chapter 5 folder on the CD-ROM. Follow the worksheet's instructions to publish your completed web.

# Chapter 6

# Investigating how ICT is used in organisations

You may find that you prefer to study this chapter after you have completed Units 2 and 3 because not only does it build on the skills you have developed in using a variety of applications such as word processing and databases but it also introduces you to topics you have not yet covered.

## What you will learn

How different applications are used in different organisations
To identify why the type of application is appropriate to the organisation's needs

## Overview

You will develop an understanding of how and why software applications are used to meet the needs of different organisations.

Through a number of case studies on a variety of small, medium and large businesses you will learn how the different applications can be used. You will also learn through these case studies that many organisations will use specific applications that:

- capture, manipulate and enhance graphic images
- automate and control processes including CAD/CAM
- monitor and record physical and environmental data for analysis and interpretation.

## Case study 1

### Producing this textbook

Producing a book and CD-ROM involves many different forms of ICT applications and hardware.

This book was written by three authors working on separate computers from their own homes. E-mails were used to communicate with the authors and the publisher and CD-ROMs used to send large files to the publisher for copy editing. The job of a copy editor is to ensure that each section of the book is produced in a standard format in a style which the designer can follow.

You will notice that a wide variety of graphical images are used to illustrate the text and make the book more interesting to read. Clip art, screen dumps, photographs, cartoons and diagrams are all used.

The authors saved all the text for the book and CD-ROM in word format using a pc. They also saved each image in a separate file in a specific format, for example tiff or bitmap. This is

essential because the book is set (creating pages that match the design) by a typesetter who works on an Apple Macintosh (MAC) computer, using specialised desktop publishing software such as QuarkXpress™. The typesetter needs to convert each file into a format that is recognised by the MAC, and ensure that the files are not corrupt.

Once the pages have been set, and proofread by an editor to make sure that there are no mistakes, they are saved as pdf's using Adobe® Acrobat®. These pdf's are saved on CD-ROM, along with the image files, and sent to a printer. The printer then downloads all the information onto their computers, which in turn calculates the size and quality of each page and how much ink is needed to print the correct colours. Most of the machinery at a printing press uses computer technology, instructing machines to print, fold, cut and bind the final product – this book!

# Continuing Education & Training Service (CETS)

The Continuing Education & Training Service (CETS) is the fourth largest provider of Local Education Authority (LEA) adult education in the country and provides day and evening classes throughout the London Borough of Croydon. There are 12 main centres and 12 sub-centres at various locations throughout the borough and good communication between staff is essential. All the main centres are linked together in a Wide Area Network (WAN).

CETS soon realised the benefits of using e-mail. Without e-mail, contacting staff who are often on the move and not always at one location proved difficult. Staff can log on to their account from wherever they are in the borough. They can even log on from home.

Using the Novell e-mail system GroupWise, distribution groups have been set up. This means that messages can be sent to the relevant group of people, for example all the staff based at the Thornton Heath Centre, or the entire organisation, without having to know each individual member of staff's name. Important notices, notification of new job opportunities and any other information relevant to the successful running of the organisation can be sent simply and quickly.

## Student enrolment

In 2002 there were over 38,000 enrolments by approximately 18,000 students on over 2000 courses. In the past, without the use of a networked information system, students wanting to enrol on courses had to go to the centre offering the course and queue, sometimes for hours. CETS' private WAN links all the centres so that people can ring or go to any centre and enrol on the course of their choice, simply and quickly. The benefits of this system are easy to understand – no long queues and people can ring the enrolment line to enrol or go to their nearest centre rather than the centre running the course. Information regarding who has enrolled is held on the student database and can be accessed from any centre in the Borough.

## Standard ways of working

It is important to CETS that everyone uses the same house style. The organisation has a special section of the network – called S-Drive – where templates for documents such as letters, memos, meeting agendas and minutes are stored (see Figure 6.1). This means that there is consistency throughout the organisation. Documents that need to be made available to the organisation as a whole are saved on S-Drive and anyone can read or use them by saving them to their own account. Importantly, however, only key members of staff have the authority to access S-Drive to amend, delete or save new files. This is necessary to ensure that files are not unintentionally changed or deleted.

All important policies and procedures are stored on this drive so that all staff can access them at any time.

*Figure 6.1 CETS's S-Drive stores standard documents such as agenda and memo forms*

## Financial control

CETS has a budget of over £8 million so it is essential that expenditure is monitored closely. The Finance Manager used Excel to set up a budgetary control system which all managers who are budget holders can use. CETS accesses Croydon Council's accounting system – Oracle – from which summary information is extracted on to Excel worksheets for each budget on a monthly basis. Transaction sheets, created in Excel, giving full detailed information for each individual transaction back this up. Excel is also used to record and control the banking and petty cash procedures. To assist in processing the transactions from these spreadsheets the Finance Manager has also used advanced aspects of Excel, such as creating macros using Visual Basic Application (VBA) programming.

## The CETS guide

CETS produces a guide giving details of all courses offered which is distributed free three times a year to all households in the London Borough of Croydon (see Figure 6.2). The guide is created 'in-house' together with the Borough's Press and Publicity Department on an Apple Mac computer using the desktop publishing software QuarkXpress. As well as producing the guide, this software is used to create the termly newsletter to CETS staff and other leaflets. Photos that are used in these publications are manipulated, either from scanning or direct from a digital camera, using Adobe® Photoshop® software. They are stored on CDs and kept as a library.

*Figure 6.2 The CETS guide is produced using desktop publishing software*

## Website

CETS' website is continuously being updated. People are able to search for the course they want online and can download the CETS guide in PDF format in full, or relevant pages only if they wish. More and more people are using the Internet to search for information and by having course details easily available online, people living outside the Borough who may not necessarily receive a copy of the guide through their door can easily access information about CETS courses.

A feedback form allows people to send any comments electronically. All job vacancies are posted on the website and potential applicants are able to download all the relevant details about a job as well as a copy of an application form. Not only is this of benefit to the applicants, but it also reduces the number of phone calls CETS staff receive requesting job packs. As yet, people are not able to apply for jobs online, nor can they enrol online, but CETS is keen to develop the website to allow this to be done in the future.

## PowerPoint® presentations

The Head of Service, Ian Jones, uses a special PowerPoint® presentation called 'All About CETS' which is shown to new staff when they join the organisation. This presentation is also shown at special events, such as for special study visits from other organisations, when visitors can learn more about the organisation. Ian Jones says:

*'By using PowerPoint® to present information about our organisation we are able to give a far more professional approach than we were able to in the past. We find that, provided we follow the guidelines for well-designed PowerPoint® presentations, they can be more inviting, attract more attention and be more effective in delivering a message than using overhead transparencies.'*

## Learning centres

CETS has four learning centres at different locations in the borough. Students can use computers to take Learndirect courses and log on

Figure 6.3 CETS' learning centres home page

to UK Online (see Figure 6.3). The centres are Learndirect centres and branded UK Online centres. In 2001–2 over 800 students studied on Learndirect courses at a CETS learning centre. Students with little or no knowledge of ICT are encouraged to do UK Online taster sessions. Students can then join a CETS course or a

Learndirect course. Many students who do UK Online taster sessions become more at ease with using the Internet and e-mail with the result that they are able to use other software to support their studies with far more confidence.

*Source:* Continuing Education & Training Service (CETS).

## Activity

Print the file: **ORG Worksheet 1** from the Chapter 6 folder on the CD-ROM. This activity requires you to identify the purposes for which CETS use different software applications in their business.

## Case study 3

### Reed Executive PLC

Many large commercial organisations have their own private WAN which link offices, shops or branches throughout the country or world. An example of an organisation with its own private WAN is the recruitment Human Resource (HR) and training consultancy, Reed Executive PLC. Reed was set up in 1960 when Alec Reed, then aged 26, opened the first Reed branch in Hounslow, West London (see Figure 6.4). He started with just £75 and worked alone for a year. The company now has over 2500 co-members (staff) and sales of £406 million in 2001. Reed has 250 branches throughout the UK and Ireland and has a private WAN connecting them.

Figure 6. 4 Reed's first branch

Reed describes a WAN as a private network that connects different geographical locations, allowing them to share information electronically, whether this is through e-mails, Internet traffic or database transactions, and so on. In the past, this was run over leased telephone lines. Nowadays, the company uses broadband technology, which has increased the speed and amount of data that can be transferred by 3000 per cent!

Without anyone leaving the office, Reed's IT Department is able to provide support to solve IT problems which its branches may have. Currently, 50 people are employed in IT, including 18 who staff a helpdesk to answer queries from consultants throughout the network.

The single WAN network holds details of over a million contacts from both employers seeking staff as well as current job seekers. Reed's 2000 or so recruitment consultants have access to the network through the PC on their desks. Branches are able to exchange information about vacancies and possible people to fill them.

Reed does a full back-up every night, using industry standard tape drive technologies such as Digital Linear Tape (DLT) and Ultrium to store all the material safely off-site.

## Website

Reed's Internet recruitment site, can be viewed through www.heinemann.co.uk/hotlinks – click on Reed. It was created in 1995, when it was one of the first UK job sites on the world wide web (see Figure 6.5). Nowadays, 24 staff are involved in the management of the website. The staff are continually looking for ways to improve the user experience for both job-seekers and recruiters.

The hosting of the site is outsourced to Attenda, a hosting and server management company. Unusually, the website invites all

Figure 6. 5 Reed's Internet recruitment site

recruiters to post details of their vacancies on to the site for free. More jobs mean more job-seekers registering their interest and applying, working on the theory that 'a crowd attracts a crowd'. Over a million people visit the site each month to search through over 100,000 current opportunities for the one that's right for them to apply to. Reed keeps potential applicants updated with the latest job vacancies by sending them an e-mail or text message. In 2002 Reed sent 3.5 million SMS text messages and over 12 million e-mail alerts to job-seekers.

Reed knows that recruiters want fast access to the right job-seekers, and the company attracts more of the right job-seekers to jobs they are handling on behalf of their client employers through the Reed website.

In addition to sourcing the right people to fill permanent and temporary vacancies through the website, Reed offers 'end to end' recruitment managed services over the Internet. This means that the administration of the whole process of taking on a new recruit, from setting up the first interview to submitting an invoice for the fee due when the person starts work can all be done electronically. What's more, both Reed and the company involved can access a continually updated screen showing what stage each job opportunity and individual job-seeker has reached.

Reed also helps people find temporary work. Each temporary worker has to fill in a timesheet every week and have it signed off by the manager at the organisation in which he or she is working so that Reed can send the person the correct wages. Traditionally, this was organised through a paper timesheet form, which is filled out in triplicate. However, nowadays, over a third of Reed's temporary workers use a special electronic form instead, through Reed's specially developed OnTime system, which puts their timesheet on the Internet. This saves everyone involved (the temporary worker, the organisation the person is working for and Reed itself) time and money.

The Internet has transformed the way Reed works, allowing it to do much more for both employers and job-seekers.

*Source:* Reed Executive PLC.

## Denne Construction and The Horizon Housing Group

Denne Construction and The Horizon Housing Group have recently built some new houses using a building system that relies on computer-aided design and computer-aided manufacture (CAD/CAM). This is the first time that this technology has been used to manufacture and fabricate light steel frame housing on site in the UK.

Each house's steel frame was manufactured on the building site as and when it was required. A transportable computer-operated machine tool formed the sections of the frame from strips of steel. The sections were then riveted together to form frames from which the houses were constructed. The houses were finished by using traditional brickwork for the outer skin of the external walls and plaster board on the inside. The completed houses look and feel like traditionally built houses.

To manufacture the frames, the computer operator highlighted the particular part that was required and the machine tool automatically manufactured the individual sections. The specification for each part was stored in the computer program.

A building system of this nature has many advantages. For example, production and assembly of the parts can be controlled to meet specific requirements of the building project. The frame can be manufactured to a consistent quality which will reduce wastage. The building company does not have to wait for materials to be delivered and it does not have to find the space to store large quantities of building materials on site. The whole process of construction is faster. A typical development like the one carried out by Denne would take 34 weeks. A similar project using traditional methods of construction might take 42 weeks. All of this can help lead to a reduction in costs.

The initial cost of the fabrication equipment is relatively low. This system also avoids the need for a centralised factory and the transportation of completed frame sections that would otherwise be required. The skills to use this system can be learned fairly quickly.

Of course, there are disadvantages too. It is necessary to have an adequate area on site to locate the necessary housing for the machine tool and to assemble the frame. The builder also has to adapt to a different way of working.

However, over the coming years we are likely to see more and more examples of this exciting new method of building construction.

Figures 6.6 and 6.7 show the development of the houses. The steel framework forming the walls and roof is clearly visible. The frame has been covered with traditional cladding materials. Figure 6.8 shows the finished houses.

Figure 6.6 The steel-frame house under construction

Figure 6.7 The outer layer of brickwork and the roof have been added

Figure 6.8 The finished houses

*Source:* Denne Construction and The Horizon Housing Group

# Case study 5

## Satellite navigation

My husband and I were driving to the south of France for our holiday, but the journey was unexpectedly delayed and we could not reach our destination in time, so we needed to find a place to stop overnight.

In this situation you would normally have to choose a town and hope to find a suitable hotel with a vacancy. In the past, we have used the Michelin guide, which lists hotels, but we still had to find the location, which can be quite difficult when you may be tired, it may be late at night and you may not speak the local language.

Now, with satellite navigation technology that can be fitted to your car, you have the means not only to find a hotel, but you can be confident you will be directed right to the front door!

This is how it works: From the Start menu, select Address Book (see Figure 6.9) which takes you to the Guidance menu, where you first choose the country from a list and then the city by typing in the letters (see Figure 6.10).

Having identified the city, you can then request Points of interest (see Figure 6.11) at the destination, which gives an alphabetical selection ranging from airports to tourist information. We clicked on Hotel (see Figure 6.12), which provided a list of hotels in Chalon Sur Saone (see Figure 6.13).

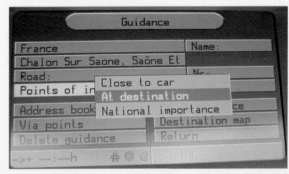

*Figure 6.11 Select Points of Interest from the Guidance menu*

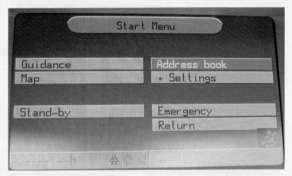

*Figure 6.9 Select Address Book from the Start menu*

*Figure 6.12 Select Hotel*

*Figure 6.10 Guidance menu*

*Figure 6.13 List of suggested hotels*

Having searched the database of hotels, we selected the Best Western, Saint Regis, and were able to obtain the full address and phone number (see Figure 6.14).

The computer then identifies the route and giving verbal and visual instructions, directs you to the front door of the hotel. At all times you are able to follow your position on the map. The scale can be varied to show the approach to a city or the exact location of the street you are looking for (see Figures 6.16 and 6.17).

*Figure 6.14 Satellite navigation system provides the selected hotel's address and phone number*

We phoned the hotel to check whether a room was available, the cost for the night and then made the reservation. We confirmed that we would be arriving in about an hour. Now, all that was required was to select OK which took us back to the destination screen and then select Start Guidance (see Figure 6.15).

*Figure 6.16 This image shows a large-scale view of the approach as you come into the city*

*Figure 6.17 In close up you can clearly see street names. The circular symbol shows the exact position of the hotel*

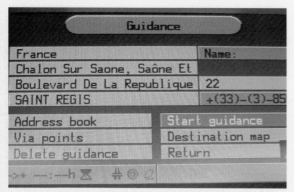

*Figure 6.15 Select Start Guidance from the Guidance menu*

# Computer Cab

Computer Cab is London's largest licensed taxi fleet offering a 24-hour service seven days a week throughout Greater London (see Figure 6.19).

*Figure 6.19 All of Computer Cab's taxis use a GPS system*

For the past six years the company has been using a satellite navigation system called Mobistar that uses a satellite that was put up for the Gulf War in 1992. Every taxi in its fleet of 4000 has a Global Positioning (GPS) system installed.

When an operator receives a booking for a cab he or she inputs the details into the computer, which in turn will find the nearest cab to the pick-up point and automatically dispatch the job to that cab. The computer in the cab has a screen so the driver scrolls through to get all the details of the job. The only time the voice channel is used to contact the operator is when a driver has a query. An operator can track onscreen any one of Computer Cab's fleet while it is doing a job.

Operators have a map come up on the screen and they can see exactly where the cab is, and also the destination and pick-up point, enabling the operator to gauge how long the cab will take to reach the customer (see Figure 6.20). Also the computer in the cab has a swipe device so that drivers can

*Figure 6.20 A Computer Cab operator views an onscreen map*

take credit cards just as a store would do. Using this technology, Computer Cab handle over 13,000 bookings a day.

*Source:* Computer Cab PLC.

# Croydon libraries

The London Borough of Croydon has 13 libraries, which are linked together via a wide area network (WAN). If you are visiting one of the branches and you wish to check the availability of a book, you can search the library's computerised library catalogue. Not only will you find out whether the book is available, you will be given details of which branches stock it and whether or not the book is on loan. Access to the library catalogue has been extended to allow borrowers to access the library catalogue via the Internet. This means that, if you have access to the Internet at home, you can find out which of the branches, if any, stock a book you need for your studies and whether or not it is currently out on loan – all without leaving home!

The Central Library has a self-issue terminal installed to save queuing at busy times.

Borrowers place their library ticket under the scanner and the computer will record the number. They then have to place each library book under the scanner and the computer will record the number and then print out a receipt which also records the date when books have to be returned.

Croydon libraries also offer free Internet access and a range of ICT learning opportunities to members of the public. At the Central Library, there is a 'Net Corner' where 15 machines are available on a first-come first-served basis. An automated booking system has been installed whereby users take a ticket from the ticket machine that informs them which terminal to use and allocates them a log-on code. Each user can have 30 minutes at one time using a machine. Five minutes before the end of this period, a warning message will be given that the session is drawing to an end so that users have time to finish off their work before the PC automatically logs the user out. This facility is extremely popular and over 1500 people use the machines each week.

Each Croydon library has public access computers, which provide:

*Figure 6.21 Net Corner in Croydon Central Library*

- free access to the Internet and online learning
- e-mail
- word processing, spreadsheets, databases and self-teaching programmes on how to use them
- access to all local and national government information
- access to the vast amount of information available on the Internet whether it is for health, leisure, welfare, education or culture
- access to learning packages in the library.

The People's Network (see page 220 for more about The People's Network) will allow Croydon libraries to treble the number of PCs available for Internet access and increase the bandwidth from 2 MB to 10 MB.

The Central Library has a CCTV enlarger available to enable the visually impaired to view the text of books, articles or important documents. The library also has a Kurzweil machine that scans text and 'reads' it back.

Source: Croydon Libraries.

The People's Network (see page 220 for more about The People's Network)

## Case study 8

# Trivalley Construction Limited

*Figure 6.22 Steve*

This is Steve. Steve and his business partners, Matt and Gary, have recently set up a building company, Trivalley Construction Limited. The company specialises in the construction and refurbishment of buildings and also undertakes electrical maintenance and inspection works on behalf of British Gas.

The type of work that the company does ranges from the construction of simple extensions to private houses, larger extensions to school buildings and restoration and refurbishment work to commercial properties including offices.

Steve, Matt and Gary have employed an Office Manager, Paul, to handle the administrative side of the business. Paul has a standalone computer system to help him with his work.

- He uses word processing software for general office correspondence.
- Invoicing, billing and accounting are handled with the aid of spreadsheet software. For example, Paul produces at least 20 invoices a day, sometimes as many as 500 a month.
- He uses a database to keep a record of customers and uses the data as a source for mailmerge letters.
- He also uses project management software to produce weekly and monthly planning sheets so that the company can programme its workload and future business projects.

After setting up the company, one of partners' first tasks was to find a company to design a new business logo and stationery for them. Since none of the partners is experienced in design, they employed a specialist company called Real World Design. Real World Design came up with several ideas for the logo and after Steve, Matt and Gary decided on the final design, the stationery was produced.

*Figure 6.23 Real World Design's suggested designs for Trivalley Construction's logo*

The partners also wanted to set up a website and had a meeting with Real World Design to discuss their requirements. The main things to be considered were as follows:

- To have a website that was unique. Steve, Matt and Gary felt they could probably have produced something for themselves using a basic web page application, but they wanted something distinctive.
- They did not want standard clip art in the web pages but illustrations to do with their business.
- The website must appeal to their target customers. They needed to strike a balance between the small domestic client and the larger commercial organisation.
- The cost.

Following this meeting, the design team produced an outline scheme. The partners decided to go ahead with the new website and had further meetings with the design company. A few weeks later, Real World Design produced the finished website (see Figure 6.25).

*Figure 6.25 Trivalley Construction's website*

Once the website was ready, Trivalley Construction had to register with an Internet service provider (ISP) in order to get Internet access. As soon as this was finalised, the design company installed the software and arranged for the website to go live.

Now that it is up and running, Trivalley Construction is keeping an eye on the number of visits (hits) to the site and hoping it will generate more business for the company. The partners will be reviewing the website regularly to ensure the

TRIVALLEY CONSTRUCTION LTD
CROWN LODGE • CANTELUPE RD
EAST GRINSTEAD • WEST SUSSEX • RH19 3BJ
TELEPHONE: 01342 315444 • FAX: 01342 303300
Web: www.trivalley.co.uk
Email: info@trivalley.co.uk

*Figure 6.24 Trivalley Construction's stationery*

information is up-to-date and, over the next few months, are planning to extend the website to include illustrations of completed projects, information about current projects and details of the services the company can provide.

In the meantime, the partners are also considering the installation of a small local area network (LAN). Paul is finding the preparation of the invoices very time consuming and is looking at ways to make his invoicing work more straightforward. He is considering the possibility of purchasing a specialised accounting package or a bespoke invoicing system.

*Source:* Trivalley Construction Limited and Real World Design

## Activity

 Print the file: **ORG Worksheet 2** from the Chapter 6 folder on the CD-ROM. This activity requires you to evaluate the effectiveness of the Trivalley Construction's web site.

## Case study 9

### Magpye Publications – Industrial Networking

# Building control system takes the guesswork out of dealing with the British weather

ABB's intelligent building control system i-bus BB is helping Cadbury Garden and Leisure at Congresbury, near Bristol, to maintain optimum growing conditions whilst ensuring customers are provided with a comfortable shopping environment

AS ONE OF THE SEVEN CENTRES in the Garden and Leisure Group, Cadbury Garden and Leisure is one of the largest and most prestigious garden centres in the country, attracting an average of 1.2 million visitors each year and offers a state-of-the-art all-weather gardening and leisure experience.

Maintaining ideal conditions is the job of ABB's intelligent building control system. The system, supplied and commissioned in conjunction with the electrical contractor, Express Electrics, provides complete control and automation of the building's thermal shade, roof ventilation and lighting systems via information received from ABB's purpose built, multi-functional weather station which continually monitors any changes in sunlight, rain, temperature, wind speed and direction.

Peter Martin, Building Development Manager for the Garden and Leisure Group comments: "When faced with the unpredictable British weather, ABB's i-bus EIB system is the obvious answer to all our needs."

ABB's i-bus EIB technology incorporates a single two-wire control cable linking individual system components that trigger or execute programmable commands ensuring complete design flexibility. Individual electronic micro-processor units such as shutter actuators, timers and power supply, not only

perform several functions independently but also communicate with each other via a single bus. System configuration and commissioning is achieved by connection of a PC at any point of the system via a serial interface, utilising specialist software.

**Important benefits** Kevin Henman, ABB sales engineer explains: "Flexibility, material savings and a reduced fire risk due to the minimal usage of cabling are important benefits resulting from the design of ABB's i-bus EIB technology. Large garden and leisure facilities such as Cadbury Garden and Leisure benefit from a truly flexible control system such as this, which will automatically respond to continual changes in the weather."

ABB and Express Electrics were able to offer additional security and cost-saving benefits to Cadbury Garden and Leisure. These included automated control of external security lighting, links to the underfloor heating and fire detection system, internal lighting control including the management of the graded lighting system installed in the newly-built pet and aquatic department and the timed operation of all retail lighting areas.
ABB
h145@industrialnetworking.co.uk
ENTER h145 ON ENQUIRY CARD

The Cadbury Garden and Leisure centre at Congresbury near Bristol attracts some 1.2 million visitors per year. ABB's intelligent building control system maintains ideal conditions, whatever the weather

*Source:* Industrial Networking and Open Control, June 2002

**Activity**

▷ Print the file: **ORG Worksheet 3** from the Chapter 6 folder on the CD-ROM. This activity requires you to identify the advantages of using a modern computer control system.

## Case study 10

# Photocopy Service Technician

Roger Spiller is a Service Technician for a photocopying company. Each day he travels from home to customers to remedy faults on their photocopying machines. In recent times, there has been an enormous change in the way he communicates with head office.

### Old system

Each evening he would be told by telephone the details of his first call for the next day. When that job was completed as soon as he left the customer, using a coded system, he phoned in giving:

- details of the problem
- the action taken
- time taken
- parts used.

Before mobile phones, Roger would have either asked customers if he could use their phone – not all customers were willing for him to do this – or found a public call box. Sometimes it wasn't easy to find a public phone or if he did, the phone was not working. Once mobile phones became available, this particular problem was solved.

### New system

These days Roger uses a Siemens Pocket PC S45, a hand held PDA (Personal Digital Assistant). He almost never phones into Work Control – all communication is done using the PDA, which has a main menu:

- Messages in
- Messages out
- Messages seen – jobs completed
- Kept – any messages you wish to retain (see Figure 6.26).

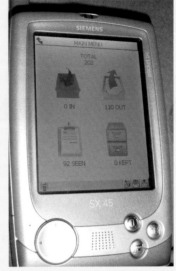

*Figure 6.26  Siemens Pocket PC SX45 main menu*

The first call for the next day is received the night before by selecting 'In'. The call is 'selected', which brings up another screen giving:

- full details of the customer
- the nature of the problem
- history of the machine (see Figure 6.27)
- its location at the premises.

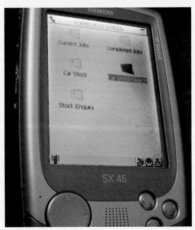

*Figure 6.27  Roger's PDA gives a history of the machines he services under 'Completed jobs'*

All this information on the machine is logged in the database against its serial number – the unique reference.

On arrival at the customer's premises, Roger accesses the next screen where he enters how long it took to get to the site and his arrival time. At this stage, he will also be given details of the next call. If he feels the job will take more than the average time, he can inform Work Control which will confirm whether they want him to do the next call or whether the job has been passed to someone else.

On completion of the job Roger presses the Send button, which accesses a series of screens to input:

- parts used
- parts to be ordered
- any other information which may be useful in the future.

### Does Roger prefer the new system?

'Yes, definitely although I admit when it was first proposed, I had reservations.'

### What are the benefits?

*'I have the whole history of the machines for the past three to four calls, so even before I arrive at the call, I have a much clearer picture of what is required than was possible in the past. It is also really useful to know the exact location of the machine, especially in a large organisation as you may be surprised how hard it can be to find someone who knows exactly which machine needs repairing and where to find it!*

*'The PDA also includes an address book and the facility to send and retrieve e-mails. The Technical Supervisor leads a team of engineers and he keeps us informed of developments by e-mail. Also the PDA contains a complete list of stock I have in the car, and I can keep in contact with the stores so that as items are used, a replacement order is automatically generated (see Figure 6.28). If I need a special part for a job, I can order it as a request and the part will be delivered the next day.'*

*Figure 6.28 The PDA gives Roger details of the stock he holds in his car*

*'If this isn't enough the PDA acts as a mobile phone, by plugging in a lead with ear phones and a mouthpiece to the USB port and pressing a button to activate the phone screen (see Figure 6.29). You can even attach a printer or a bar code reader to the PALM.'*

*Figure 6.23 Roger can use the PDA as a mobile phone*

## Palmer McCarthy

Palmer McCarthy is a small firm of Chartered Certified Accountants based in Croydon which has been in business over 70 years. The staff of ten regularly use computers in their work. They have a small local area network (LAN) using the star topology where each terminal is connected directly to the file server. The network was installed by a specialist IT company. One of the partners makes any changes to the system as required and deals with any problems. In the last three years the firm has not had to call in outside assistance for network failure.

Staff regularly use Microsoft® Office software, as well as special tax return software called Taxpoint, which allows them to submit tax returns electronically to the Inland Revenue. Viztopia, a special accounts preparation software package allows them to produce accounts far quicker than before computers were used. IT has increased the firm's ability to respond to time pressures and information requests in addition to increasing the amount of work that staff can handle. IT has therefore increased the profitability of the firm.

E-mail has allowed the firm to have instant contact with a large number of its clients and the Internet has been invaluable for obtaining tax information from the Inland Revenue and Customs & Excise, as well as information regarding charity accounting from the Charity Commission. The staff can download important circulars on tax issues directly from the Inland Revenue's website.

Palmer McCarthy has not as yet created a website to promote its business. Traditionally, new business has come through word of mouth and recommendation of by existing clients. The partners have yet to be convinced that the work and investment required to ensure that a website is kept up-to-date and maintained will be covered by any new business that the site may generate. They feel strongly that having no web presence is better than having an out-of-date, poorly maintained website.

*Source:* Palmer McCarthy

## Congestion charging in central London

If you live near or in London, you will not be surprised to learn that traffic congestion in the capital is the worst in the UK and among the worst in Europe. In fact, average speeds in the centre of the capital are now lower than 10 mph! It is believed that London loses £2 million to £4 million each week because of the time lost caused by congestion. In an effort to overcome traffic congestion and to try to encourage people to use other forms of transport, in February 2003 the London Assembly introduced congestion charging.

Drivers are required to pay £5 per day if they wish to drive in central London between 7 am and 6.30 pm Monday to Friday. A network of 203 enforcement cameras, similar to CCTV-type cameras used at ports and airports have been sited throughout the centre of London. These cameras provide high quality video-stream signals

Figure 6.30 *Central London congestion charging zone icon*

to an Automatic Number Plate Recognition (ANPR) computer system.

Two types of cameras are used, one taking colour images that show a vehicle in its surroundings, and a monochrome (black and white) camera used to read number plates. These cameras use 'X-wave technology' which enables them to see better in poor light conditions. Captured images are sent back to the ANPR system from which data is generated showing the exact time and date that the images were taken. Images from both cameras are stored together with the information from the ANPR reader in case the information needs to be compared.

The images are then automatically matched against a database of drivers who have registered to pay. Drivers who have not registered to pay by midnight of that day, will then be sent a penalty notice after the number plates are checked against the Driver and Vehicle Licensing Agency (DVLA) database.

## Case study 13

### Holiday home rental

One of the co-authors of this book is a co-owner of a holiday home on the Costa Blanca, Spain. When the owners purchased the property they needed to find an effective way of marketing the property. They decided that the Internet was the most suitable medium for doing this. Their first step was to purchase a domain name. This was done very easily via the website Simply. By using this site the owners found that a Costablanca-holidays name was available and purchased the domain name for a small fee for a two-year period. To view these sites, go to www.heinemann.co.uk/hotlinks and then click on Simply or on Costa Blanca holidays.

The next step was to design a website. They were anxious to keep the site simple, but informative and found that by using FrontPage, they could create a suitable site quickly and

with little effort. They found that by using a digital camera and downloading the images to their computer they could add images to the website to illustrate the property. As yet they have not purchased Adobe® Photoshop® to manipulate the images, but have found that Microsoft® Photo Editor has been sufficient to meet their needs.

By using the Resize option within this software, large picture files can be reduced in size in order to ensure that download time is reduced.

Another software package, PaperPort, was used to adjust the colour, tint and brightness and contrast of images.

Once the web was completed, it was published – www.simply.com provided a suitable web hosting plan and avoided using alternative cheaper or free web hosting plans which often

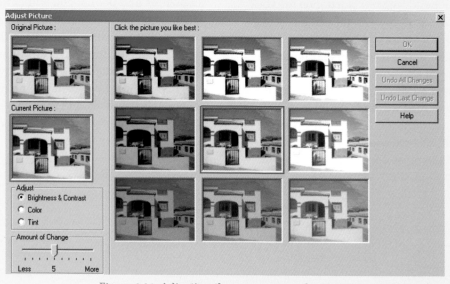

*Figure 6.31 Adjusting the appearance of an image using PaperPort*

result in irritating banners unrelated to the website being displayed.

After the website was published, it was then necessary to ensure that Internet users would find the site when searching the Internet. Most search engines allow website owners to submit their site so that the URL is added to their index. Some search engines may require a fee for this service, but others such as Google do so for free. However, these search engines will not guarantee that all sites will be listed.

Having submitted the website, it took a little over six weeks for the site to begin appearing on searches. User statistics have shown that whereas in March 2002, the average number of visits to the site was seven a day, this increased to 52 a day in January 2003 (see Figure 6.32).

The owners have found that for minimal cost in terms of marketing, they have been able to successfully rent out their accommodation by having their own website. Booking requests are received both by e-mail and by telephone, and most of the communication between the clients and the owners is undertaken through e-mail. Booking forms are e-mailed to prospective clients, who then return them in the post with payment.

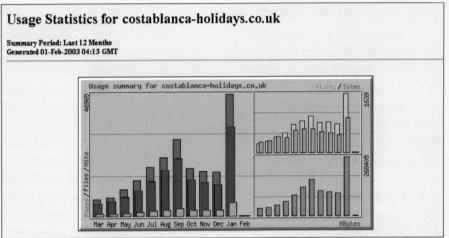

**Usage Statistics for costablanca-holidays.co.uk**

Summary Period: Last 12 Months
Generated 01-Feb-2003 04:13 GMT

*Figure 6.32 Numbers of visits to the Costablanca-holidays website March 2002–January 2003*

When you are building your portfolios for your Applied GCSE assessments you will be required to use a variety of information sources, including the Internet, and most importantly to acknowledge them. When the authors carried out their research for this book and the case studies for this Chapter, the information was sourced from a variety of sources including searches on the Internet, personal and business contacts, newspapers, magazines and books. You will notice that the source is acknowledged at the end of each case study and at the relevant point in the book, as well as on the acknowledgements page (see vi). Take care to do the same in your own studies.

This chapter has given you an insight into a variety of businesses and the different ways that computer technology assists organisations in their day-to-day activities.

# 7

# Developing business documents

After studying this chapter you should be able to:

- produce documents in styles that suit your purpose
- produce documents in styles that suit your readers
- choose and apply standard document layouts
- improve the accuracy and readability of the documents you create.

In this chapter you will learn how to create and compose a variety of documents using styles, types of information and layouts that suit their different purposes. You will study a range of authentic documents used in organisations, and compare them with the style and layout of the documents you create.

## What you will learn

Language style
Document style
Presentation techniques

## Overview: Business documents

If you could look through the filing system of any organisation or company, you would find all sorts of documents stored in countless files.

The documents would include:

- letters
- memos
- faxes
- e-mails
- reports
- newsletters
- agendas and minutes of meetings
- web pages
- hard copies of interactive presentations
- data capture forms
- invoices
- financial plans
- database reports.

If you studied several of these documents, you would probably notice that some were written and presented in a very formal style while others were more informal, both in the language used and in their presentation. This is because different documents have different purposes, and they use different styles to achieve those purposes. For example, an invitation to attend a job interview is not likely to be presented in the same way as an invitation to an 18th birthday party – see Figure 7.1.

> 2 Lodge Road
> Wayfield
> ER6 4KN
>
> 1 May 2003
>
> Mr M Gates
> 12 Green Lane
> Wayfield
> ER3 7JB
>
> Dear Mr Gates
>
> I refer to our recent telephone conversation and confirm an appointment has been made for you to attend my 18th birthday party on 18 May 2003 at 20:30 hours. Please telephone to confirm you are able to attend.
>
> On arrival, please ask for Miss Harris.
>
> Yours sincerely
>
> *Eleanor Harris*
>
> Eleanor Harris

> **Come for an interview for the IT Technician vacancy**
>
> **Place:** Jude's office
> **Date:** 12 May 2002
> **Time:** 10.30 am
>
> **RSVP**

*Figure 7.1 Both the invitation and letter have been produced in styles that do not fit their purpose. An invitation to attend for interview will usually be formal and a birthday party invitation is generally informal*

When you go to work your future employer will expect you to have good general qualities as well as the professional skills needed for a particular job. As you progress through your career, you will be competing for jobs with several other people who have the same or similar professional qualifications. When this happens, the employer looks hard at those general qualities – qualities like good IT skills, being someone who works hard, being a fun person to work with and having good communication skills.

The communication skills your employer will look for are in speaking and listening, and especially, in writing. Most business organisations rely on written communications for the majority of their work and you will almost certainly be responsible for producing your own correspondence when you go to work.

Good writing mostly depends on choosing the best style for the type of document you are producing. There is a wide range of different document types you may need to write, including:

- a letter responding to a complaint
- a glossy advertisement for a new product
- an e-mail to a company asking for information on a product
- a memo to the sales team discussing a new product
- an interactive presentation about a new business enterprise
- a table of results for a special sales promotion
- a report on the sales promotion
- minutes of a meeting of the sales team
- an invitation to a business function
- a telephone message taken for a colleague.

## The starting point

For any document to be effective it needs careful planning and the points you must consider are:

- the purpose of the document
- the target audience
- writing style and tone
- presentation and layout
- accuracy, clarity and consistency.

You will find it very useful to start collecting business documents which come into your home.

## The purpose of the document

Each of the documents in the list above has a specific purpose, and this purpose affects the writing and presentation style. The purpose of a formal letter responding to a complaint is to try to sort out the problem. The purpose of the glossy advertisement is to sell the product. The purpose of the table of results for the sales promotion is to make the results clear to understand.

Throughout the writing process, you must always think about the purpose. Each word, sentence, and paragraph should contribute towards the purpose you have in mind.

## The target audience

The next question you need to ask yourself is: who is going to read your document? Is it a customer, colleagues or the general public? A customer receiving a letter responding to his or her complaint would expect a formal reply using language that he or she can understand, that is, without technical language or jargon. On the other hand, a memo to the sales team discussing a new product might be highly technical. A note to a colleague passing on a telephone message will be informal while an advertisement, designed to appeal to a wide audience, must be eye-catching and to the point.

## Writing style and tone

Once you know the purpose of a document and who is likely to be reading it, you should be able to decide on the most suitable writing style and tone.

You would almost certainly choose different writing styles and tone for a letter of complaint, a thank you letter for a birthday present, an advertisement or a children's story. Choosing the right language style is essential to ensure the document sends the right message.

The basic choice of language style is formal or informal. For example, a letter applying for a job should be written in a formal style. The style has to help achieve the purpose of the document, which is to encourage the reader to consider your application. It would not be an appropriate place to make a joke or to use the informal phrases that are often used in conversation. A letter that starts with 'Dear Sir, I am writing to you to apply for work in your organisation' is likely to create a very different impression to a letter that begins with 'Hi, I'd really love a job with you lot!'.

On the other hand, if you are inviting people to a party, then 'Hi, I'd really love you to come to my party!' is more informal and friendly than 'Dear Friend, I would be most pleased if you could attend my party'. The slightly more formal style is not wrong if it creates a tone that is right for your purpose. A formal party invitation may be the right choice for a wedding invitation, for example.

The difference between formal and informal styles is not clear-cut. Imagine it as a line with 'very formal' at one end and 'very informal' at the other, with varying amounts of each in between. To help you choose the style for your document, look carefully at other similar documents you come across. Always keep your document purpose and reader(s) in mind, then you should have no difficulty in getting started.

Sometimes, however, no matter how hard you try to find the right words, they don't seem to go down on paper the way you would like. If that happens, try saying out loud what it is you are trying to write. Usually, that will help the words and ideas to flow. Write down what you said and then look over your words to see how you might improve them. There are tools within software that can help you to improve your writing style (see below).

## Presentation and layout

Any document that is produced on behalf of an organisation presents an image of that organisation to the person receiving it. Whether it is a letter sent by a single employee or the Annual Report produced by the board of directors, the image presented by the document is very important and you should take great care to plan the layout and structure of all your business documents.

## House style

Often, organisations have a house style for their documents, which must be followed at all times. A house style aims to present a standard, easily recognisable look to an organisation's documents. This look or image gives customers (and employees) a sense of good organisation and efficiency, of everybody working together to produce a high quality product or service.

Many organisations invest a lot of money in their house style as the foundation of their printed or published image. If you have received different letters from the same organisation, compare the layout. You will notice that, although different people in different departments may write them, they all have the addresses, dates and references in the same position and all use the same font. The same is true for logos – they are always in the same place, and are the same colour and shape.

If you compare business letters sent from a variety of different organisations, you will see that they too are all very similar. This is because most business documents follow standard styles so that if you were asked to produce a business letter, a memo, an agenda for a meeting or a report, you would be able to do it without any difficulty. Fortunately, most software has tools to help you with the presentation of documents. Standard templates are available for letters, memos, faxes, invoices, reports, web pages and presentations – you will learn more about these in the following pages.

## Accuracy, clarity and consistency

By now, you will be familiar with the spell checker and should be using it as a matter of routine. However, most applications have additional tools to help you present documents that are accurate and can be clearly understood. These include:.

- AutoCorrect
- the grammar checker
- the thesaurus.

## AutoCorrect

The AutoCorrect feature will automatically detect and correct errors as you type. For instance, if you type 'adn', as soon as you press the space bar, AutoCorrect will replace what you have typed with 'and'. See what happens when you type 'amkes' rather than 'makes' or —> or <=> or, on a new line, === followed by enter or return!

If you accidentally leave the Caps Lock on at the beginning of a new sentence, AutoCorrect will turn this 'tHIS EXAMPLE' into 'This example', or if you forget to capitalise the first letter of Monday or Tuesday, AutoCorrect will put it right for you.

AutoCorrect also ensures that every line in a list will start with a capital letter, which can sometimes be annoying if you want lower case. (DBD Worksheet 1 looks at AutoCorrect in more detail.)

## Grammar checker

The wavy green lines that appear under text point out possible errors in grammar in a similar way to the wavy red lines that show spelling errors. The grammar checker tool is available to help you produce accurate work such as making sure the subject and verb agree or checking you have not confused similar words.

For example, if you typed 'What course was Ellie and Grace doing at college?', the grammar checker would suggest changing 'was' to 'were' because the verb of a sentence must agree with the subject in number and in person (see Figure 7.2).

The grammar checker will also indicate errors in capitalisation, incorrect punctuation and incorrect spacing between words.

A word of advice – the grammar checker is an excellent aid to accuracy but use it with some caution because in some instances what you have typed will be perfectly acceptable and will not benefit from being changed.

## Thesaurus

The thesaurus is a list of words organised into groups of words with similar meanings. It is useful if you are trying to find an alternative word, perhaps because you have used the same word twice in one sentence, or if you are trying to find a better word.

Look at the following example:

'The Students' Association shop wants to ensure the correct textbooks are in stock to ensure students can purchase them without delay.'

The word 'ensure' has been used twice and there may also be a better word for 'correct'. By using the thesaurus we are able to come up with the alternatives shown in Figure 7.3.

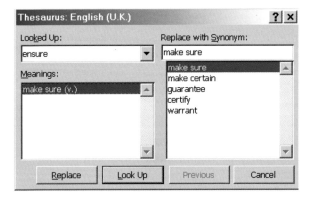

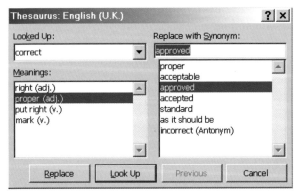

*Figure 7.3 The thesaurus facility offers a choice of alternative words*

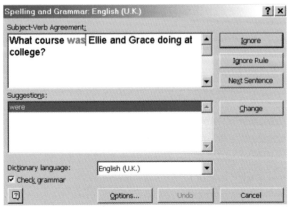

*Figure 7.2 The grammar check tool*

'The Students' Association shop wants to make certain the approved textbooks are in stock to ensure students can purchase them without delay.'

The revised sentence is much better.

Becoming familiar with, and using these tools will help you to produce a professional looking document. However, the tools alone will not ensure your documents are accurate and you must make the final check by carefully proof-reading every document that you produce. Always make sure that what you have written is accurate, clear to understand and says what you intended it to say.

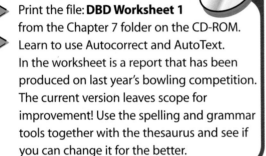

**Activity**

▷ Print the file: **DBD Worksheet 1** from the Chapter 7 folder on the CD-ROM.

▷ Learn to use Autocorrect and AutoText. In the worksheet is a report that has been produced on last year's bowling competition. The current version leaves scope for improvement! Use the spelling and grammar tools together with the thesaurus and see if you can change it for the better.

## Choosing the right document style

Organisations use different styles of documents for different purposes. These include:

- business letters
- memos
- faxes
- agendas and minutes of meetings
- reports
- publicity materials
- web pages
- presentations
- data capture forms
- financial plans
- database reports.

## Templates

Most software applications offer a feature – Templates – that can help you produce the right style of document. For example, in word processing software there are templates for letters and faxes, memos, reports, publications and web pages. In spreadsheet software there are templates for invoices, orders and expenses. Presentation software offers a wide variety of templates, including those for company meetings, marketing plans and selling products. In web page software there are templates that will help you create a website to suit your purpose.

In all software applications, you access templates through File, New. In word processing software you will be presented with a Templates dialogue box similar to the one in Figure 7.4.

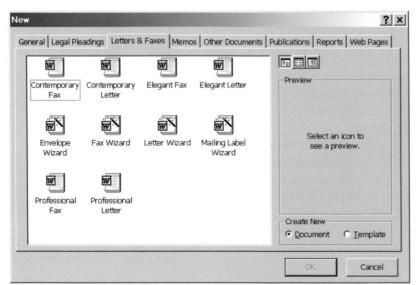

*Figure 7.4 The Templates dialogue box*

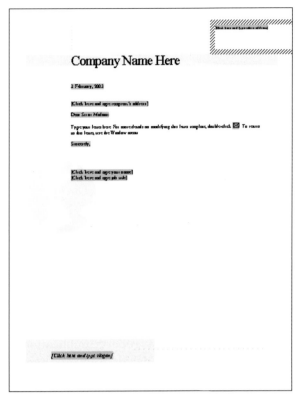

*Figure 7.5  A letter template*

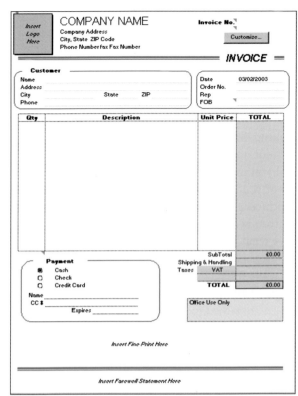

*Figure 7.6  An invoice template*

From here you can select the appropriate tab and choose a template. Figures 7.5 and 7.6 show some examples of templates in word processing and spreadsheet software.

There will be opportunities to use templates in the activities on the following pages.

## Business letters

Some organisations have templates set up in their house style that employees are expected to use if they are writing letters, but many organisations rely on their employees' knowledge to write a business letter.

A business letter is a formal, written communication from one organisation to either another organisation or an individual. Look at the letters in Figure 7.7 which have been sent from the student shop at Jubilee 6th Form College.

Study both the layout and content of the letters. They contain features that you will find on most business letters:

- the letters contain similar details

- they are presented in a fully blocked style with open punctuation
- each letter has a beginning, a middle and an ending
- the language is formal.

Look more closely at the presentation of the formal business letter to Heinemann in Figure 7.8.

## Layout and presentation

- Every line starts at the left margin – this is called **blocked style**.
- The only punctuation is within the body or content of the letter. Notice that there are no commas or full stops in the reference or addressee details or after the opening or close – this style is called **open punctuation**.
- The postal town in the recipient's address is shown in capital letters with the post code underneath (or two spaces away if space on the page is tight).
- Clear lines are left throughout the letter to separate the different sections. In most cases one clear line is sufficient but in order to leave enough space for the

**JUBILEE 6TH FORM COLLEGE STUDENT ASSOCIATION**

Festival Walk
Wayfield
Midshire
ER2 2AD

Telephone 01952 502002
Fax 01952 502003
E-mail ass@jubilee.ac.uk
www.jubilee.ac.uk

Our Ref 2003/020

19 September 2003

Heinemann Educational Publishers
Halley Court
Jordan Hill
OXFORD
OX2 8EJ

Dear Sirs

NEW BOOK ORDER

Further to my telephone call to your office today, I enclose my order for the following titles:

10   AVCE ICT Student Book (2nd Edition)
5   Researching Language (2nd Edition)
10   Modular Mathematics for AS and A Level
10   AS and A2 English Literature
15   GCSE ICT for Edexcel

I look forward to receiving the books within the next 7 days.

Yours faithfully

*Salim Hassan*

Salim Hassan
Shop Manager

Enc

---

**JUBILEE 6TH FORM COLLEGE STUDENT ASSOCIATION**

Festival Walk
Wayfield
Midshire
ER2 2AD

Telephone 01952 502002
Fax 01952 502003
E-mail ass@jubilee.ac.uk
www.jubilee.ac.uk

29 September 2003

Miss Eleanor Harris
2 Lodge Road
WAYFIELD
ER6 4KN

Dear Miss Harris

AVCE ICT STUDENT BOOK (2ND EDITION)

I refer to your visit to the Student Association shop on 18 September and am pleased to inform you that the AVCE ICT Student Book is now available priced £16.99.

Please bring this letter with you when you come to collect your book.

Yours sincerely

*Salim Hassan*

Salim Hassan
Shop Manager

*Figure 7.7 Business letters*

---

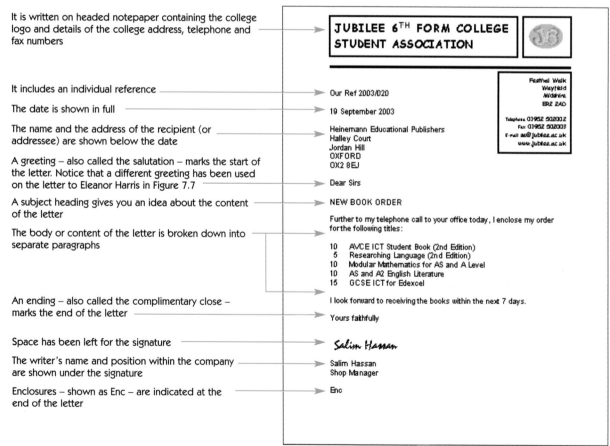

It is written on headed notepaper containing the college logo and details of the college address, telephone and fax numbers

It includes an individual reference

The date is shown in full

The name and the address of the recipient (or addressee) are shown below the date

A greeting – also called the salutation – marks the start of the letter. Notice that a different greeting has been used on the letter to Eleanor Harris in Figure 7.7

A subject heading gives you an idea about the content of the letter

The body or content of the letter is broken down into separate paragraphs

An ending – also called the complimentary close – marks the end of the letter

Space has been left for the signature

The writer's name and position within the company are shown under the signature

Enclosures – shown as Enc – are indicated at the end of the letter

*Figure 7.8 Common features of business letters*

signature, five clear lines should be left. If a letter is short, it is advisable to leave more space – the spaces between the reference, date, addressee and greeting may be increased as long as the spacing is consistent. Within the letter itself you must keep to one clear line.

- The complimentary close must match the opening salutation. Did you notice that the two examples in Figure 7.7 are different?

## Golden rules

Here are a few rules to remember:

- If you start with Dear Sir/Madam, you must close with Yours faithfully.
- If you start with Dear Mr/Mrs/Miss/Dr followed by a name, you must close with Yours sincerely.
- You must always use a capital Y for Yours and lower case f or s for faithfully or sincerely.
- You do not normally start a letter with Dear Janet or Dear John unless you know the person well and would use his or her first name in conversation.

## Content

The first paragraph of a letter introduces the topic. You may be referring to a telephone conversation, a letter you have received or an advertisement you have seen. You are likely to start a letter with an opening sentence that begins like this:

- Thank you for your letter dated …
- I refer to our recent telephone conversation …
- I am writing to enquire …
- With reference to your advertisement in the Wayfield News of 10 June 2003 for …

The middle paragraph(s) expand on the reason for writing.

The final paragraph concludes the letter and often starts with a sentence like this:

- Please contact me if you would like further information …
- I look forward to hearing from you …
- Thank you for …
- We will contact you again in due course …

## Style of language

In both of the examples in Figure 7.7 the message is clear and the tone is pleasant and courteous.

Some organisations expect their employees to use the first person plural – we and us – if a letter is sent on behalf of the organisation. If you were writing a business letter as a private individual, you would use the first person singular – I and me.

**Activity**

> Print the file: **DBD Worksheet 2** from the Chapter 7 folder on the CD-ROM. This worksheet gives you the opportunity to write two business letters.

## Memos

A memorandum, or memo as it is usually called, is a document used for internal communication within an organisation. Since the communications are all within the same organisation, there is no need to send formal letters from one person or department to another. A memo cuts out the unnecessary detail of a letter and concentrates on the message. Look at the memo in Figure 7.9.

---

### Memorandum

**To:** Nicola Davey
**From:** Michael Nicholas
**Date:** 10 October 2002
**Subject:** Proposed Ski Trip – 18–25 February 2003

Before I give my approval for the proposed skiing trip during February half-term, I would like to meet with you and staff accompanying the students in order to discuss procedures to ensure students' safety.

I am available the week after next, except Tuesday. Please contact my office to arrange a convenient date and time.

---

*Figure 7.9 A memo*

What do you notice about the content and presentation of the memo?

- It has a heading 'Memorandum' which is clearly visible.
- It is produced in fully blocked style – everything is aligned to the left.

- In this example, one line space separates the heading from the main body of the memo.
- The content of the memo is brief.
- Unlike letters, there is no salutation or complimentary close. On a memo these are unnecessary since people in the same organisation are usually on friendly terms and can be expected to know each other.
- The memo is unsigned.

With the growing use of e-mail, information of a general nature that was previously sent to all employees by means of a memo is increasingly sent via e-mail.

**Activity**

▷ Print the file: **DBD Worksheet 3**
▷ from the Chapter 7 folder on the CD-ROM. In this worksheet you will use a memo template and produce your own memo to the manager of the student association shop.

## Faxes

A fax, or facsimile, is a means of sending a copy of a document from one fax machine to another via the telephone system. A computer is not an essential piece of equipment if you wish to send a fax, whereas it is vital if you wish to send e-mail via the telephone system. However, with the right software you can send a fax electronically from one computer to another without feeding the document through a fax machine. The cheaper cost of a fax machine therefore makes it attractive, especially for small businesses.

A document containing text and/or pictures is fed through a fax machine, converted into electronic form and transmitted down the telephone line. The receiving fax machine interprets the electronic data and prints a copy of the original document. Once printed, the data on the receiving fax machine is lost and only the hard copy remains.

It is general practice to send a fax cover sheet as the first page in any fax transmission so that the person receiving the fax knows how many pages to expect. Figure 7.10 shows a fax cover sheet.

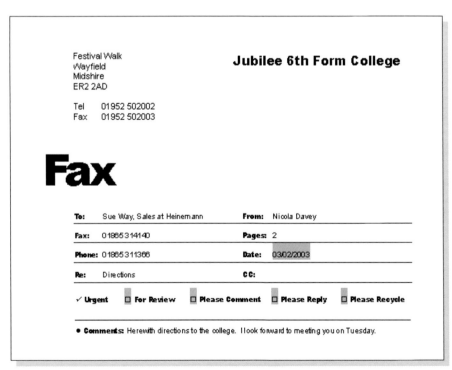

*Figure 7.10 A fax cover sheet*

## Agendas and minutes of meetings

When you go to work, or if you are on the committee of any sports or social club for example, from time to time you are very likely to attend meetings. A meeting provides a group of people with the opportunity to discuss topics of common interest. Some meetings are rather informal and are arranged at short notice and some meetings are more formal and will be arranged some time in advance. The more formal meetings often follow standard procedures and use standard documentation.

### Agendas

When you receive notification of the date, time and place of the meeting you will probably also receive a list of the subjects that will be discussed at the meeting. This is called an agenda. A typical agenda will look similar to the one in Figure 7.11.

Apologies, minutes of last meeting, matters arising from the minutes, any other business and date of next meeting are usually standard to all agendas. The items in between will vary from meeting to meeting.

### Minutes of meetings

While the meeting is taking place, somebody makes notes of what is discussed and agreed, and from these notes it is the person's responsibility to prepare the minutes of the meeting. The minutes record the decisions taken at the meeting and any action that must be taken as a result of the decisions and by whom.

Figure 7.12 shows the minutes that were produced following the Students' Association meeting on 15 October.

The items in the minutes follow the same order as the items on the agenda. Anything not on the agenda is discussed under 'Any other business'. In addition, minutes always record who was present at the meeting and list the people who sent their apologies.

**JUBILEE 6TH FORM COLLEGE STUDENTS' ASSOCIATION**

**Notice of Meeting**

**15 October 2002**
**5.30 pm**
**Room 163**

**AGENDA**

1. Apologies
2. Minutes of last meeting
3. Matters arising from the Minutes
4. Election of new President
5. New equipment in the gym
6. Proposed ski trip to France
7. Any other business
8. Date of next meeting

*Figure 7.11 An agenda*

| | Action |
|---|---|
| **MINUTES OF THE MEETING OF THE JUBILEE 6TH FORM COLLEGE STUDENTS' ASSOCIATION** | |
| **15 October 2002** | |
| **Present:** Nicola Davey (President)<br>David Westgate<br>Salim Hassan<br>Faye Church<br>Tamal Aakel | |
| **Apologies for absence** were received from Kate Medwin | |
| **Minutes of last meeting**<br>The minutes of the last meeting were agreed. | |
| **Matters arising from the minutes**<br>David Westgate said that the flyer promoting special offers in the Student Union Shop had been well received and that sales resulting from these offers had been very encouraging. | |
| **Election of new President**<br>Nicola Davey's year in office ends on 31 October. Nominations have been received for Helen Brett and Gary Deaves. The election for the new President will take place on 28 October. Salim Hassan agreed to prepare suitable posters. | SH |
| **New equipment in the gym**<br>The new exercise cycles, aerobic stepper and treadmill have proved very popular. David Westgate will organise induction sessions to encourage more students and staff to use the facilities. | DW |
| **Proposed ski trip to France**<br>The Principal would like to discuss issues concerning student safety and a meeting has been arranged for 21 October at 1630 in his office. Nicola Davey, Tamal Aakel and Kate Medwin will attend as they will be accompanying the skiing party. | ND/TA/KM |
| **Any other business**<br>Faye Church outlined details of Rag Week 14–18 May. She has approached one or two members of staff to enlist their help in coordinating the activities. Faye will report on progress at the next meeting. | FC |
| William Old has agreed to perform at the next Valentine's Day Party. | |
| **Date of next meeting**<br>18 November 2002 | |

*Figure 7.12 Minutes of a meeting*

## Reports

A report is usually prepared following a detailed investigation into something. The investigation might be necessary for one of many reasons, for example in order to find a way to put right a problem, to look at the possibility of introducing new working practices or to give information following a business trip.

Reports are usually divided into four sections:

- Introduction – briefly explains the purpose of the report.
- Methodology – provides details on how the investigation was undertaken.
- Findings – records what the investigation revealed, that is, what the author found out about existing systems/practices. This section is often broken down under different headings or divided into sub-sections.
- Conclusions/recommendations – the final section considers everything that has been found out. Where appropriate, the report will suggest suitable action that can be taken to improve or sort out a situation.

A report is usually numbered using a system known as decimalised numbering:

1 xxxxxxxxx
2 xxxxxxxxx
   2.1 xxxxxxxxx
   2.2 xxxxxxxxx
3 xxxxxxxxx
   3.1 xxxxxxxxx
      3.1.1 xxxxxxxxx
      3.1.2 xxxxxxxxx
   3.2 xxxxxxxxx
      3.2.1 xxxxxxxxx
      3.2.2 xxxxxxxxx
4 xxxxxxxxx

### Activity

▶ Print the file: **DBD Worksheet 6**
▶ from the Chapter 7 folder on the CD-ROM. You will use the report you worked with in DBD Worksheet 1 to learn how to use the decimalised numbering system.

## Publicity materials

In order to attract attention, an event, product or organisation needs publicity. This might involve an expensive advertising campaign on TV or a poster on a notice board. During a general election, the main political parties use billboards to get their message to the electorate whereas a small or local organisation might rely on an advertisement in a local newspaper. The message might be saying 'buy me', 'watch me' or 'visit me', but it will usually be short, to the point, eye-catching and designed to persuade the reader.

For example, the Marketing Department at Croydon College used the slogan 'Of course you can!' in a recent publicity campaign during the college's enrolment period. As shown in Figure 7.13, the slogan appeared on a variety of advertising sites, on trams and buses in the town and on the college building itself. The purpose was to encourage prospective students to go to the college and enrol. The theme continued on the college website and other publicity material.

*Figure 7.13 Croydon College's 'Of course you can!' campaign advertised on a tram in the town centre*

It is likely that you might have been or will shortly be looking at local schools and colleges with a view to moving into further education after taking your GCSEs and, as a result of this, you will collect publicity material from the different places you visit. This will probably be in the form of prospectuses. As you look through them, try to identify what it is that you particularly like about one prospectus more than others. Look also at flyers that come through your front door or the loose inserts in magazines. Any of these might give you some ideas when producing your own publicity material.

What made you choose a particular fiction book from the library? The chances are you chose it because you liked the cover. What prompts you to choose designer shades as opposed to similar sunglasses found in any local high street chemist shop? It is quite likely that you have been influenced by publicity material.

Be aware of everything that is around you and you will appreciate that publicity material is a powerful marketing tool that can produce great results if care and thought go into producing it.

## Web pages

In Chapter 5, you looked at creating a website using a text editor and HTML and also using an authoring tool – FrontPage®. As you will learn throughout your course, the Internet is a very important marketing tool, but a poorly designed website could lose a company business, rather than attract business.

It is important therefore to make sure that your website looks good and is easy to use. A well-designed website should present the organisation's image and be user friendly.

### Designing a website

- Plan your site on paper before starting to set it up. You should produce a structure diagram (see page 64) showing how all the pages will link together and also how each page will appear.
- It is tempting to use as many advanced features as possible. Just because you can include video clips and blinking text, it doesn't mean that you should! Sometimes too many features will detract from the information you want to put across.
- Don't use too many fonts on one page and use well-known ones. Not everyone will have the same fonts on his/her computer.
- Use graphics with care. Too many will slow the download time and frustrate visitors.
- Make sure that the site is easy to use and any instructions are clear.
- Ask a friend to look at your site. He or she may point out something obvious that you have overlooked.
- Look at other sites – they can give you ideas of what to do and what not to do.

## Presentations

You learned how to create a presentation using multimedia software in Chapter 4. The ability to create a good, attractive and interactive presentation using software such as PowerPoint® is invaluable. A company holding a sales conference will probably use a PowerPoint® presentation to present information. These presentations will almost always use the company house style, for example the company logo, colours, and so on.

When designing a presentation it is important to think about the following:

- Plan the content of the presentation first by creating a storyboard as described in Chapter 4. Your aim is to have a clear and understandable presentation. Add any special features after you have created the basis of the presentation and try to avoid using too many of these features at one time.
- Proof-read your presentation carefully – poor spelling or grammatical errors will spoil the end result. It is important to remember that when proof-reading, most people unintentionally read what they *expect* to see.
- Avoid using too many technical terms or abbreviations – your audience may not be familiar with these.
- Each slide should have one aspect that catches the audience's attention first – headings are best in a larger font than the remainder of the text. Remember that you will need to use a font size that people will be able to read easily. Font size 24 or above is a good size. Font size 12 or 14 may be fine for a handout, but you would need extremely good eye-sight to read the words if you are sitting at the back of a room!
- Avoid using all capital letters – these are more difficult to read. When you are out and about, look at road signs – you will notice that they usually use both upper and lower case letters rather than all capital letters.
- Take care when using colours. Sometimes too many or the wrong colours can make a slide difficult to view. If you cannot view an

object easily in the Black and White option from the View menu, then it will not be easy to view in full colour.

- Use words carefully. You may find, for example, that pictures or graphs are a much better way of communicating than text.
- Use sounds carefully. Inappropriate use of sounds can be distracting and spoil an otherwise good presentation.
- If you intend to include moving images or videos, make sure that the equipment you are using will allow the presentation to be seen properly and not be spoilt by being jerky or slow.
- If using preset timings for the transition of slides, make sure that the timings are set at a realistic pace. Changing slides too slowly can be just as annoying as slides changing too rapidly.
- Keep the content interesting and to the point – a presentation with too much information may bore the audience and you will lose their attention.

### Fact file

Most people read what they expect to see. Try writing the following words exactly as you see them, and then ask a friend to read them aloud to you:

Paris in the the Spring

How many people read 'Paris in the Spring' instead of 'Paris in the the Spring'?

### Activity

> Print the file: **DBD Worksheet 9**
> from the Chapter 7 folder on the CD-ROM. The worksheet contains an example of a slide for you to comment on.

## Data capture forms

Data capture forms are used for all sorts of purposes (see Chapter 3, page 50) – arranging car, house, travel or health insurance, ordering goods, opening a bank account, obtaining a young person's identity card or passport, completing a tax return. Almost certainly at some time you will have completed a form. It might have been an application form for college or a driving licence. In these cases much of the data you provided will be the same, for example name, address, date of birth, but other details will be different. The college application form will be interested in your school grades; the driving licence authority will check whether you have any physical problems that would make you unsafe to drive.

Sometimes the data is given over the telephone and at other times, the data is hand-written on a paper form. Forms should be easy to complete, with the boxes or spaces indicating what is meant to be written in them. The design and layout of a paper form is very important and can make a difference to the accuracy of the data and how easy it is to read what has been written.

### Activity

> Print the files: **DBD Worksheet 10**
> and **DBD Worksheet 11** from the Chapter 7 folder on the CD-ROM. DBD Worksheet 10 includes an example of a college application form. DBD Worksheet 11 shows an alternative layout for the application form.

## The invoice

When buying something in a store, the customer may choose to pay either in cash or with a debit or credit card. Businesses operate in a different way. A business will place an order for goods or services with a supplier; the goods are delivered with a delivery note confirming what items have been included. The customer checks that the order is correct and signs the delivery note (see Figure 7.14). The invoice – a statement showing how much is owed – is sent separately to the accounts department (see Figure 7.15). Payment is requested within an agreed time, usually within 30 days of the order.

Most invoices include the following details:

- supplier's logo, address, phone and fax numbers, e-mail and possibly web address

**Select Stationery Ltd**
Unit 6
Wayfield Business Park
WAYFIELD
ER4 7JN

**DELIVERY NOTE**

Tel: 019 8777 4050     Fax 019 8777 4051     Email: Select@weconnect.co.uk

| Name: | Jubilee 6ᵗʰ Form College | Invoice No. | 1453 |
| Address: | Festival Walk | Invoice Date: | 12/3/00 |
| Town: | 44 Merryview Way | Order No: | 10002 |
| Post Code: | WAYFIELD | Dispatch Date: | 29/01/-- |

| Quantity | Description | Catalogue Ref: |
|---|---|---|
| 20 | File - Lever Arch | 401602 |
| 35 | Highlighters - jumbo size - 6 pack - assorted colours | 300780 |
| 75 | Post-It cube 76 x 76 mm 325 sheets | 355206 |
| 100 | Ruler - 30 cm | 232204 |
| 60 | Sellotape | 232202 |

Received by: _____     Date: _____

*Figure 7.14 Delivery note*

**Select Stationery Ltd**
Unit 6
Wayfield Business Park
WAYFIELD
ER4 7JN

**INVOICE**

Tel: 019 8777 4050     Fax 019 8777 4051     Email: Select@weconnect.co.uk

| Name: | Jubilee 6ᵗʰ Form College | Invoice No. | 1453 |
| Address: | Festival Walk | Account No: | JC899 |
| Town: | 44 Merryview Way | Order No: | 10002 |
| Post Code: | WAYFIELD | Date: | 12/03/-- |

| Catalogue Ref | Description | Quantity | Unit Price | TOTAL |
|---|---|---|---|---|
| 401602 | File - Lever Arch | 20 | £ 0.87 | £ 17.40 |
| 300780 | Highlighters - jumbo size - 6 pack - assorted colours | 35 | £ 2.19 | £ 76.65 |
| 355206 | Post-It cube 76 x 76 mm 325 sheets | 75 | £ 3.59 | £ 269.25 |
| 232204 | Ruler - 30 cm | 100 | £ 0.33 | £ 33.00 |
| 232202 | Sellotape | 60 | £ 0.96 | £ 57.60 |
| | | | Sub Total | £ 453.90 |
| | | | Discount | £ 6.81 |
| | | | Vat | £ 79.43 |
| | | | Total | £ 526.52 |

*Figure 7.15 Invoice*

- customer's details
- references such as the customer's account and order number, the invoice number and VAT registration number
- the date
- details of the items ordered or services provided
- cost of each item
- VAT if applicable
- total amount to be paid.

Nowadays, orders are often placed by telephone. Businesses usually confirm the order in writing, by sending a purchase order form. Individual shoppers also order by telephone but don't usually confirm the order. Have you ever ordered items from a catalogue by telephone? You will be asked for the unique catalogue reference, which is entered directly into the computer. The reference is stored in a Lookup table, the computer immediately searches for any data related to that reference and then automatically inserts the data into the appropriate place on the screen. This saves time as the administrator does not have to refer to a long price list, and reduces the risk of errors. If the Lookup table is accurate, then the correct item will be ordered. Figure 7.16 shows Select Stationery's Lookup table. Figure 7.17 shows its invoice addressed to Jubilee 6th Form College.

| STATIONERY LOOKUP TABLE | | |
|---|---|---|
| Catalogue Reference | Item | Trade Price Excluding VAT |
| 232 201 | Eraser | 0.30 |
| 401 601 | File - A4 Ringbinder | 0.66 |
| 401 602 | File - Lever Arch | 0.87 |
| 300 780 | Highlighters - jumbo size - 6 pack - assorted colours | 2.19 |
| 300 781 | Highlighters - pocket size - 6 pack - assorted colours | 1.94 |
| 351 341 | Notebook - spiral bound | 0.43 |
| 351 340 | Notepad - A4 Ruled - 80 sheets | 0.87 |
| 297 141 | Pencil | 0.31 |
| 297 145 | Pencil sharpener | 0.66 |
| 297 144 | Pens - Hybrid Gel - 6 pack - assorted colours | 4.29 |
| 297 143 | Pens - Rollerbal - 4 pack multi assorted colours | 3.89 |
| 297 142 | Pens Flexi-grip Retractable - 4 pack assorted colours | 2.98 |
| 297 146 | Pens stick - 12 pack | 1.19 |
| 355 207 | Post-It cube 50 x 50 mm 400 sheets | 1.69 |
| 355 206 | Post-It cube 76 x 76 mm 325 sheets | 3.59 |
| 245 602 | Pritt stick large | 2.59 |
| 232 203 | Ruler - 15 cm | 0.27 |
| 232 204 | Ruler - 30 cm | 0.33 |

*Figure 7.16 The Lookup table*

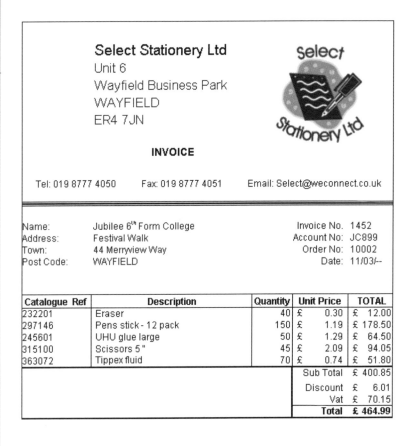

**Select Stationery Ltd**
Unit 6
Wayfield Business Park
WAYFIELD
ER4 7JN

**INVOICE**

Tel: 019 8777 4050      Fax: 019 8777 4051      Email: Select@weconnect.co.uk

| Name: | Jubilee 6th Form College | Invoice No. | 1452 |
|---|---|---|---|
| Address: | Festival Walk | Account No: | JC899 |
| Town: | 44 Merryview Way | Order No: | 10002 |
| Post Code: | WAYFIELD | Date: | 11/03/-- |

| Catalogue Ref | Description | Quantity | Unit Price | TOTAL |
|---|---|---|---|---|
| 232201 | Eraser | 40 | £ 0.30 | £ 12.00 |
| 297146 | Pens stick - 12 pack | 150 | £ 1.19 | £ 178.50 |
| 245601 | UHU glue large | 50 | £ 1.29 | £ 64.50 |
| 315100 | Scissors 5 " | 45 | £ 2.09 | £ 94.05 |
| 363072 | Tippex fluid | 70 | £ 0.74 | £ 51.80 |
| | | | Sub Total | £ 400.85 |
| | | | Discount | £ 6.01 |
| | | | Vat | £ 70.15 |
| | | | Total | £ 464.99 |

*Figure 7.17  Select Stationery's invoice*

```
TESCO

                                    £
WATERCRESS                        1.19
MUSHROOM CLS/C
0.255 kg @   £2.38/ kg           0.61
ORG BCH CARROT                    1.49
GINGER 125G                       0.59
FINEST PEPPERS                    1.39
SPROUTS 500G                      0.95
ORGANIC TOMATO                    1.39
CORIANDER                         0.69
ORGANIC TOMATO                    1.39
BABY POTS LSE
1.085 kg @   £1.79/ kg           1.94
ONION SHALLOTS
0.405 kg @   £2.29/ kg           0.93
ORG AVOCADO                       0.79

TOTAL                           13.35
VISA DEBIT                      13.35
CHANGE DUE                       0.00

CLUBCARD STATEMENT

CLUBCARD NUMBER 63400400028947955*
POINTS THIS VISIT                  13
TOTAL UP TO 04/10/01              279

FREE DELIVERY ON EVERYTHING FROM OUR
            WINE WAREHOUSE

Choose from our entire range by the case
Don't worry if you're not sure, we'll
  help you make the right selection and
       also deliver to your door.
Visit our New Online WINE WAREHOUSE at
            www.tesco.com
   but hurry, offer ends 13/10/01

OPEN 24 HOURS

Monday 08:00 until Saturday 22:00

     Sunday 10:00 - 16:00

          THANK YOU
    FOR SHOPPING AT TESCO
           ABINGDON
   STORE TEL (01235) 707400
 PHARMACY TEL (01235) 550332
GARDEN CENTRE TEL (01235) 707444

 If you have any comments about today's
  shopping trip, please let me know

     DANNY MANSFIELD
    CUSTOMER SERVICE
         MANAGER

6/10/01  17:06  2008  006  1004  9184
```

*Figure 7.18  Till receipt*

Nowadays supermarket till receipts provide much more detail than they used to. At one time, the receipt showed only the price of the item and the total bill, but now a description of the item is included as well as the price. If some items are on special offer, such as two for the price of one, that also shows on the receipt as a multisave item – see Figure 7.18.

This is possible because the barcode is the reference in the Lookup table. When the price of a product changes or a special offer is introduced or finishes, the data in the Lookup table is changed, without having to change price labels on each individual item.

**Activity**

▷ Print the file: **DBD Worksheet 12** from the Chapter 7 folder on the CD-ROM. The worksheet explains how to complete an invoice using a lookup table.

## Financial plans

Many people at work are paid monthly, direct into their bank account. They earn more or less the same amount each month. They have fixed expenses each month, such as rent or mortgage and travel costs, but some months there are extra bills, such as the cost of a holiday. To overcome the problem of earning the same amount each month, but needing more cash in some months, many people save some of their earnings each month so that the money is available when required. This is an example of financial planning.

Businesses are no different. Think about a company manufacturing toys. The biggest selling period, that is, the period when a toy manufacturer *earns* the most income, is in the months leading to Christmas. The company's biggest period of *expenditure* (spending), however, is probably in the spring and summer. Therefore, it is vital to plan the company's

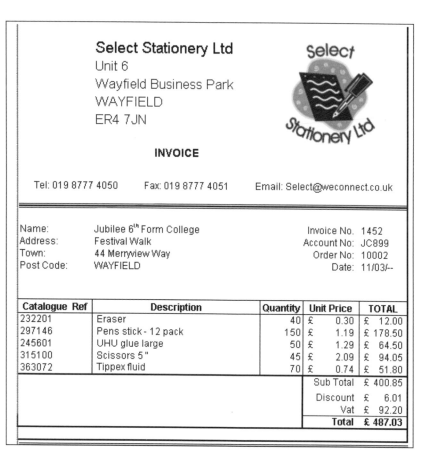

**Select Stationery Ltd**
Unit 6
Wayfield Business Park
WAYFIELD
ER4 7JN

**INVOICE**

Tel: 019 8777 4050      Fax: 019 8777 4051      Email: Select@weconnect.co.uk

| | | | | |
|---|---|---|---|---|
| Name: | Jubilee 6th Form College | | Invoice No. | 1452 |
| Address: | Festival Walk | | Account No: | JC899 |
| Town: | 44 Merryview Way | | Order No: | 10002 |
| Post Code: | WAYFIELD | | Date: | 11/03/-- |

| Catalogue Ref | Description | Quantity | Unit Price | TOTAL |
|---|---|---|---|---|
| 232201 | Eraser | 40 | £ 0.30 | £ 12.00 |
| 297146 | Pens stick - 12 pack | 150 | £ 1.19 | £ 178.50 |
| 245601 | UHU glue large | 50 | £ 1.29 | £ 64.50 |
| 315100 | Scissors 5 " | 45 | £ 2.09 | £ 94.05 |
| 363072 | Tippex fluid | 70 | £ 0.74 | £ 51.80 |
| | | | Sub Total | £ 400.85 |
| | | | Discount | £ 6.01 |
| | | | Vat | £ 92.20 |
| | | | **Total** | **£ 487.03** |

*Figure 7.19 Invoice showing the increased cost if VAT is increased to 23 per cent*

finances carefully, to ensure that enough money is available in the business when the raw materials needed to make the toys have to be bought.

However, financial planning in a business context is more complex. Not only is it necessary to plan for the short term, businesses usually plan for the longer term, perhaps the next three to five years. Clearly, it is quite difficult to predict future sales and plan expenditure accordingly. Take, for example, the fashion industry. Fashion shows for winter clothes take place in the spring or summer before, and vice versa. Store buyers have to try to decide which will be the most popular lines. In a country like the UK, where the weather is so unpredictable, this can result in having large quantities of stock left at the end of the season, which the stores are then forced to sell at bargain prices.

This is where the power of the spreadsheet is invaluable. A financial plan can be set up in the spreadsheet to calculate the expenses and work out the minimum sales required to break even, that is, to cover all the costs of making a product. Once the basic plan has been set up, the impact of possible changes can easily and quickly be identified. For example, imagine that a business has heard a rumour that the government is going to increase the rate of VAT to 23 per cent. This would have an huge impact on it. The company might wish to find out how much money will be involved if the rumour proves to be true. By changing the rate of VAT in the spreadsheet, the additional cost can be shown. Compare the invoice for Jubilee 6th Form College (Figure 7.17) with Figure 7.19 which shows the difference in cost if VAT had been increased to 23%.

## Activity

▷ Print the file: **DBD Worksheet 13**

▷ from the Chapter 7 folder on the CD-ROM. The worksheet explains how to create a financial forecast when setting up a new restaurant at Jubilee College.

## Database reports

As you learned in Chapter 3, the advantage of a computerised database is that the data need only be entered once, but a wide variety of reports can be produced from the database. Let's look at two examples: Select Stationery Ltd and Jubilee 6th Form College.

The different departments of Select Stationery Ltd use the database of customers to obtain different information or reports:

- The Sales Department records customers' orders.
- The Accounts Department uses the database to send out invoices.
- The Marketing Department uses the database to advertise promotions or special offers.
- The Sales director may wish to know information on purchases made by different customers to try to identify other pro$ucts that the customer could be persuaded to purchase.
- The Finance director may wish to check whether the cost of delivery to certain customers is worthwhile, compared to the profit made.

When students apply to Jubilee 6th Form College, the Admissions Department enters their details into the student records database and each one is given a unique student ID number. If a student then enrols at the college, he or she is given an identity badge, which may well be in the form of a swipe card, and his or her unique ID number will be linked to other database tables about courses and registers.

During the time a student attends the college, different departments or members of staff use the database to obtain different information from the various related tables.

- Admissions staff use the mailmerge facility to send standard letters giving the date and time of the student's interview and after the interview to confirm whether a place has been offered or not together with any conditions attached to the offer, such as the GCSE grades required.
- Once a student has enrolled, the programme manager for the course may use the database to provide a list of names and dates of birth for those students who took up the offer of a place. The programme manager may also use the database to obtain a student's address, telephone number or emergency contact number, or to send mailmerge letters to the whole group.
- The ID number is also linked to the register table, so that a register is generated for each class with the list of ID numbers, names and date of birth and columns to record whether each student is present, absent or late. The register may be in optical mark reader (OMR) format which is then scanned into the computer to record attendance.
- Once the attendance data are scanned into the database, reports can be generated showing the attendance record of one particular student, or the record of the whole group for one particular lesson.
- Funding from the government is dependent on students continuing their studies. Colleges have to prove that students are still attending at certain census dates in the year. Therefore, the Finance Department uses the register data to confirm which students are attending on these census dates.
- Some colleges use security gates where each student has to swipe the ID card, which then allows the student to pass through the gate. If the student has left the college or has been suspended, the ID number will be blocked by the security staff, which then prevents the barrier opening when the card is swiped. In the event that a particular student has caused trouble, the security staff enter details of the problem into the computer, which then generates a report in the form of an incident log. The report is sent to the relevant programme manager, who then has to take up the matter with the student concerned to decide what action, if any, should be taken.

All these different kinds of reports are made possible because the student's ID number is linked to different tables within the student records database. The layout of database reports is covered in page 54.

# Unit 2

# ICT systems in organisations

Most organisations use ICT in some areas of their work. In this unit you will find out about:

- how and why organisations use ICT
- the main components, or parts, used to design an ICT system
- how ICT systems are designed and implemented.

You will learn how to design, implement and test a system and represent it graphically.

## What you will learn

- **8** How and why organisations use ICT
- **9** The main components
- **10** How ICT systems are designed and implemented

# Chapter 8

# How and why organisations use ICT

This chapter looks at:

- the four main functions of business – sales, purchasing, finance and operations
- how different departments communicate and exchange information, internally an$ externally.

## What you will learn

The needs of organisations
Functions of organisations
How organisations use ICT

## Overview

Before you can understand how and why organisations use ICT, you need to be aware of the different types of organisations, how they are structured, the typical departments and what the function of those departments is. Although some organisations are very small, and it may be that one person performs the role of a large number of people in quite separate departments, the same basic structure and functions will apply.

## The needs of organisations

There are three main types of organisation:

- commercial
- industrial
- public service.

Commercial organisations exist to sell a product, for example clothes, household goods, insurance, and to make a profit. Industrial organisations process raw materials or manufacture goods and also aim to make a profit. Public service organisations, as the name suggests, offer a service to the public and are not profit making.

One thing all these organisations have in common, however small or large, is the need for clear and accurate information, which nowadays is usually provided via an ICT system. The needs of a small business may require only a limited use of ICT, whereas a large organisation will have more varied needs that are met by use of ICT systems. It is vital for every organisation to identify its needs, so that an effective ICT system is designed and implemented. Needs will change over time so this process is ongoing.

## Activity

▷ Print the file: **OS Worksheet 1** from the Chapter 8 folder on the CD-ROM. This worksheet will help you to check out commercial, industrial and public service organisations.

## Functions of organisations

Large organisations are divided into different departments which carry out the four main functions of business:

- sales
- purchasing
- finance
- operations.

## Sales

All organisations must *sell* goods or services to other organisations or individuals – their customers. In most cases, customers pay for the goods or services, but in some cases, services are provided 'free'. A patient going to an NHS hospital for an operation does not pay directly for the treatment, although he or she will pay indirectly through taxes. It is important to treat customers well. If a business fails to do this, then it will lose its customers, which is bad for business. If an organisation cannot sell its goods or services, or no one wants them, then the organisation will go bankrupt or cease to trade.

## Purchasing

All organisations must *buy* goods and services from other organisations – the supplier. Examples of goods and services are:

| Goods | Services |
|---|---|
| Raw materials from which products are made | Cleaning |
| Components, or parts | Accountancy skills/auditing |
| Products bought in bulk and resold | Legal advice |
| Goods needed to run the business, e.g. stationery, furniture, food for a staff canteen | Banking |
| | Decorating/repairs |

*Examples of goods and services*

Just as a business must treat its customers well, it would expect to be treated well by its suppliers. If, for example, you receive poor service, the wrong goods arrive or are not on time, you will find another supplier. If, however, the supplier is efficient and courteous, you may even be prepared to pay more, which is good for the supplier's business.

## Finance

Collecting the money and paying the bills is an essential part of any business. All organisations undertake a variety of financial functions and a large company will have an Accounts Department that deals with a range of financial matters, such as paying:

- for goods/services received and obtaining payment for goods/services sold
- VAT to the government and claiming VAT refunds
- staff salaries into individual bank accounts

- income tax to the Inland Revenue and National Insurance contributions to the Department of Social Security
- pension contributions to the pension fund
- for gas, electricity, telephone, rates, rent.

This department will also be responsible for keeping the company accounts.

One of the main roles of the finance director is to ensure that enough money is coming into the business, before money has to be paid out. The efficient operation of an organisation plays an important part in good financial control.

### Activity

▷ Print the file: **OS Worksheet 2** from the Chapter 8 folder on the CD-ROM. This worksheet will help you to check your understanding of the functions of organisations.

## Operations

The operations function involves carrying out the main business of the organisation.

### Industrial organisations

In an industrial organisation the operation of the business relates to what is produced and how it is produced. For example, a factory producing cars will purchase steel for the body of the car and a wide variety of other components, or parts, such as tyres, in-car audio systems, mirrors, glass, instrument panels, steering wheels, carpets – the list is endless. It is essential that the Operations Department ensures that all these components are available as needed, without having too much stock (stock being held has to be paid for and until goods are sold, no money is received). It is equally important that the right models are produced in suitable quantities. For example, more of the *inexpensive* models are sold, so it would be unwise to make too many of the *expensive* models.

The general rule for all industrial organisations is to match what is made to the orders received and to ensure no delay in production because some components have run out, while large supplies of other components are held in stock. Products must be ready on time and should work correctly, so the Operations Department is also responsible for the quality of the product.

An industrial organisation must also think about designing new products or modifying existing ones to keep them up-to-date. Why do you think car manufacturers continually change their models and add new features? They want people to buy new cars. Similarly, the construction industry has to draw plans and write specifications of the materials to be used in the construction of a new building. Design, planning and specifications are all part of the operations function of an industrial organisation – see Figure 8.1.

Figure 8.1  *The operations function in an industrial organisation*

## Commercial organisations

The operations function in a commercial organisation involves providing goods or a service – see Figure 8.2. Many of the same aspects apply as in an industrial organisation. For example, if you go to a clothes shop, you would not expect it to sell only one size of jacket. The majority of people come in the 'average' range of sizes, so it is sensible to have more items in these sizes and fewer in the very small or very large categories.

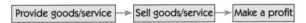

Figure 8.2  *The operations function in a commercial organisation*

A commercial organisation offering a service rather than a product also has to ensure the service matches the needs of the client. For example, if you have booked a flight through a travel agency, you expect a seat to be available on the plane when you arrive at the airport. Operations staff should ensure that the information they are using is correct, that is, there is space on the flight and that your booking is recorded and your ticket issued.

## Public service organisations

The main function of a public service organisation is to provide a service, for example schools and colleges provide education, doctors and hospitals provide health care, the Inland Revenue and Customs and Excise collect taxes – the latter may not seem much of a service, but if taxes are not collected, then the other services cannot be provided.

## Other aspects of the operations function

In all three types of organisation the operations function may also include personnel, administration, computer services and, very often, transport.

The operations function is concerned with the smooth running of the organisation, and to run smoothly each department of an organisation is dependent on information received from or sent to other departments.

## How organisations use ICT

Organisations use ICT to:
- communicate effectively internally and externally with suppliers and customers
- manage and control a production process
- manage finance – including payroll, budgeting/forecasting, transactions and reporting
- manage stock control
- market products and services efficiently.

## Communicate effectively

All businesses need to communicate internally and externally. If the organisation is small, perhaps just one office with two or three staff, most of the internal communication is likely to be verbal. A large organisation with many departments will also use written communication such as e-mails, memos, reports.

External communication between the organisation and its customers or suppliers will be verbally, either face to face or by telephone, and written, through e-mails, fax, business letters and reports.

It is essential that the flow of information within the organisation is effective. In a small office, this could be as simple as using a proper message pad, rather than scraps of paper or, worse still, relying on memory when taking telephone messages for a colleague. In a large organisation information must pass easily and efficiently from one department to another. Let's consider the flow of information between Select Stationery Ltd and Jubilee 6th Form College's bookshop.

The buyer in the bookshop places an order with Select Stationery, its supplier. This may be by phone, fax or e-mail, and is then confirmed by a purchase order sent out from the college's Purchasing Department, a copy of which goes to the Accounts Department – see Figure 8.3. When the goods are delivered, a delivery note will be included with the order to confirm what goods have been delivered. This delivery note

is checked to ensure the contents of the order are correct and passed to the college's Accounts Department so that it knows the goods have to be paid for.

At Select Stationery the order is received by the Sales Department, which then enters the details into the computer – the electronic data processing system – which checks electronically for stock. This generates (produces) a duplicate delivery/advice note for the warehouse, which will arrange for the goods to be sent to the college's bookshop. The details of the order are transferred electronically into the customer's account. When the goods are delivered their receipt is confirmed by the customer signing the duplicate copy of the delivery note. The Accounts Department at Select Stationery will then send an invoice (bill) to the college's Accounts Department.

These transactions may also be made electronically via the computer.

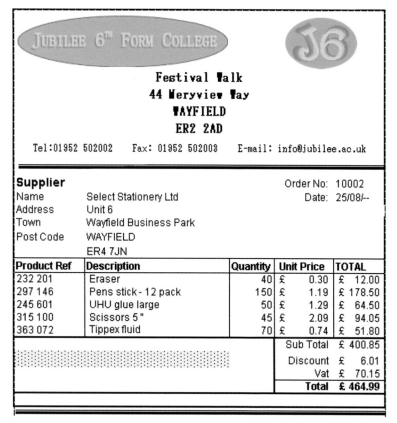

*Figure 8.3 Purchase order from Jubilee 6th Form College*

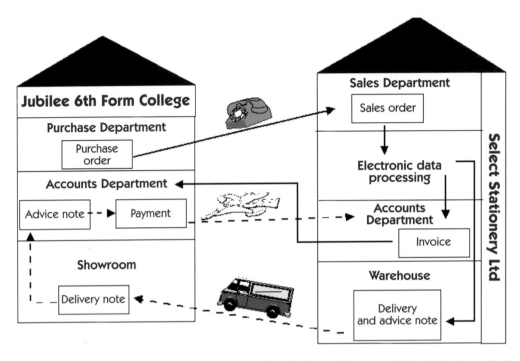

*Figure 8.4 Flow of information between Jubilee 6th Form College and Select Stationery Ltd*

Figure 8.4 shows one example of information flow. Other examples include:

- records of staff sickness, hours worked, that are passed to the Wages/Salaries Department so that the payroll can be calculated
- details of students used by the:
  - Admissions Department to record applications
  - Registrations Department to record actual enrolments
  - Examinations Department to register students with the awarding body, e.g. Edexcel, AQA, OCR, and record results
  - Records Department to track attendance
  - Finance Department to claim funding.

The essential factor in communication is that every employee knows and understands the methods and systems to be used in relation to his or her responsibilities.

In most organisations the information flowing between departments still relies on an employee making a decision about who to talk to or who to send the information or request to. This may lead to problems because the information may be sent to the wrong person or incorrect details passed on, the person receiving the information may be absent and not able to deal with it, or in certain cases an employee may send the information on and never receive a reply.

Let's look at a simple example of this.

A sales representative working in a company has to submit his monthly expenses claim. He will complete the expenses form, pass the form to the sales manager who will authorise or reject the claim when she is next in the office.

The sales manager then sends authorised claims to the Accounts Office.

There are two accounts clerks, one who raises cheques when the claim is over £20, the other who is responsible for cash payments for claims under £20. Claims are often sent to the wrong accounts clerk which can delay the process.

The sales representative is never quite sure where the claim is in the system and when payment is ready.

This has led to computerised systems to manage the flow of information. These are usually known as **business process management** or **work flow systems**. If such a system is used in the company, the following procedure could apply:

The sales representative completes his monthly expenses claim on his computer on a standard form. Once it is completed, he clicks on the Submit button.

The claim will then go directly to the sales manager for authorisation. If the sales manager is away on business, the system has been set up to automatically redirect the claim to the sales director.

Whoever authorises the claim, he or she would click on the Authorise button and the claim will be analysed by the system and sent to either the accounts clerk responsible for cheques or the accounts clerk responsible for cash payments.

Once the cash or cheque payment has been prepared the accounts clerk can click on a button to send a notification to the sales representative that the cheque or cash is ready for collection.

In a typical system such as this the sales representative can check on the progress of his claim at any time without having to speak to anyone.

## Activity

▷ Print the file: **OS Worksheet 3** from the Chapter 8 folder on the CD-ROM. In this worksheet you will create a flow chart to illustrate the sales representative making his expenses claim.

## Manage and control a production process

The modern industrial organisation uses computer-aided design/computer-aided manufacture (CAD/CAM) software in the design and manufacture of products ranging from kitchen sinks to suspension bridges, from making a plan of a house to a pattern for a dress. This enables designers and engineers to develop new products and test them before investment is made in expensive new machinery.

Architects and designers have transferred their skills in technical drawing using a drawing board to the computer (see Figure 8.5). This enables them to produce clear, detailed drawings quickly and accurately. Changes in the design can be made without the need to produce completely new drawings. Three-dimensional (3D) CAD software will turn the drawing into virtual reality, enabling the client to take a virtual tour of the new building – a very powerful tool if you are trying to persuade backers to invest in a project. On a smaller scale, kitchen, bathroom or bedroom planners use virtual reality to 'show' a customer what his or her new fitted room will look like.

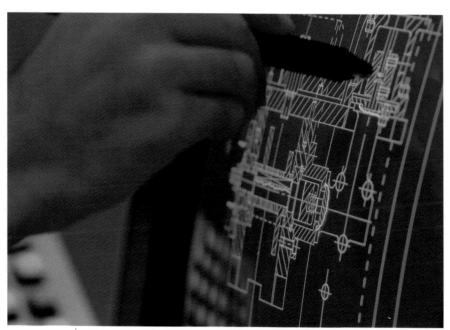

*Figure 8.5 The modern architect designs with the aid of a computer*

Designers from other professions have benefited from CAD, too – fashion designers can visualise their clothing in different fabrics and different colours. CAD software is also used in the design of sports equipment such as racing cars, yachts, skis, and sports wear such as ski wear or football boots. Computers can work out the maximum speed or durability of new designs and new materials. This is called **computer modelling**.

Large projects such as the development of new shopping malls or office buildings can be designed within a fixed budget using computers. Computers support management of such projects, comparing actual costs with projected costs. This provides project managers with information that enables them to keep projects within budget and timescale.

*Figure 8.6 Technical drawing and computer graphics are combined to produce a model of a car*

Let's look at the way CAD and CAM might work to produce a new car:

1   At the design stage, technical drawing and computer graphics are combined to produce a model of the car (see Figure 8.6).
2   The car model is tested before the first car is built to find out, for example, how it will perform in a road crash. The design will be modified (altered) to overcome potential problems, and tested again on video display screens until it has the best mix of features. This includes simplicity of production and manufacture, and the cost of production is also considered.
3   Shared databases are then used to integrate the car's CAD information with CAM processes to produce precision designs for the dies that are made before mass production begins, resulting in better quality products.

CAM engineers also use computer modelling to work out the best manufacturing procedures for the factory. For example, if the brakes and the gears are made of the same materials and require some of the same machine tools, these might be manufactured first. The factory would then change production over to frames and welding, then to spraying and finishing. This process continues on to testing and handling the finished product.

During manufacture machines are often used to do the jobs that humans used to perform. As well as simple, routine tasks such as body welding in a car factory, they can control complicated sequences of operations without the need for people (see Figure 8.7). For example, operators used to connect all telephone calls. Now, automatic telephone switching equipment selects the route and connects calls.

*Figure 8.7 No need for humans – robot arms weld a car body*

## Manage finance

### Payroll

A payroll system is used to work out employees' wages or salaries. It will calculate:

- the gross pay – that is, the total pay before deductions
- the amount of income tax to be deducted
- National Insurance contributions
- pension contributions
- the net pay – that is, the amount the employee actually receives.

Finally, the system will also print out the employees' pay slips (see Figure 8.8).

Employees are paid either in cash, by cheque or by credit transfer direct into their bank account. The payroll system can:

- print out a list of cheques required
- print out the actual cheques
- print a list of the credit transfer details for the bank.

The most up-to-date payroll systems can transfer the credit electronically direct to the bank account of the employee.

The payroll system will also:

- produce P60s (certificate of pay, income tax deducted and National Insurance contributions for the year)
- produce P45s (certificate to show pay, tax deducted and National Insurance contributions to date, issued when a person leaves or changes jobs)
- give a complete listing to the Inland Revenue at the end of the year.

### Budgeting/forecasting

In Chapter 7 you looked at financial plans and the advantages of a spreadsheet to businesses in their budgeting and forecasting of income and expenditure. Refer back to DBD Worksheet 13 and the spreadsheet you created for the college restaurant financial plan. Notice how the profit increases as more meals are sold. This is because the fixed costs remain the same.

Once the break-even point (when the income earned from a product equals the costs of producing it) has been worked out, forecasts can be made to predict how much profit will be made if more goods are sold. Some costs will not change or may increase only slightly, for example the original design costs, the cost of running the premises (rent, rates, gas, electricity, telephone, salaries). To manufacture more goods will require the purchase of more parts, but the income earned from the extra sales will bring greater profit.

On the other hand, if sales are lower than predicted, the forecast can be adjusted to show how much the loss will be if no action is taken. Once that amount is worked out, decisions can be made on how to reduce expenditure. This may mean making some staff redundant, or taking other actions such as spending less on publicity.

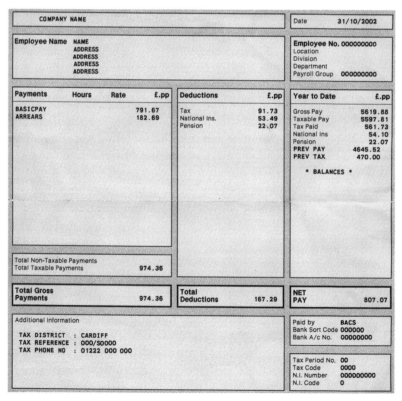

Figure 8.8 A payslip

## Transactions

Every day businesses are dealing with millions of transactions which need to be recorded into their computer system. A transaction could be paying a bill, enrolling at college, booking a holiday, and so on. Let's consider the transactions involved in buying the weekly groceries. Supermarket chains such as Sainsburys and Tesco have a central warehouse which receives stock from their suppliers. The goods are then distributed to the local branches. A customer goes into the shop and buys the groceries. The transactions involved are as follows:

- customer buys the groceries
- each item is scanned at the checkout and listed on the till receipt
- the bill is totalled
- customer pays the bill.

## Reporting

Each transaction generates a number of reports:

- At the end of the day, all till receipts are summarised giving a total value for everything sold, which should match the total of all cash, cheques or debit receipts in the tills.
- All the sales for the day for each product are totalled into one report which is sent electronically to the central warehouse.
- When stock falls below the re-order level an order is generated electronically to the supplier.
- The supplier delivers the goods – reported in the delivery note.
- The supplier sends an invoice to the customer.
- The customer makes a payment to the supplier.

> ### Activity
> Print the file: **OS Worksheet 4** from the Chapter 8 folder on the CD-ROM. The worksheet will help you to check your understanding of transactions and reporting.

## Manage stock control

The stock of a business is all the goods it has for sale. Stock control is how the stock is managed. It is important:

- to know as accurately as possible what is in stock
- to have enough stock so that the business does not have to turn customers away
- not to have too much stock.

It is bad for a business if it runs out of stock a customer wants, but it is also bad for profits to have a great deal of stock which is not selling.

The use of a computer database to record stock levels provides an accurate picture of what is in stock all the time. As already mentioned, when an item is sold the bar code is scanned, the details are automatically input into the stock control database and the item is deducted from the total available. This means that store or factory managers can check how much stock they have left, which items are running low and which are selling well. It is also possible to build in a 'low stock warning', and some computer systems are programmed to automatically reorder goods when stock falls below a certain level

Before computers, the only way to check the stock was to count each item individually, a very time consuming process. However, although it may appear intelligent, a computer database can provide information based only on the data fed into the system. Therefore, wastage and theft are not recorded, so from time to time it is still necessary to check that what is actually in stock matches computer records.

## Market products and services efficiently

The purpose of the Marketing Department is to promote the products and/or services of the organisation. In other words, it has to try to persuade individuals or other businesses that its products or services are better than those of its competitors.

Marketing methods include:

- sending out advertising flyers
- distributing leaflets
- advertising in papers, magazines, on billboards, on television, radio or at the cinema, on videos and CDs
- attending business fairs, e.g. wedding fairs where businesses providing the various products/services used at weddings such as car hire, clothes, venues, photographers, will have stands and show what they have to offer
- special promotions – e.g. buy one get one free
- word of mouth.

Think about how you learned about your school or college. What made you choose the one you are attending instead of others in your area?

The use of ICT has made it so much easier to produce professional advertising quickly, effectively and, in some cases, cheaply, which has led to the explosion in direct mail. Whichever marketing method is used, a cost is involved, so it is important to ensure that this is more than covered by increased income.

In small organisations marketing may be undertaken by the Sales Department, whereas large organisations will have a separate Marketing Department.

# The main components of ICT

This chapter looks at all the components, or parts, that make up a computer system, as well as the software needed to run it. It also considers data security and how computers can be linked to form networks.

## Overview: ICT systems

If you were to conjure up an image of an ICT system in the workplace, you would probably picture something like the one shown in Figure 9.1.

Figure 9.1 ICT system in an office

However, as you have seen in Chapter 8, there are many other situations where people use ICT systems in their work (see Figure 9.2).

These ICT systems all look very different and handle a wide range of tasks, but they all work in much the same way:

1   Data is entered into the system.
2   A processor acts on the instructions received.
3   The result of the instructions is output.
4   The data is stored.

This sequence is known as the **information processing cycle** – see Figure 9.3 (overleaf).

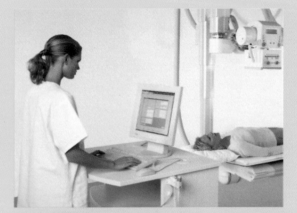

Figure 9.2 ICT systems in the workplace

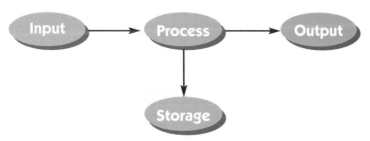

Figure 9.3  *The information processing cycle*

# Hardware

A computer system is made up of a number of components, or parts, including:

- input devices to enter data into the system
- a processing unit to manipulate, or handle, the data
- output devices that display the data
- storage devices that save the data
- ports and cables that join the system together.

Figure 9.4 shows a typical computer system comprising keyboard, mouse, monitor, printer and tower. This is often referred to as a personal computer or PC. Let's look at each of its components in more detail.

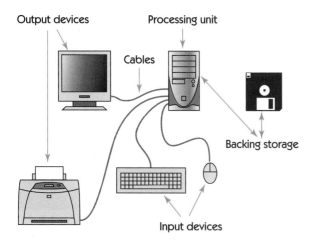

Figure 9.4  *A personal computer*

## Checkpoint

**PC** stands for personal computer.

# Input devices

Input devices provide the means of entering data, commands and programs into the computer's central processing unit (CPU). They include:

- keyboard
- mouse
- tracker ball
- scanner
- optical character recognition
- optical mark reader
- magnetic stripe reader
- bar code reader
- digital camera
- touch screen
- graphics tablet
- microphone
- sensors.

## Keyboard

The keyboard is the most recognisable input device. It is used to enter data or commands into the computer. Touching or pressing a key sends an electronic signal to the computer's processing unit and the signal is interpreted (read) as a character or function.

As you saw in Chapter 1, the computer keyboard is similar to an ordinary typewriter keyboard, but with extra keys for specialised functions.

The first six keys on the top row of the alphabetic characters spell QWERTY and this is the name used to describe the standard layout of most typewriters and keyboards. In the early days of manual typewriters, the hammers that swung up to strike the print ribbon tended to get stuck together if the typist went too quickly. The original design was therefore based on mechanical considerations designed to slow the typist down, rather than on efficiency, and the letters most frequently used were put as far apart as possible. Over the years, suggestions to modify the design have been unpopular and so it remains very close to its original form (see Figure 9.5).

Some keyboards come with added keys for using the Internet and others have an integrated wrist support. Ergonomic keyboards have been developed to reduce the risk of repetitive strain injury to workers who use keyboards for long periods of time. Keys rely on finger pressure rather than hand movement and the keyboard has been split in two sections so that users' wrists are in a more natural and comfortable position (see Figure 9.6).

*Figure 9.5 A traditional keyboard*

*Figure 9.6 Ergonomic keyboards*

### Concept keyboard

The **concept**, or touch-sensitive, **keyboard** is probably familiar to you from your time in primary school. It consists of a plastic surface where keys are replaced by designated areas which are programmed to input commands into the computer (see Figure 9.7). Overlays are put on the keyboard with symbols to indicate the areas and the commands are activated by pressure.

*Figure 9.7 A concept keyboard*

The concept keyboard is ideal for the young or disabled who cannot manipulate a standard keyboard and it is also useful in situations where, for example, dirt or liquids could damage a conventional keyboard. You have probably seen them in use in fast-food outlets – the assistant presses the printed overlay to select the customer's choices of food and drink.

> **Checkpoint**
>
> A **concept keyboard** is an input device with a flat surface covered with a printed overlay that is touched in order to carry out the actions printed on it.

### Mouse

A mouse is a device that enables you to interact with the computer screen. The standard mouse comprises casing, buttons and a base (see Figure 9.8). The casing is designed to fit between the fingers

*Figure 9.8 A mouse*

and thumb of one hand with the bottom of the palm resting on a mat or other surface. The bottom is flat and has a 'multidirectional detection device', usually a rubber ball. The top generally has two buttons and, nowadays, most also have a wheel for scrolling or zooming.

You control the movement and position of the on-screen cursor (or mouse pointer) by moving the mouse around on the desk. To select an item, you position the mouse pointer and press one of the mouse buttons. This produces a 'mouse click'. You might have heard the terms 'double click', 'click and drag' and 'drag and drop'. These describe actions you perform with the mouse such as picking up an icon by clicking the left button and holding the button down while you drag the icon elsewhere on the desktop (or screen).

Dust and dirt on the rubber ball can cause the mouse to stick or hang. If this happens, clean the ball by wiping gently with a cotton bud dampened with water.

In recent years, the design of the mouse has developed and today you will find several alternative, more technologically advanced designs of mouse readily available, including the following:

- In the **optical mouse** the rubber ball has been replaced with an optical sensor that detects motion on the desktop. A tiny digital camera takes pictures of the surface beneath the mouse (at a rate of up to 1,500 pictures per second) and these pictures are translated into movement of the cursor on the screen. The sensor works on most non-reflective surfaces – even your lap – and as there are no moving parts, the mouse moves smoothly.
- The **cordless mouse** relies on digital radio technology to send signals to a digital receiver. Radio waves enable communication with the CPU from a distance of up to 2 metres regardless of anything which might be in the way.

## Tracker ball

A **tracker ball**, sometimes called a **rollerball**, is like an upside-down mouse that allows the user to point and select items on screen by rotating the ball with the fingertips, rather than pushing a mouse around a desktop. It requires very little space to operate and is often used with CAD software. You might find a tracker ball used on machines in public places such as the one illustrated in Figure 9.9 which is used for designing and printing business cards.

Figure 9.9 This machine is used to print business cards. The rollerball is just below the keypad

## Scanner

### Flatbed scanners

The most popular type of **scanner** is a flatbed scanner which works in a similar way to a photocopier (see Figure 9.10). The document to be scanned is placed face down on a flat bed of glass and the lid is closed. The sensor moves across (scans) beneath the glass reading the words, symbols or graphics as a pattern of light and dark or colour, which it translates into a digital signal that the computer can store and manipulate. The scanned image is displayed on screen where it can be resized, colours can be changed or imperfections removed. The edited image can be imported into another document or saved ready to be retrieved at a later date. The quality of the image is dependent on the resolution of the scanner – the higher the resolution, the sharper and clearer the image.

A scanner that has optical character recognition (OCR) software is able to scan text so that it can be edited (see below).

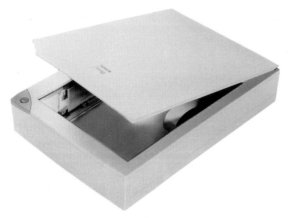

*Figure 9.10 Flatbed scanner*

> **Checkpoint**
>
> A **scanner** translates graphics, words or symbols on a printed page into digital signals that are recognised by the computer.

### Handheld scanners

Handheld scanners perform the same job as flatbed scanners, but as they are usually only a few centimetres wide, the amount of information that can be scanned is limited (see Figure 9.11). They are rolled across the document to be scanned, but the image produced is generally of a poorer quality to that produced by a flatbed scanner.

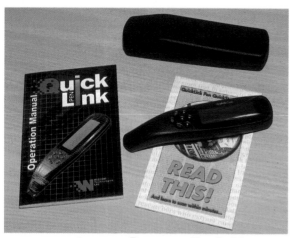

*Figure 9.11 Handheld scanner*

## Optical character recognition (OCR)

Some scanners also offer optical character recognition whereby OCR software can identify written or printed characters individually and convert them to their digital equivalent. The scanned text is displayed on screen and can be edited in exactly the same way as text that has been directly keyed in. However, it is not uncommon for some letters to be misread, particularly if the original text is of poor quality, so text scanned in this way needs very careful proof-reading.

## Optical mark reader (OMR)

An optical mark reader is a scanning device that reads pencil marks from a specially designed form or document. It is often used for questionnaires, multiple-choice answer sheets and even the national lottery (see Figure 9.12). The optical mark reader scans the sheet and the computer is able to process and analyse the results very quickly. Imagine an answer sheet for a multiple-choice test. Scanning and analysing the sheet with the aid of a computer is very much faster than it would be if, for example, your teacher was checking the answers.

*Figure 9.12 The lottery ticket terminal uses OMR to produce lottery tickets*

## Magnetic stripe reader

If you have a bank account, you will almost certainly have a card with a magnetic stripe on one side (see Figure 9.13). Information about your account is magnetically stored on the black stripe and when you 'swipe' the card, the

Figure 9.13 The magnetic stripe on
the back of a debit card

Figure 9.14 Bar codes on product labels

stored information is read by a magnetic stripe reader. For example, when you insert the card into a cash machine the magnetic stripe reader reads the data stored on the strip and knows which account is being accessed. To check the identity of the user, you are asked to enter your personal identification number (PIN) and the computer compares the PIN with the stored data.

If you watch people going to work in many office buildings, you might see them using swipe cards to operate turnstiles or doors in order to get into the building. This is a security measure to ensure that only employees can enter. Companies need to protect the vast amounts of valuable data on their computer systems and it is essential to protect unauthorised users gaining access.

Magnetic stripe readers are widely used with electronic point of sale (EPOS) terminals in shops. When a customer pays for goods with a credit card or debit card the card is swiped and the amount is automatically paid either by the credit card company or directly from the customer's bank account. Debit and credit cards have a space for a signature on the reverse and the shopkeeper must check that the signature the customer signs on the slip matches the one on the card.

Stolen or lost cards should be reported to the bank or credit card company as soon as possible. Stolen card numbers are programmed into the computer and if someone tries to use the card, the shopkeeper will automatically receive a message to contact the bank or credit card company. These measures are in place to try to reduce fraudulent use of stolen cards.

## Bar code reader

Most items offered for sale in shops will have a bar code printed on them (see Figure 9.14).

A bar code is a strip of vertical bars of varying widths that provides a unique reference code for the product. Groups of bars represent individual digits and most bar codes are made up of 12–13 digits. The last number is called a check digit. The computer applies a set of calculations to the individual digits and the final answer should equal the check digit. This ensures, or double checks, that the correct details have been entered. If a mistake is detected, an error message is generated.

Next time you are in the supermarket, watch the assistant scanning the shopping. He/she passes the bar code in front of a red beam of light. The light scans the bar code and the data is interpreted (read) through a decoder. The reference is matched to the stock list in the computer system and the appropriate price and description are displayed on the display screen and printed on your bill. Have you noticed that sometimes when an item won't scan, the assistant has to key the number in manually? This explains why the numbers are always printed beneath the vertical stripes. If the assistant enters an incorrect bar code the calculation will not match the check digit and an error message will be displayed. If that happens the bar code numbers must be entered again.

A great advantage of using a bar code system is that any price change only needs to be made to the computer system and not each individual item. The computer system can be programmed to recognise specific bar codes and therefore shops can offer customers special deals such as 'buy one get one free'. The computer will recognise the matching bar codes and will automatically deduct one price from the bill.

Next time you go to your local library look closely at your library ticket and inside the front cover of the library books. Do they have bar codes? The bar code on your ticket recognises you as a member of the library and the bar code in the book identifies a particular copy of the book. When you borrow a library book, both your ticket and the book are scanned. The library computer system can then match the borrower with the book. When you return the book it is scanned again and the computer system removes the link between you and that book. This enables the system to keep track of books on loan and to generate letters automatically to remind members that their books are overdue.

## Digital camera

A digital camera looks very similar to a traditional camera, but most have a facility that enables you to view the image on a small LCD (liquid crystal display) screen built into the camera. As soon as you take a picture, you can view it on the screen and, if you don't like it, you simply delete it. This is very different to a traditional camera where the image is recorded on film that must be processed before the image can be viewed.

With a digital camera, light intensities are converted into digital form that can be stored on a memory card or memory stick. With the use of a computer, the digital image from the data file can be viewed on screen and edited with photo imaging software. It can then be imported into a document or printed on special photographic quality paper and will look the same as a traditionally processed photograph.

## Digital camcorder

Digital camcorders work in a similar way, but the video footage is stored on a small camcorder tape. Video editing software makes it possible to edit the footage in a professional way by adding voice-overs, special effects, titles or fading in and out of scenes.

## Webcam

Another type of digital camera is the webcam (world wide web camera). A webcam automatically records an image every so often rather than continuously. The time lapse can be seconds, minutes or even hours. The image is then viewed through a web page. Webcams have many uses, for example to monitor traffic conditions or to promote holiday areas. Look on the BBC website (Just go to www.heinemann.co.uk/hotlinks and click on BBC) to see examples of traffic conditions in major towns and cities. Alternatively, check the websites of holiday destinations and you are likely to find webcams promoting the area.

## ● Snapshot

**Philip Morris, IT Manager, Chester Zoo**

Phillip Morris faces unusual problems in his job as IT Manager at Chester Zoo. For example, when the zoo installed a webcam in the monkey enclosure the monkeys didn't like the IT engineers invading their territory and pelted them with fruit! Once the camera was installed it too became a target for bricks and grass thrown by the monkeys.

There are 110 terminals throughout the zoo – many of them outside in the animal enclosures. The zoo keepers use the computers to share information about animal feeding and welfare, but the terminals get covered in dust and mud and frequently need air blasting to get them clean.

Computers have taken over jobs formerly done manually. For example, in egg keeping, by monitoring the evaporation of water and humidity there is an increased chance of a successful hatch.

The zoo has a new EPOS system and is considering the installation of a new computerised gate system and the creation of a database system for membership records. This would remove many of the current paper-based systems.

*Source: Computing, 14 February 2002.*

## Touch screen

A touch screen allows the user to interact with the computer by touching the screen on a display menu. This breaks an infrared light beam and generates an electronic signal that identifies the location on the screen. Alternatively, the screen is covered with a touch-sensitive transparent panel and the force of the touch completes a circuit (acting like a switch). Computer software interprets the signal and performs the required operation.

You are most likely to come across touch screens in public places. For instance, BT is installing multimedia kiosks in many public places. You can use the touch screens to access the Internet, send e-mails or choose ring tones for your mobile phone, for example (see Figure 9.15).

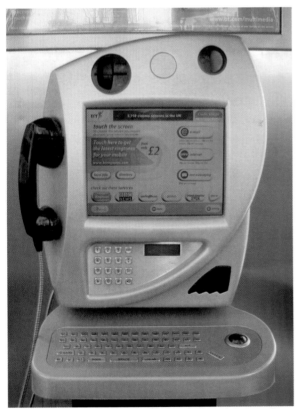

*Figure 9.15 A multimedia kiosk with touch screen and telephone*

### Checkpoint

A **touch screen** allows data to be input into the computer in response to touch.

## Graphics tablet

A graphics tablet – sometimes called a digitising tablet or digitiser – is used for freehand drawing and sketching and is especially useful for tracing drawings. It is used along with a cursor (puck) and/or a pen (stylus) (see Figure 9.16). The tablet contains electrodes that detect the movement of the cursor or stylus and the movements are translated into digital signals that are sent to the computer.

*Figure 9.16 A graphics tablet with puck and stylus*

## Microphone

Microphones are sensors that detect sound. Some microphones are used with voice recognition equipment that translates spoken words into digital signals for the computer. The computer is able to match voice patterns with those stored in the system. If you wanted to use voice recognition software, it would probably be necessary to record your commands several times over so that the computer is able to recognise your spoken voice and respond.

## Sensors

In a computerised control system, **sensors** are used to detect environmental conditions such as temperature, light, humidity or pressure. The data is not entered manually via the keyboard or mouse. Instead, an electronic signal registering the current condition, or state, is sent to the computer and, if necessary, the computer program will respond. For example, in a heating system, if the temperature falls below a pre-set level, the computer will react by producing a signal to activate heaters to bring the temperature back to the pre-set level. When the level is reached the computer will generate an instruction to turn off the heaters.

One advantage of using sensors is that they can operate 24 hours a day for 365 days a year in all weathers and under any condition. Sensors are not only used for control programs, they can also be used to gather data which is then stored on the computer. This is known as data logging. For example, data recording daily temperatures, rainfall, wind speed and hours of sunshine, and so on, are gathered (or logged) in order to produce weather statistics.

**Checkpoint**

A **sensor** is an input device used to measure a physical quantity.

## Processing unit and associated components

The main processing unit of a computer system is usually housed in a tower, mini-tower or desktop case.

Within the casing are the various components involved in processing. They include:

- the central processing unit
- memory
- motherboard

In addition are the various components which link all parts of the computer system together:

- ports
- modem
- network card
- display.

Each component has an important job to do.

### Central processing unit (CPU)

The central processing unit (CPU) or processor is the part of a computer that controls all the other parts. It is often thought of as the computer's brain.

The key role of the central processing unit is to:

- carry out instructions within the software
- handle control signals
- perform arithmetic and logic operations.

The CPU is a microprocessor – a chip of silicon – composed of tiny electrical switches (see Figure 9.17). The speed at which the processor carries out its operations is measured in Megahertz (MHz) or millions of cycles or pulses per second. Intel is the world's largest PC chip manufacturer and the Intel Pentium is probably the best known processor. The Intel Celeron is a cheaper chip and is often used in home computers. The world's second largest manufacturer is Athlon and the Athlon chip provides another cheaper alternative which is said to be more powerful than the Pentium.

The higher the number of MHz, the faster the computer can process information. In 1965, Gordon Moore, the founder of Intel, accurately

*Figure 9.17 A microprocessor*

predicted that the capacity of memory chips would double every 18–24 months. Late in 2000, the first-ever 1 GHz (Gigahertz) processor was introduced, and in 2002, the 2.2 GHz processor appeared. By the time you read this book there will probably be an even more powerful chip available! However, for most people with average processing requirements, a processor running at about 1 GHz should be adequate. The very powerful processors are more suitable for those who are working with large and complex graphic processing requirements.

Each time you press a letter on the keyboard, an electronic signal is generated which passes between the keyboard and the processor. The processor interprets (reads) the electronic signal and displays the letter on screen. Similarly, when you click on an icon with your mouse the instruction is carried from the mouse via the cable to the CPU, which reacts to the signal and carries out your instruction. For example, when you click the Save 🖫 button to save a data file, the instruction goes to the central processing unit where it is carried out. The CPU will interpret other instructions you give such as create an automatic backup copy, password protect or make a file read only.

Within the central processing unit, there is an arithmetic logic unit that handles all arithmetic and logic operations:

- The arithmetic unit enables the computer to add up (+), subtract (–), multiply (*) and divide (/), or perform standard arithmetic functions such as = sum, = average, = maximum, and so on.
- The logic unit handles more complex queries such as equal to (=), greater than (>) or less than (<). A typical query in a

database might be to show all girls aged over 12. The logic operators you would be using are = girls and >12.

In a computerised control system a signal from a sensor is received by the CPU and acted upon. The resulting action might be something simple like turning on a light or something more complex like activating a robot.

## Memory

The working memory of the computer, where data and instructions are stored for fast access, is found in the main processing unit. It consists of **ROM** and **RAM**:

- **ROM** (read-only memory) is a permanent memory that is available whether the computer is switched on or off. The start-up procedure when you switch your computer on is stored in ROM. It is installed when the computer is manufactured and can be read from but not over-written. This means it cannot be changed. It is the memory that brings you to the desktop whenever you switch on and from there you can access the software you want to use.
- **RAM** (random access memory) is a fast temporary working memory where programs and data are stored when the computer is running. For example, if you open your word processing software to write an essay for your homework, the document you are creating is stored in RAM while the computer processes your instructions. However, it must be saved permanently on a hard or floppy disk or it will be lost when the computer is switched off. For this reason RAM is known as volatile memory – which means non-permanent memory.

### Fact file

The terms 'to boot up' and 'booting up' are sometimes used to describe the start-up process.

The amount of memory which comes with the average computer is increasing very rapidly. In the mid 1990s a hard drive would have been about 800MB; 5 or 6 years later it was already 20GB.

### Storage capacity

The size of data or storage capacity of a computer is measured in bytes. One byte contains 8 bits – bits stands for binary digits and is the smallest unit of data that can be stored. A byte is approximately equal to one single keyboard character (letter, number or special character).

The storage capacity of a computer is normally described in terms of Kilobytes (KB), Megabytes (MB) and Gigabytes (GB). The list below will help you to compare the difference in memory size:

- bit – smallest unit of data with a value of 1 or 0
- byte – equal to 8 bits; approximately one character
- kilobyte (KB) – equal to 1,024 bytes or $2^{10}$
- megabyte (MB) – equal to 1,048,576 bytes or $2^{20}$ (equal to approximately 500 double line spaced pages of text)
- Gigabyte (GB) – equal to 1,073,741,824 bytes or $2^{30}$ (equivalent to approximately 500,000 double line spaced pages of text)
- terabyte (TB) – equal to about 1,099,000,000,000 bytes or $2^{40}$.

## Motherboard

The motherboard is the main printed circuit board of the computer that usually forms the 'floor' of the system (see Figure 9.19). All the other electrical components are plugged into the motherboard, for example the CPU and the memory. The components are linked by 'buses' which are etched into the motherboard and which carry signals from one component to another.

Figure 9.19 The motherboard

## Ports

Ports are the 'sockets' at the back of the main processor casing and are used to attach peripheral devices such as the printer, monitor, keyboard, mouse, scanner, and so on. Cables from each peripheral plug into the ports allowing data to be sent and received between the peripherals and the microprocessor.

### Serial port

The serial port has traditionally been used for connecting monitors, mice and keyboards to computers and, nowadays, is the means of transferring data from a handheld computer to a PC. Data transfer is very slow – approximately 3 hours to transmit 1 GB data.

### Parallel port

The **parallel port** transmits data in or out in parallel and is a common external port that is found on almost all PCs. This port is used to connect printers, scanners and external storage devices. PCs can be linked directly together using parallel ports but the transfer of data is slow – taking up to 30 minutes to transfer 1 GB data. This is fast enough for printers but very slow for scanners.

## Universal Serial Bus

The Universal Serial Bus (USB) is the current preferred port and is known as a Plug and Play connection. Plug and Play is a Windows system that allows peripherals to be plugged in or unplugged without having to reboot the PC. Windows has a selection of device drivers stored within its own memory and these can be installed automatically. The USB provides a much faster transfer of data than the traditional serial and parallel connection ports and it has become the standard fitting on new computers since 1997. One GB of data can be transferred in approximately 11 minutes. With an up-to-date computer system, you would probably use USB connections for a printer, scanner, digital camera and/or webcam.

The **USB2** port is new technology that will transfer 1 GB data in approximately 17 seconds. It has been designed for use with digital cameras, external hard disks and other devices that need to move large amounts of data quickly.

## Modem

If you want your computer to provide access to the Internet or e-mail, you will need a modem. Modems come ready installed on most new computers, but some computers have a separate external modem which plugs into the PC. The modem converts the computer's digital signal into an analogue signal that can be carried over the telephone network (see Chapter 11).

## Network card

Computers in schools, colleges or at work are probably connected to a network. Networks allow the sharing of resources and information by users. To access the network, each PC must be fitted with a network card. This is similar to a printed circuit board, which slots into the CPU, and contains all the necessary electronics and connections to allow the PC to link into the network (see page 156).

## Disk drives

RAM and ROM do not provide a permanent means of storing either your applications

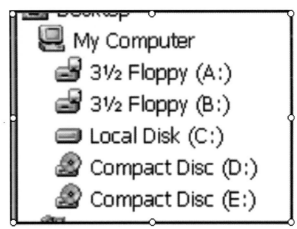

*Figure 9.20 Disk drives*

software (such as word processing, spreadsheet or database) or the data you have input and spent time working on. To store the data permanently, you need a disk drive. A disk drive is a storage device that transfers data to and from magnetic or optical disks. Your PC will probably have several drives that may be represented on the computer like this: (see Figure 9.20)

**A:** – generally the floppy disk drive
**B:** – sometimes used for the Zip drive
**C:** – the computer's hard drive
**D:** – normally for the CD-ROM or CD-RW
**E:** – the DVD drive.

You might also notice additional temporary drives (for example F:) when a digital camera or other peripheral device is plugged into the USB port. The computers you use on your networked system at school or college will probably allocate different letters to the drives.

### The hard disk drive

The hard disk drive is the storage area, rather like a filing cabinet, where all the applications software you use and documents you create are kept. It is the main permanent storage area of the computer and data can be transferred to the hard disk much faster than to a floppy disk. The hard drive houses one or more rigid magnetic disks that rotate about a central axle (see Figure 9.21). The surface of each disk is divided into a number of concentric circles or tracks which the read/write heads access. The tracks are divided into sectors.

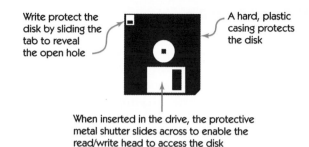

Write protect the disk by sliding the tab to reveal the open hole

A hard, plastic casing protects the disk

When inserted in the drive, the protective metal shutter slides across to enable the read/write head to access the disk

*Figure 9.22  A 3.5" floppy disk*

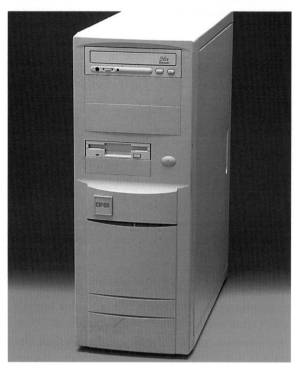

*Figure 9.21  A tower casing housing the hard drive, CD and floppy disk drives together with the CPU*

Today's hard drives are measured in Gigabytes (GB). The more expensive computers will have the largest hard drives. Hard drive capacity has increased substantially since the mid 1990s. The extra capacity is needed because complex application software, which is able to perform complicated functions, requires much greater storage space than earlier versions.

## The floppy disk drive

The floppy disk drive enables you to save files onto a floppy disk so that you can take data files between home and school or college and also make back-up copies of your data files as a security measure in case your hard drive gets damaged or your data files become corrupted.

Floppy disks are round, flat and made of a flexible material called Mylar. The disk has a magnetic surface upon which data is recorded and it is covered with a hard, protective plastic case. The disk turns in the drive allowing the read/write head to access the disk. Most PCs take a 3.5" floppy disk which can store up to 1.44 MB of data – see Figure 9.22. This is equal to about 300 A4 pages of plain text. The size of a data file containing graphic images and

complex formatting will be much larger and, as a result, will reduce the number of pages that can be stored on disk.

A floppy disk must be formatted before data can be written to it. Formatting establishes tracks and sectors into which data files are stored. The write-protect tab protects the data on the disk from accidental deletion. A write-protected disk can only be 'read from' and not 'written to'. This means the files stored on the disk can be retrieved, but they cannot be accidentally overwritten or deleted. It also protects the disk from picking up infection from a computer virus from another computer.

Care should be taken when handling disks to protect the data stored on them. If you are carrying disks to and from home and school or college, store them in a protective case to keep them clean and away from dust and moisture. The surface of the disk should not be touched (which is one reason for the hard, plastic casing) and it should be kept away from extreme temperatures. To avoid accidentally erasing the data from a disk keep it away from magnetic fields – so don't store it close to a telephone or television.

## Zip drive

The Zip drive is similiar to a floppy drive but can store 100 MB of data, at least 70 times more than a floppy. Most newer Zip disks can store as much as 250 MB. The Zip disk is slightly thicker than a floppy disk and needs a separate drive. Data is compressed, which means the size of a file, which may be too large to fit on a floppy disk, is reduced. In this way large data files can be backed up or transferred from one machine to another. Zip drives were particularly useful before it was possible to store data optically.

*Figure 9.23  Are you confused by computer acronyms?*

### PenDrives/USB Memory Sticks/Keychain drives
USB storage devices are becoming an increasingly popular method of storing data and are set to replace the floppy disk. You can learn more about these in Chapter 11, page 187.

### Optical storage
**CD-ROM** (compact disk read-only memory). This uses the same technology as CD music discs and CD players where a laser beam *reads* data from an optical disk. 'Read' is the key word here as you can only read information from a CD-ROM – you cannot store additional data on it. A typical CD holds around 650 MB of data, which is equal to about 450 floppy disks.

Nowadays, most computer software comes stored on a CD-ROM. The entire contents of a text-based encyclopaedia takes up only 25 per cent of one standard sized CD-ROM! The remainder is filled up with video sequences, animation, photographs, sound and interactive programs. The result – an interactive multimedia encyclopaedia.

**CD-R** The recordable compact disk can store about 650 MB very cheaply. Data is written to the CD-R using a special CD Writer and is permanently burned into the CD-R. Look at the back of any CD you have created and you will see a slight 'shadow' where the recording has been made. If you record music using a recordable compact disk, recordings are reproduced without any loss of sound quality.

**CD-RW** The CD-RW is both recordable and re-writable and also stores about 650 MB data. This means you can record, erase and re-record data very cheaply. More and more new PCs come with a CD-RW drive ready installed and this provides an alternative method for backing up or transporting large data files from one computer to another.

**DVD** The digital versatile disk is probably familiar to you in the format used for storing videos. It offers a much sharper image than videotape and the quality of the soundtrack is far better.

**DVD-ROM** This is the same diameter as a CD but holds nearly ten times the data – between 4.7 GB and 17 GB – making it ideal for full-length movies. If the computer you are using has a DVD-ROM drive but no CD-ROM, don't worry because you can still play CDs on the DVD ROM.

**DVD+RW and DVD-RAM** These re-writable DVDs are currently being developed. As this chapter is being written, they are in competition with each other. The DVD+RW is being sponsored by Hewlett-Packard, Phillips and Sony. It can store 3 GB per side which is a higher capacity than the DVD-RAM which can store 2.6 GB. The DVD-RAM is being developed by the DVD Consortium.

## Magnetic tape

The sort of work you do on the computer can easily be backed up on CDs for safety. However, most organisations need to back up much larger amounts of data and rely on magnetic tape to create back-up copies of the computer's hard drive.

Magnetic tape consists of a thin plastic strip with a magnetic coating to one side and is stored on a reel or cartridge. The tape is read to and written from by means of a tape drive which winds the tape from one reel to another past a read/write head. The back-up procedure is often run at night when the computer is not in use.

DLT (digital linear tape) is a form of magnetic tape and drive system used for computer data storage and archiving and can hold around 70 GB of data on a single cartridge when compressed. Another form of tape drive called Ultrium was launched two years ago and some models such as the HP's StorageWorks Ultrium 460 can store a massive 200 GB of uncompressed data per cartridge!

Access to data on tape is by **serial access**, which means that the tape must be run from one end to the other until you come to the data you might be looking for. This is similar to a videotape where you may have to run through the tape to find the programme that you want to watch. Magnetic tape is ideal as a method of backing up but not as a general storage method for files you work with everyday.

On the other hand, data files on disc on the PC can be found by **direct access**. This is similar to a music CD where you can go directly to the track you want to listen to – in other words, you have direct access to the track. If you want to open a certain data file, the computer brings up the complete file and not the bit at the end of the previous document as well.

## Output devices

When you enter text through the keyboard or select a function through an icon or pull-down menu with the mouse, you usually see the result of your action on the computer screen. The computer screen **outputs** the result of the instructions that have been **input** into the system.

The main output devices include:

- the monitor (or screen)
- printer
- plotter
- speakers
- motors/actuators.

## The monitor

A monitor or visual display unit (VDU) is the part of the computer system that displays images (characters or graphics) generated by the computer's video adapter. The image or text on screen is called **soft copy**.

The standard monitor consists of a cathode ray tube (CRT) similar to that used in television sets together with the housing or case (see Figure 9.24). They are cheap, easy to make but take up a large amount of space and do not have high definition. The size of screen is worked out by measuring the distance between the diagonal corners of the screen. Standard sizes are 15", 17", 19" and 21".

The newer flat-panel display screens or TFT LCD (thin film transistor liquid crystal display) screens take up much less desk space and give a bright, crisp image (see Figure 9.25). They are currently much more expensive than the standard monitor although, as they are becoming more popular, more manufacturers are making them and the price is falling.

The sharpness or clarity of the image on a VDU depends on its resolution. Resolution is measured in pixels (short for picture elements). The more pixels per square centimetre of screen, the better the resolution. Resolutions vary between 1024 x 768, 1280 x 1024 and 1600 x 1200 pixels. The higher the number of pixels, the clearer and crisper the display.

## Printers

If you need a permanent (or hard) copy of the information on-screen, you will need a printer. Today, most PCs attach laser or ink-jet printers, but the dot-matrix printer is useful for some printing jobs, for example when printing the multi-copy documents used to track and process orders. Laser and ink-jet printers are known as non-impact printers because no part of the printer touches the page to form the image. They print in black and white and/or colour.

*Figure 9.24 A standard CRT monitor*

*Figure 9.25 A flat-panel display screen*

The quality, or resolution, of the image is measured in dots per inch (dpi). The more dots per inch, the more detailed the output. The speed of the printer is rated by pages per minute (ppm) or by characters per second (cps) – the higher the value, the faster the speed (and, of course, the greater the cost). However, when considering the speed, you should remember that files containing graphics are more complex and will inevitably slow down the printer.

### Laser printers

Laser printers are based on the same technology as photocopiers – lasers produce an image on an electrically charged drum (see Figure 9.26). Dry ink or toner sticks to the electrical charge and is fixed by heat. They have a high resolution of 1200+ dpi, and reproduce complex graphics very clearly. They are very quiet and operate at reasonably high speeds of between 8 and 30+ ppm. Some laser printers work only in black and white – those operating in colour and at the faster speeds are the most expensive.

### Ink-jet printers

Ink-jet printers use liquid ink to spray characters onto a page (see Figure 9.27). They also offer a high resolution of up to 1200 dpi and it can be difficult to tell the difference between a print produced on a good quality

*Figure 9.26 A laser printer*

*Figure 9.27 An ink-jet printer*

ink-jet and a standard laser printer. However, they operate at much slower speeds of between 6 and 10 ppm for black and white copies and half the speed if printing colour. They, too, are quiet to operate and generally cheaper in price than a laser printer, but when used with inexpensive copier paper the ink has a tendency to smudge.

### Dot matrix

Dot matrix printers are known as impact printers because the dot-matrix print head hits (or impacts on) the paper and, for this reason, they are noisy in operation. The characters are made up of dots using a 9, 18, or 24 pin print head (see Figure 9.28). The pins hit the paper through a ribbon making patterns of dots in the shape of letters, numbers or graphics. They can print different fonts in different sizes and reproduce graphic images. The print quality depends on the number of dots in the matrix. This could be low enough to show individual dots or high enough to look almost like fully formed characters.

When Jubilee 6th Form College's bookshop placed an order with Select Stationery, it is likely that the duplicate delivery/advice note prepared for the warehouse would have been printed on a dot matrix printer used in conjunction with NCR (no carbon required) stationery. This is a set of pages (usually in different colours) with a special chemical coating. When the dot matrix print head strikes the page a chemical reaction occurs and an imprint is made on all copies.

The use of different colour pages helps ensure that the right copies go to the right places. One copy of the delivery/advice note will be used by the warehouse to make sure the right goods are picked from store and the other copy will go to the customer when the goods are delivered. Sometimes additional coloured copies may be used for the Accounts Department and for the customer's file.

## Plotter

There are two types of graph plotter:

- the flatbed plotter (see Figure 9.29)
- the drum (or rolling) plotter (see Figure 9.30).

The advantage of the drum plotter is that it can work with very large sheets of paper. Plotters are often used alongside CAD software to

*Figure 9.29  A flatbed plotter*

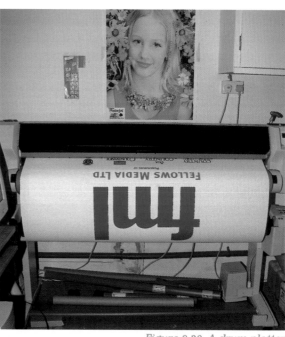

*Figure 9.30  A drum plotter*

*Figure 9.28  Dot matrix printer*

produce technical drawings where precision is essential, for example in engineering and architectural applications.

A plotter differs from a printer in that it draws images using a pen that can be lowered, raised and moved across the page to form continuous lines – a printer produces 'lines' in the form of a series of closely spaced dots. Lines and curves are drawn on the page by a combination of horizontal and vertical movements of the pen or paper. The pen (or pens in multicolour plotters) produces horizontal lines by moving along a horizontal bar. With the flatbed plotter, it is the movement of the bar that enables the plotter to draw vertical lines, whereas with the drum plotter, the paper moves.

> **Activity**
> ▷ Print the file: **COM Worksheet 1**
> ▷ from the Chapter 9 folder on the CD-ROM. Use your knowledge to identify the different parts of a computer system. Choose suitable computer systems for Bho and David.

## Speakers

Most computers are fitted with a small internal speaker that will beep to draw your attention to an error, for example if you hit the wrong key. On multimedia PCs additional speakers are

*Figure 9.31 Multimedia PC with speakers*

attached to the computer to provide better quality sound (see Figure 9.31). A sound card enables the computer to output sound through the speakers. The computer you are using probably has a Sound Blaster sound card. Sound Blaster has become the standard for most PCs.

## Motors

Computer control systems usually have a VDU attached to them so that computer programs can be monitored or changed. However, they generally do not need a printer. A more likely output device would be a motor. For example, a greenhouse would need a motor to open the window automatically if the temperature became too high or a robot would need a motor to make it move.

> **Activity**
> ▷ Print the file: **COM Worksheet 2**
> from the Chapter 9 folder on the CD-ROM and decide whether the items listed are input devices, output devices, processing devices, storage devices or ports and cables.

## Software

A computer cannot do anything on its own. It needs **software** to make it work.

While it is easy to recognise computer hardware (monitor, keyboard, mouse, and so on) because you can see it, you can neither see nor touch computer software. Some software comes pre-installed on the computer (the start-up program) and some comes on CD-ROM (operating systems and application software) that the user or computer supplier must load onto the hard drive before the computer can be used.

> **Checkpoint**
> **Software** is a set of instructions written to make the computer work.

The different types of software include:

- operating systems
- applications software.

## The ROM BIOS chip

The instructions that enable the computer to start up is permanently stored in the read-only memory chip on the motherboard. When the computer is turned on or restarted, it looks for the start-up instructions in the ROM BIOS chip. BIOS stands for Basic Input Output System and is a set of instructions that tells the computer how to handle the flow of information between the computer and its input and output peripheral devices.

## Operating systems

The **operating system** is the most important program that runs on the computer and provides the basic user interface when no applications are open – see Figure 9.32. The computer you are using probably offers you the desktop as your starting point.

The purpose of the operating system is to:

- schedule tasks
- recognise data input from the keyboard, mouse or sensor
- keep track of the directories and files on the disks
- control peripheral devices such as the printer.

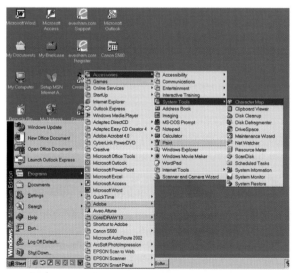

Figure 9.32 *A typical user interface. The operating system recognises the instruction given when you click on the Start button and brings up a selection of programs you can run*

This makes the operating system the foundation on which applications software such as word processing and spreadsheet programs are built. The most common operating systems for PCs are MS-DOS and systems that use Windowing Environments such as Windows 2000 or Windows XP. Apple Macs have a different operating system known as the Mac OS.

> ### Checkpoint
> The **operating system** is the software program through which all application programs run.

## MS-DOS

MS-DOS was developed by Microsoft® and introduced as a standard operating system in all IBM-compatible computers from the early 1980s. For many years, it was the most popular system in use. MS-DOS stands for **M**icro**S**oft **D**isk **O**perating System. It controls many internal computer functions such as how to process information, how to manage files and how to interpret commands. For this reason, it is described as a 'command led' system. DOS is difficult to work with because commands have to be typed in an exact way and there are too many different codes for the ordinary everyday user to remember.

### MS-DOS Prompt

Have you noticed the MS-DOS Prompt  listed in the Accessories menu? Many computer users don't know what it means or what it does. Click on it and you will find yourself in the command prompt – see Figure 9.33.

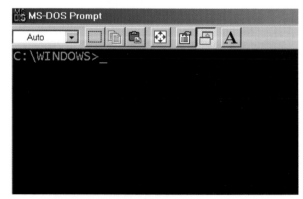

Figure 9.33 *MS-DOS Command prompt screen*

When the command prompt C:\> is displayed the command processor is waiting for a command. For example, typing 'dir' at the command prompt and pressing Enter will display the contents of the current drive/directory. For most people, what is shown on-screen may look confusing and generally only experienced programmers and technicians work with DOS.

## Windows

Windows was first introduced in 1985 and is now the most popular PC operating system. The name comes from the computer term 'windowing environment' which is an operating system that can divide the screen into independent areas called windows. Each window has its own frame that can usually be resized and moved around on the screen. Individual windows can contain different software applications, documents or messages, or even their own menus or other controls (see Figures 9.34 and 9.35).

### Graphical User Interface

To the average computer user, the advantage of Windows is its Graphical User Interface (GUI – say 'gooey') which is a user friendly method of showing information on screen graphically. It lets you start programs, select menus, choose commands and other options by using the mouse to click on the menus or icons. You do not need to know the complicated commands required by DOS.

### Directories, folders and files

Directories and folders are created through the operating system and the commands to rename, delete or move files are acted upon by the operating system. For example, to copy a file from the hard drive to a floppy disk, use My Computer and drag and drop the file from one folder to another.

### Loading software

If you have ever loaded software from a CD-ROM onto a computer, the operating system generated the instructions that took you through the steps and automatically allocated an area on the hard drive for the software to be stored.

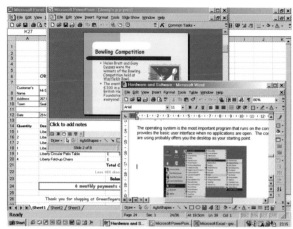

*Figure 9.34  The windows environment. In this example there are three different applications running in their own windows at the same time. The advantage is that you can work in one window, refer to another and switch between windows*

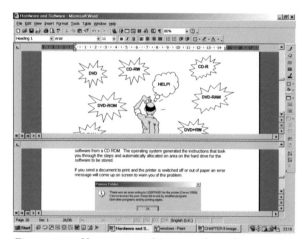

*Figure 9.35  If you are working on a long document in Word, for example, you can split the screen into two windows and work on one end of the document while looking at the other*

### Error messages

If you send a document to print and the printer is switched off or out of paper, an error message will come up on-screen to alert you (see Figure 9.36). This message is produced by the operating system.

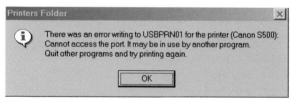

*Figure 9.36  Error message produced by the operating system*

## Applications software

In Unit 1 you learned how to use a selection of software applications or software packages. These are programs designed to help users perform certain types of work by manipulating (handling) text, numbers and graphics, or all three together. All the popular software applications are now written to work in the Windows environment. This is helpful for the computer user because the applications look very similar on-screen and this makes it much easier to work with different software applications.

The various types of applications software include:

- word processing
- spreadsheets
- databases
- desktop publishing
- graphics.

## Word processing

Word processing enables you to manipulate text-based documents, for example you can enter text, edit and format it, change the presentation, and so on. The simplest features make typing and basic editing tasks such as deleting and inserting easier. The more complex ones check your grammar, help you find alternative words, allow you to include graphics or calculations created in another program in your text and merge documents with data files. You will probably use word processing software to present your coursework for ICT and possibly some other subjects.

## Spreadsheets

Spreadsheets are used to process numbers and they are particularly useful for financial forecasting. Spreadsheets are divided into cells that can contain text, numbers and formulae and the cells can be formatted to display their contents as whole numbers or currency, and so on. Spreadsheets can automatically produce charts and graphs to display trends and make comparisons clear. These can then be imported into word processed reports or presentations.

## Databases

A database contains data. The database allows you to process the data in various ways to produce information. For example, the database in a video store contains the names and addresses of members and the titles of videos. It can manipulate this data to produce information to show which member might have a particular video on loan or how many times that video has been borrowed. This information helps the store offer a selection of videos that will appeal to the public.

The database in Jubilee 6th Form College stores details of all the students and their courses. It produces information on students' progress and achievements. This is very important to the college because the funding it receives is calculated on student numbers and achievement.

## Desktop publishing

A desktop publishing (DTP) package is more sophisticated than word processing software because it has the capability of producing complex page layouts. For example, the text to be included in a newsletter would be created in a word processing application, spell checked, edited and saved. It would then be imported into the DTP program together with graphics that would have been created in a graphics program.

Newspapers and magazines are produced using DTP software. To achieve the best results from a DTP application, the user needs a high resolution monitor and colour laser printer.

You have already seen in Unit 1 that it is not essential to have DTP software in order to produce newsletters or brochures because word processing software has many of the features of desktop publishing programs. For instance, text formatting enables you to change the font size and style, page layout features make it possible to change the page orientation (portrait or landscape) and put the text into columns, and graphics features allow you to add lines and borders and position and resize graphics.

## Graphics

Most PCs now have a graphics card installed which allows the computer to display pictures. Graphics software includes:

- paint programs
- illustration and design programs
- presentation graphics, e.g. charts and graphs
- animation software
- CAD software.

Graphics software comes in two formats:

- bitmap
- vector.

## Bitmap and vector images

A bitmap image is made up of small squares called pixels which can be edited pixel by pixel but, when enlarged, the image loses its sharpness. Paint and photo editing programs are typical examples of bitmap applications. Vector graphics packages represent images by designating coordinates and drawing lines or geometric shapes in relation to them. A vector graphic is stored as a file containing instructions for drawing it and can be enlarged or reduced without losing quality. Drawing packages are examples of vector graphics.

Figures 9.37 and 9.38 show the components of the Jubilee 6th Form College logo copied into both bitmap and vector software and enlarged. Can you see the difference?

Figure 9.37  A bitmap image loses its clarity (sharpness) when enlarged

Figure 9.38  A vector image keeps its sharpness when enlarged

### Checkpoint

**Pixel** stands for picture element.

## JPEG and GIF formats

It can be confusing trying to understand the difference between the various file formats available for graphic images. The most common way of storing an image on a PC is as a bitmap, that is, as a grid of pixels. However, the more detailed the image, the larger the file size and when a graphic is intended for the Internet the larger the file, the longer it will take to download. To overcome this problem, files are compressed so that they can be transmitted as quickly as possible. The following are the two file formats suitable for the Internet and e-mail:

- A **JPEG (.jpg)** image is best for photographic images to be viewed on the web or to be sent via e-mail since it supports a maximum colour depth of 24 bit or 16.7 million colours.
- A **GIF (.gif)** format supports a maximum colour depth of 8 bits or 256 colours and is ideal for web graphics and animations but not photographs.

Both JPEG and GIF images can be interlaced, that is, a low-resolution representation of an image can be downloaded first which will then be gradually replaced by a more detailed version, giving the illusion of faster downloading.

## TIFF and Windows bitmap formats

The two other graphics formats that you will probably come across are **TIFF (.tif)** and **Windows bitmap (.bmp)**.

TIFF files support 24 bit or 16.7 million colours and so are the preferred format for desk top publishing, print and photography uses. The file sizes can be very large, particularly images that are large enough to fill an A4 page, which may be many megabytes in size, and so a very powerful PC is needed to handle the files efficiently. A TIFF image is compatible with both PCs and Apple Macs. In the publishing and art worlds, the Apple Mac is generally preferred to the PC and the TIFF is the preferred format.

**Bitmap** files with the .bmp format are specific to Windows and cannot be viewed easily on other operating systems. Windows has traditionally used bitmap images for small graphics, desktop icons and tiled backgrounds for desktop wallpaper. They support 24 bit colour depth and are therefore equally as good as TIFF files for quality, but they cannot be compressed and they create very large files. Files created in Paint are typical bitmap files.

## Utilities programs

Utility programs help computer users recover data that has been lost as a result of damaged disks, virus attack or accidental deletion. They provide diagnostic and measurement routines that check the performance of the system and are built into the memory to continually monitor the executable files (the main applications) for any damage or change. If any change is detected, the file is prevented from being run and a user message is given. The increasing use of the Internet and e-mail has greatly added to the risk of picking up a virus and anti-virus software is essential in order to scan files, detect and remove viruses from both hard and floppy disks. The process of removing a virus is known as disinfecting.

If you transfer data between your computer at school or college and your computer at home (or even a friend's computer), it is advisable to check that your anti-virus software is up-to-date. New viruses are continually being produced and they could miss detection if you are using out-of-date anti-virus software.

## Setting up the system

A new home computer system is delivered in separate boxes and must be put together before it can be used. Exactly the same happens in business, only there will probably be a lot more boxes to unpack!

### Stay safe!

There are some very important safety issues you should remember whenever you are working with a computer system. Whether you are connecting the components, testing the system or simply sorting out a loose connection, *always* follow these safety rules:

- Connect all the power cables to the rear of the system unit *before* plugging them into the wall outlet or power strip.
- To avoid damaging a computer, *never* plug in or unplug a cable when the system power is on.
- *Never* handle a live connector – it could kill you.

## Cables and connectors

The computer won't work unless all the different components are connected together. If you look at the on-screen display when the computer boots up, you might see messages such as 'keyboard detected' or 'mouse initialised' that show the main processing unit is trying to locate the keyboard and mouse. In other words, the central processing unit is trying to establish, or set up, a communication link with the peripheral devices and this communication takes place through the cables that connect the system.

It is fairly straightforward to set up a system as hardware connections on desktop and tower cases, and on portables, are all standard. Newer computers are colour coded to ensure the right connections are made, for example a green plug goes into a green socket for the mouse and a purple plug goes into a purple socket for the keyboard. Just in case the user may be colour blind, easily recognisable symbols are printed on the casing, for example a mouse symbol shows where to plug in the mouse.

The cables connecting the keyboard, mouse, VDU, and so on, should be attached before plugging into the main electricity supply to make sure the system powers up and runs properly. At this stage, any accessories such as printers or scanners can be connected. This keeps things simple, so if there are any problems, they will be easier to deal with.

It makes sense to plug your devices into a surge protector because electrical surges and voltage spikes can cause serious damage to computer systems. Surges and spikes are momentary over-voltages of up to several thousand volts that last a few millionths of a second. In the event of a power failure, reconnection might result in a power surge.

## Installation

Once you have the basic system connected, powered up and running smoothly, you are ready to install the software and prepare the system for use. Almost all systems come with the operating system pre-installed and configured. From this point, you may have to install drivers for the display, the printer and any other peripherals, as well as the applications software.

Device drivers are programs that enable a computer system to communicate with a device. A printer driver, for example, translates computer data into a form that is understood by the specific type of printer you have connected. In most cases, device drivers also manipulate the hardware involved in sending data to the device.

When you are installing new applications software, the program set-up usually asks if you would like it to create a new directory (or folder) in which to store the new program. It also suggests a name and shows the path. For example, if the program is called Sportsman, it might suggest c:\ sportsman\.

## Testing

The installation and set-up is only successful once you have tested it thoroughly. Testing means being able to perform each of the following actions without any problems:

- powering up
- accessing applications software
- entering, saving, retrieving and printing data.

### Powering up

When you power up you should hear the hard disk beginning to spin and see the monitor flicker into life. If nothing happens, switch off the computer and check the power cables to make sure they are still plugged in securely. If you are using a surge protector, make sure it is switched on. If you can hear the power supply fan whirring, but nothing shows up on the monitor, make sure the monitor is turned on. You may also need to check and adjust the monitor brightness control.

Keeping a system in good shape has a lot to do with the way you power up and down. Here are some tips:

- Power up the monitor first, then each of the accessories before you switch the system on

– this causes fewer devices to pull on the same power source at the same time.
- Avoid turning the system on and off frequently.
- Never turn the system off when the hard drive indicator light is on.
- Once you have shut down the system, do not turn it back on again until the hard drive has come to a complete halt.
- Whenever you restart the system, use the reset button rather than the power button.
- Always close whatever programs you are using and shut down the system before switching off.
- If you use an extension lead, never turn the system on and off from the extension lead switch.

## Accessing applications software

If the software has been loaded successfully, you should be able to open it from Start, Programs and by selecting the program you want or by clicking on the appropriate icon on the computer desktop.

To ensure that each application is functioning correctly, test it using the following procedure:

1 Open the application.
2 Type 'Test1' with your initials and the date.
3 Save the file as Test1 with any appropriate extension.
4 Exit the application.
5 Re-open the application.
6 Open the file.
7 Print a copy.
8 Save and close the file.
9 Exit the application.

Your computer is now set up, but before you start using it make sure that any cables are safely tucked away and do not cause a hazard for anyone to trip over. You will find more advice on working safely in Chapter 13.

## System configuration

The system will be set up with standard settings which, for most people, will be quite satisfactory. However, some people will find the system much easier to use if some small adjustments are made. This is called configuring the system. For example, the left-handed user will find the mouse more comfortable to use if the button functions are reversed. Someone who is colour blind might find certain desktop colours difficult to make out. Experienced typists might like to give more functions to the keyboard to avoid interrupting their work to use the mouse. Some may like to work with the ruler in inches and others in centimetres.

Changes to system configuration can be made:

- by creating data directories or folders
- through the Control Panel
- through the pull-down menus
- through style sheets.

## Creating data directories or folders

When software is installed on a computer the operating system ensures that directories/folders are created to keep all the relevant program files together. It is equally as important to create directories/folders to separate data files from program files. If you do not do so, you will end up with a very long, muddled list of data files.

Imagine a filing cabinet with everything thrown in – how difficult it would be to find anything (see Figure 9.39). A computer without directories/folders is similar to a disorganised filing cabinet.

A tidy filing cabinet will have drawers labelled and inside the drawers, files are used to separate the papers into subjects.

In computer terms, think of the drawer as a directory (or folder) and the hanging files as sub-directories. The use of directories/folders results in data files being in the right place and therefore easy to find, edit, view and manage. There is also less likelihood of accidental deletion of program files.

You should have set up suitable folders for your own GCSE work when you were looking at the Preparatory Unit. If you haven't already done so, do it now before your computer becomes too disorganised!

Figure 9.39  A computer without directories or folders is like a disorganised filing cabinet

## Security

Once an organisation has installed a new computer system, it needs to give careful thought to system security in order to protect its investment – not only the investment in hardware but also the data stored on the system. Threats to computer security may come from within an organisation or from outside. Security of computer systems is therefore a major issue, not only because the equipment is very valuable, but so is the data within the system. It might even be argued that the data is more valuable, than the equipment because it can be difficult or impossible to restore, whereas hardware and software are replaceable.

## Theft

The most obvious threat is theft of the computer equipment and peripheral devices such as microchips, keyboards, printers or even floppy disks. Most organisations now restrict access to buildings and issue staff with photo identity cards that must be shown or swiped in order to gain entry. Visitors are usually required to sign in, wear a visitor's ID card and be escorted by a member of staff while on the premises.

Once within the building, some internal doors are kept locked and can be opened only by the use of swipe cards or alarmed keypads. Sometimes computers themselves are also alarmed or under closed-circuit television (CCTV) surveillance.

## Data security

When you use your school or college computer system you probably have to log on with a special number and password. When you enter your password it is almost certainly coded and you will see a series of asterisks on screen ******. The reason for this is to make sure nobody learns your password so they cannot access your data files. The password helps to keep your data secure, so it is important to keep it secret.

When choosing a password it is important to select something you will remember but not something that is going to be obvious to someone else. For example, try to avoid using your name, that of your favourite football team or pop idol, and so on.

The same rules apply in business. Any organisation using computers has a responsibility under the Data Protection Act to make sure its computer systems are secure. You will find that most companies use a system of login IDs and passwords and that many systems automatically call for changes to passwords at regular intervals. This is to ensure that passwords remain confidential. In this way, if somebody has found a way into the system their access would only be for a limited time.

A database manager has the responsibility for managing a large and complex system and for making sure that data is accurate, up-to-date and secure. The design of the database might restrict access so that only relevant information is available to database users. This means that junior members of staff can only gain access to less important data while more senior staff will have access to all or most of it. Management of the system also ensures that only certain staff are able to enter or amend data in the system while others will be able to read it but not change it. Imagine a situation where anybody could change the data – how could you ever be sure that the data was reliable?

Some databases have time-restricted access that limits the time the user has to find information. Special software is used to provide an 'audit trail' to show which user has logged onto which files and for how long. This is a way of checking whether anyone has accessed information they are not authorised to see.

The security of data being transmitted is guaranteed by coding data before it is transmitted. You will find a similar dialogue box to the one shown in Figure 9.40 by choosing Tools, Options, Save (or use File, Save As and select Tools, General Options).

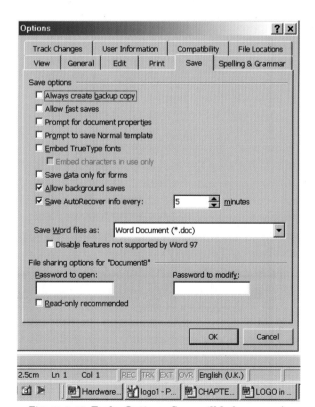

Figure 9.40 Tools, Options, Save will help you secure your own data files. Other ways to do this include creating back-up copies, AutoRecover, Passwords and Read-only files

## Backing up

Has your computer frozen or stopped responding to your instructions in the middle of a task for no obvious reason? Sometimes it is because the system is being asked to do more than it can handle and your only option is to display the Task List by pressing Ctrl + Alt + Delete in order to close any programs that are not responding and hope that your work will be recovered. If you save your work regularly, however, this should not be a problem because you could revert (go back) to the saved data file and continue your work. Unfortunately, if the problem was caused by hard drive failure, you wouldn't be able to reboot your computer and carry on with your work, even if you had saved it. This is why it makes sense to regularly back up your data files.

Hard drive failure and the loss of data that this might involve could spell disaster for any organisation that relies on the computer to process its day-to-day functions such as purchasing, stock control, accounting, production, and so on. Loss of data means loss of business. Protection of data is therefore an essential operation within any organisation. The obvious way to protect data is by regular backing up of the system.

Although a floppy disk or CD might be a suitable method of back-up for your coursework, most businesses use magnetic tape to back up the vast quantities of data they use (see page 144). Back-up is generally carried out overnight when the system is not busy and the back-up tapes (together with the original software) are usually stored in special 'disaster-proof' safes. For safety and security reasons, these are generally stored away from the main business premises so that if the premises are destroyed, the tapes and software would still be safe. In this way, the business can recover data and resume trading. Although the organisation might not have a record of every transaction since the last back-up, it would not lose everything.

Less valuable data might be kept in a locked filing cabinet and, in some cases, as an added precaution, the filing cabinet is bolted to the floor.

Nowadays, more and more people use laptop computers as well as the main company computer system. Backing up data stored on the main computer will not help if the data is only on a laptop which might get damaged, lost or stolen and it is therefore just as important to ensure that data on a laptop is saved both internally on the hard drive and externally on a floppy disk or CD.

Remember, even if you have set your computer to back up your work automatically, the back-ups will be on the hard drive, so if the hard drive crashed you would lose both your original work and the back-ups. The answer is to save your work *regularly* on *both* the hard drive and disk or CD.

The table on page 157 shows the advantages and disadvantages of the two most popular methods of backing up – digital tape and CDs/DVDs.

### Fact file

It is advisable to back up (or copy) data files on a secondary storage medium such as floppy disk or tape drive to provide a secure copy in case the original becomes unusable.

## Computer networks

Electronic communication plays an important role in business, home and your school or college life. Cable television is a form of network. If you use a cash-point machine to draw money from your savings account, you are using a network. When you are surfing the web you are using the world's largest network. Nowadays, it would be unheard of for businesses with branches throughout the UK, such as Sainsbury's and Marks & Spencer, not to use networks to communicate with each other. Jubilee 6th Form College has an annexe at Clifton on the outskirts of Wayfield. In order to communicate between both sites, the college depends on network communication.

| Method | Advantages | Disadvantages |
|---|---|---|
| Digital tape | Cheap to manufacture<br>High capacity (one cartridge the size of a videotape can hold Gigabytes of data)<br>Tape can be erased and reused | Fragile – tapes are mechanical and are liable to wear and breakage<br>Magnetic fields can wipe a tape or cause major damage to stored data |
| CD/DVD | CDs are a fraction of the size of most tape formats and require little storage space<br>Writable and re-writable CDs now cost less than floppy disks<br>Not sensitive to magnetic fields, water, sunlight or heat, but can be scratched | Writing speeds can be quite slow<br>Storage capacity is less than many tape back-up systems – CDs hold 650–700 MB while DVDs can hold about 4.7 GB |

Source: *Computing*, 28 February 2002

*Advantages and disadvantages of backing up on digital tape and CD/DVD*

## What is a network?

A network is several computer systems linked together so that facilities such as printers, storage, computer programs, and so on, can be shared. When computers are linked together like this, it is very easy to exchange information between them. A home computer is probably a standalone system, whereas your school or college will usually have a network. Networks can be either wide area networks (WANs), which link systems over a large geographical area, or local area networks (LANs), which link systems over a much smaller area.

### Local area networks

A LAN is a group of computers linked together over one small geographical area, usually one building, an office in a building, or across several buildings on one site. Your school or college will probably have a local area network. The LAN can consist of just two machines connected together (you could do this at home if two members of your family both have home computers). Alternatively, it may consist of a large number of computers located in several buildings.

Usually, if the distances involved are less than two kilometres, the network is a LAN. The system will be connected together using the organisation's own cabling. Most LANs are connected to a powerful machine called a **server**. There are a number of ways in which the LAN can be linked, but each different network configuration (layout) is known as a **topology**. You will learn more about common network topologies on pages 163–4.

Sometimes, in very large organisations a LAN will include mini or mainframe computers, very powerful computers, which are nowadays usually connected to normal PCs. However, in the past these would have been connected to a number of 'dumb' terminals (a dumb terminal has no processor or hard drive). These were very popular until PC costs reduced and servers became more powerful. As important data is still often stored on a mainframe, organisations may choose to link these systems to a modern network which consists of a number of PCs connected to a server. The server is not used by any one person, but contains one or more hard drives, which can be accessed very quickly by the other PCs on the network.

### Wireless local area networks

New technologies are being developed all the time. There are now systems which use radio signals and infra-red for networking without cables. Wireless local area networks (WLAN) are more flexible than a traditional wired network and can transmit and receive information through the air, walls and ceilings. Many schools and colleges are using wireless networks so that students can use laptop computers in any classroom and still log on to the network to do their work.

## Servers

The most common servers are **file servers**, but larger networks may have servers that have different uses. A network may have a **print server** (sometimes the file server and print server will be the same) and a **web server**, for example.

The file server provides central disk storage for the users of a network. It identifies each user's files separately, and will not allow another user to access them. Files are **downloaded** from the file server to the workstation, and **uploaded** from the workstation to the file server. Users will be able to access their files from any workstation on the network. You have probably experienced this at school or college – although you may like to sit at the same workstation in a classroom, it is not necessary as you can access your files from any machine.

A file server may also have a shared drive (sometimes called the pool drive) where all users can access files. Your school or college may have a shared drive, where teachers can save files that they want all the students to have access to. Look back at Case study 2 in Chapter 6 (page 85) which describes how the Continuing Education & Training Service (CETS) has a shared drive where standard documents are kept.

A web server is a computer connected to the Internet. Browsers can access the web server to find and display different pages of a website. A website is published on a web server (see Chapter 5).

The print server is responsible for controlling requests for printing. As each print request is received, it is placed in a print queue and once the previous request has been completed, it starts the next one.

This is quite a complex topic, so let's look at a simple diagram to represent printing. In Figure 9.41 the arrows represent the flow of information between the network components.

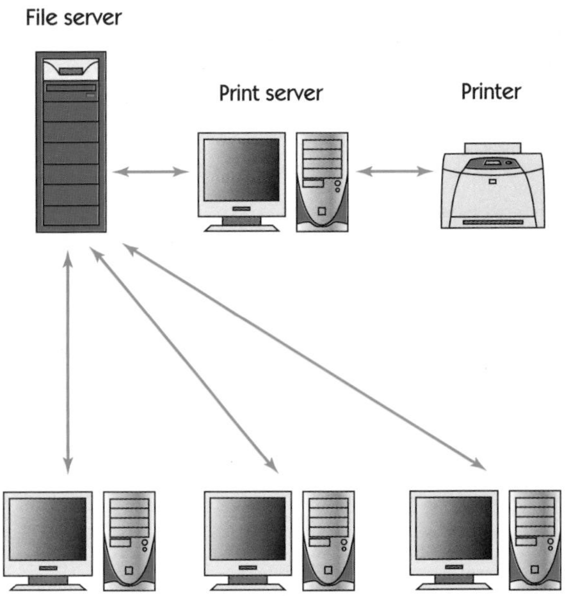

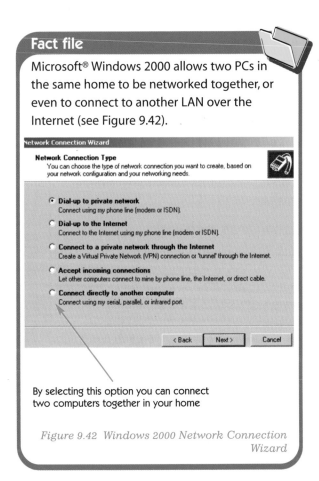

Figure 9.41  Flow of information in a local area network

### Fact file

Microsoft® Windows 2000 allows two PCs in the same home to be networked together, or even to connect to another LAN over the Internet (see Figure 9.42).

By selecting this option you can connect two computers together in your home

Figure 9.42  Windows 2000 Network Connection Wizard

### Peer-to-peer networks

Not all LANs are server-based networks. There is another type called peer-to-peer networks. These are very simple networks that do not have a machine which is used only as a server, but have several computers linked together to share resources such as files, printers and scanners. This type of network needs to be in one general location, such as a room or several rooms on one floor of a building, and can be difficult to manage. It is not generally recommended to install a peer-to-peer network when there are more than ten machines.

## Wide area networks

A WAN consists of computers connected together over a wide geographical area, usually over two kilometres and even worldwide. Communication over a WAN can be by telephone lines, satellite or microwaves. Many organisations such as banks and companies such as Virgin Megastore will have their main computers located in one place, usually the head office, and will connect with their branches by means of telephone wires. A company will have to use links for a WAN provided by telecommunication companies such as BT or Mercury and pay charges for these services.

The original telephone link – the Public Switched Telephone Network (PSTN) – operated at low speeds, but more recently high-speed networks have been built. Public Data Networks (PDNs) are specifically for **data** transmission, whereas the Integrated Services Digital Network (ISDN) carries voice, data, images and video through a single **digital** line. With the PDN and ISDN systems, it is no longer necessary to convert the signal into **analogue** forms for transmission. The difference between digital and analogue transmission is discussed later in this chapter.

### ADSL

Asymmetric Digital Subscriber Line (ADSL) is the latest telecommunications technology that allows very rapid data transmission along a normal telephone line. ADSL gives a continuously available, 'always on' connection. This service, which is much faster than an ISDN system, is available to more and more telephone exchanges in the UK. You will learn more about ADSL in Unit 3.

### Types of WANs

There are two types of WANs:

- public wide area networks
- private wide area networks.

Public WANs are available to most of the public, usually through telephone and cable television networks, whereas private WANs use privately owned or rented lines and may be accessed only if you are a subscriber to the system. The best known examples of public WANs are the Internet and cable television.

Many large commercial organisations have their own private WAN which links shops or branches throughout the world or country.

In Chapter 6 you learned how two very different organisations – CETS and Reed Executive plc use private WANs in order to carry out their day-to-day business.

---

**Find out …**

- Are the PCs you use at school or college connected in a LAN?
- If so, how many computers are linked?
- How many servers are used in the system?
- If there is more than one server, what types are used?

---

## Advantages of a networked ICT system

- Expensive peripherals such as printers and scanners can be shared among several users.
- Software can be shared – it is cheaper to purchase a 'network software licence' for the number of machines using the software, than buying individual licences for standalone machines.
- It is convenient to store data and software on one machine, the server, and for all users to access the data through the server. Files can be accessed from any PC without having to pass disks between users. This

also avoids having to duplicate information. It is very difficult to ensure that each standalone PC holds up-to-date, accurate information, whereas shared data in a network enables every user to have access to the latest information, and data is updated only once.

- Messages can be sent almost instantly to users on the network, whether the network is a LAN or a WAN, even if the message is being sent across the world. This facility is known as **e-mail** (see Chapter 5).
- It is possible to control users' access rights. Users are issued a login name and password (usually by the person in charge of the network – the network manager) before they can access the network. This means only people who are allowed to can access data which helps to ensure that neither the copyright nor data protection laws are broken. The network manager can limit the data and software which individual users or departments can access by setting read/write privileges on files.
- It is easier to manage backing up of data on a network. The network manager will be responsible for regular backing up of data. Also, all the data is stored in one place – on the file server. The more closely monitored back-up procedures are, the less likely that files will be lost.
- Software is the same throughout the network and can be loaded centrally on the server. Also, the network manager can easily ensure that no illegal software is being used if software is installed on the server. There is an organisation called the Federation Against Software Theft (FAST). You will lean more about this in Unit 3, Chapter 13.
- The network can be maintained and supported centrally. Software is installed once on the server rather than having to be installed on each separate standalone computer. Problems can be solved centrally by the network manager, without leaving his or her desk to go to the user's machine. Have you ever had a problem at school or college with your computer,

which has been corrected 'remotely' by the network manager? This may have been when you had difficulty logging on, for example.

## Disadvantages of a networked ICT system

- The equipment needed to run a network – cables, network interface cards, servers and the rental of telecommunication links – can be expensive. A standalone system may be cheaper.
- Only certain people should have access to the nuts and bolts of the system. For a network to be maintained properly, one or more specialists will probably need to be employed to manage the system as most people would not have the expertise. This is usually a network manager and his or her assistant(s), depending on the size of the network. As a cheaper alternative, a small business may pay for a specialist company to provide network support when required.
- A network relies on the file server working properly. A problem with the server affecting data transmission can have a disastrous impact on an organisation. Important information will not be able to be accessed and tasks may have to be done manually. Have you ever experienced problems because 'the network is down'? This could be because there is a problem with the server.
- Security can be a problem, especially when the network is connected to the Internet. Viruses can be introduced onto the network, from a user's floppy disk, by downloading a file from the Internet or from receiving and opening an infected e-mail. There is also a danger of hacking, a topic which you will learn about in Unit 3. A closely monitored security policy should be implemented to ensure that everything is done to make the system as secure as possible.

Figure 9.43 Fibre optic cable

## Network components

As you have learned, a network links together a number of PCs to share facilities such as software and printing. Communication across the network can be achieved by microwave or satellite link, necessary to send signals over long distances for a WAN, or by cable, which would be typical in a LAN.

Networking is not just about connecting computers together with cables, although cables usually play an important part. A network requires components, or parts, such as network connectors, network interface cards (NICs), special software, PCs (known as clients) and in a server-based network, at least one server.

### Cables

The type of cable used to connect a network affects the speed and accuracy with which it operates and the ease of installation – a very thick cable being difficult to place in and along walls. Popular cable types include the following:

- Fibre optic cable (expensive to install) – this is a very fast method of transmitting data, giving data transmission speeds greater than 1 Gigabit per second or 1000 million bits per second over great distances. Fibre optic cable communicates the data by pulses of light instead of electricity and is less liable to distortion (see Figure 9.43).
- Unshielded twisted pair – this is similar to telephone wire, is cheap, has high transmission rates and is small in size so that cables are easily sunk into cabling

ducts. It comes in different categories with different data transmission speeds, the latest has speeds of 1 Gigabit per second, but is very expensive.
- Coaxial cable – this is the same type of cable that is used for connecting a television aerial to a television set and, at one time, was the most widely used network cabling as it was inexpensive, light, flexible and easy to work with.

### Fact file

Signals transmitted via ordinary telephone lines become weaker and weaker over long distances. They therefore have to be amplified (made stronger) at intervals and are affected by electrical interference causing crackling on the line. The idea of communicating by sending light pulses down a tiny strand of glass was first thought of in 1966, but it was not until 1977 that BT transmitted along a fibre-optic link. The glass core of the fibre-optic cable is as fine as a human hair – about 0.05 mm in diameter. The glass which makes the fibres is a very pure form of silica, so pure in fact that if it were made into a window 20 km thick (the distance between Bristol and Bath), you would still be able to see through it clearly!

### Servers

As explained above, most LANs are server based, the server being a powerful computer used for the storage and distribution of data around the network. Nowadays, many PCs are capable of acting as a server, but it is better to use one that is designed specifically for the job. A server can have multiple central processing units, large banks of hard disks and the capability to cope with hardware failures without the end user even noticing. For example, some servers are equipped with two power supplies so that if one goes down, the server can switch to the other. Most servers allow an external tape drive or optical disk drive to be connected for backing up the system.

## Workstations

A workstation – sometimes called a client –  is a single-user PC connected to the network. It can be either an ordinary PC, with a disk drive and a processor, connected to the network or a semi-dumb terminal with a less powerful processor and perhaps no disk drive.

## Network interface cards (NICs)

In order to access the network, each PC, including the server, must be fitted with a network interface card (see Figure 9.44). This is a printed circuit board, which slots into the motherboard, and contains all the necessary electronics and connections to allow the PC to link into the network.

## Connectors

These are used to connect network cables to PCs or other devices. A network interface card will have connectors on it for network cables.

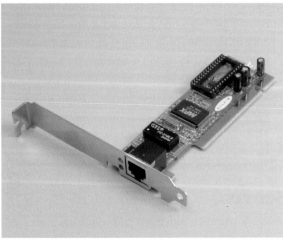

*Figure 9.44 A network interface card*

## Operating system

As you learned earlier in this chapter, in addition to applications software, computers also require an operating system which:

- controls the loading and running of programs
- controls the use of peripherals such as disk drives and printers
- makes the hardware easier to use and helps the operator decide what to do by displaying simple messages on screen, e.g. printer out of paper
- allows formatting of disks and files to be renamed, copied and backed up
- maintains a directory of files stored on disk
- makes sure no problems arise but tries to overcome them if they do.

Microsoft® Windows 98 or Windows Me are operating systems primarily designed for the home user. Many networks in business use Windows NT, or the newer Windows 2000 as their operating system. Windows 2000 comes in two categories: Professional edition for the network workstations and Server edition for the network servers. Other examples of network operating systems include Novell, UNIX or Linux.

As well as the above facilities, network software can:

- produce a log of the programs as they are run, recording who has used the computer, for how long and what they did
- charge the appropriate account if the user is paying
- organise the use of hardware and software facilities, ensuring that everyone has a fair share, but giving precedence to those users with a high priority over those with low priority
- maintain network security.

### Fact file

You can buy a server with several hard disks that are known as 'hot pluggable'. This means that the server has a bank of hard disks on the front that can be removed and swapped over without turning the machine off.

## Network topologies

### Checkpoint

The **network topology** is the way in which the **nodes** in a network are arranged. A node may be a computer or another device such as a printer. The way in which the network is arranged affects the way in which it operates. There are three common topologies in use: the bus, ring and star networks.

### Bus network

In a bus network all the nodes (devices) share a single cable with the ends **terminated** using a **terminator** – see Figure 9.45. The messages are transmitted in either direction from one point along a single bus from any PC to any other. Problems arise when more than one user wishes to send a message at the same time. To overcome this, the workstation checks first whether the bus is busy. If it is, then the station has to wait. Also, a problem with a bus network can be caused, not by a fault in the system such as the cable breaking, but by someone accidentally unplugging one of the leads from the back of the PC. This type of problem can be hard to find – it is usually the last computer to be checked that is causing the problem!

A bus network is cheap and easy to install. Extra workstations can be added without disrupting the network, and it is also fairly easy to find faults in the cable. However, if there is a problem with the cable, the whole network fails, and if too many workstations are attached to the network, performance is slow.

### Ring network

A ring network is similar to a bus network with the ends joined up, and may or may not depend on a central file server (see Figure 9.46). All the computers within the network can communicate with each other, but messages are transmitted in only one direction, which provides fast, simple transmission. A **message token** (a unique

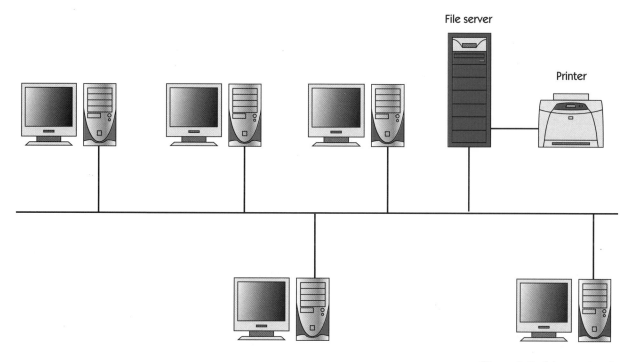

*Figure 9.45 A bus network*

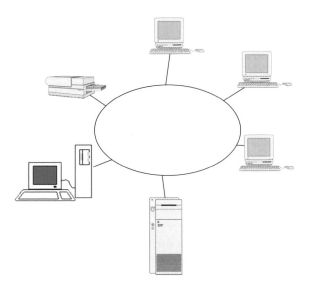

Figure 9.46 A ring network

A star network has a good, reliable performance even when the network is busy and is less likely to suffer faults than other topologies. This is because each workstation is served by its own cable. A breakdown in one cable does not affect the other stations, and it is simple to add workstations without interfering with the network

However, as cable can be a major cost of a network, a star topology may be expensive to install. Also, if the hub or server breaks down, then the whole network is affected.

reference) addressed specifically to the destination computer is sent around the ring. Each node checks the token address, with the addressed node accepting the message.

The advantage of ring networks is that they provide equal access for all computers with even performance, even with large numbers of users connected to the system.

The drawback of a ring network, just as with the bus network, is that if there is a fault at any point in the system, the whole network breaks down. A disadvantage of a ring network is that network reconfiguration will disrupt the operation of the network. Although cheap to install, because of the disadvantages, ring networks are less popular than they used to be, particularly for large networks.

## Star network

The main difference between a star network and a bus network is that each node is connected individually to a central point to which the server would be connected (see Figure 9.47). When this type of network was first used, computers were connected to a centralised mainframe computer or file server. Nowadays, most star networks are connected to a **hub**.

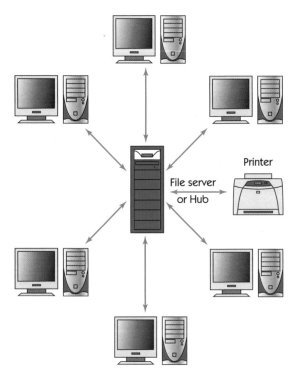

Printer

File server
or Hub

Figure 9.47 A star network

## Combination networks

It is becoming more common to find more than one type of computer network linked together on one site. An example of this is the **star bus** network. The star bus is a combination of the bus and star topologies. In a star bus topology there are several star topology networks linked together with a bus network.

This type of network is often used in schools or colleges where each classroom has its own star network with a hub at the central point and the hubs are joined to the main server by the bus network.

## Find out ...

- What network topology does your school or college use?
- Does your school or college use a combination of different topologies?
- Draw a diagram of the network, identifying the main components.

## Activity

▶ Print the file: **COM Worksheet 3** from the Chapter 9 folder on the CD-ROM. This worksheet requires you to correctly identify three different network topologies.

## Network protocols

Electronic communication works only if the receiving machine understands the signals coming from the sending machine. They both have to use the same 'language' or follow the same set of rules. These rules are known as the protocols.

To illustrate this point, when home video recording was first introduced three systems came on to the market: VHS, Betamax and Philips. All were able to record programmes and play them back, but tapes for one system could not be used in machines designed for the others. They were using different protocols. People found it a nuisance not to be able to play tapes from any system on their machine. Eventually, because VHS was licensed to more video cassette recorder manufacturers, there were more and more machines able to play VHS tapes, and the popularity of Betamax and Philips 2000 systems declined rapidly. Nowadays, there are many manufacturers of domestic video recorders, but they all use the VHS system (protocol).

Similarly, there are many manufacturers of computer equipment, but there is no total standardisation for the computer industry and different companies use different protocols.

In data communication and networks, there are many protocols or rules to ensure that when messages are transmitted electronically, they arrive at their destination, any errors being detected and corrected. To enable correct, accurate communication, settings, or parameters, need to be agreed by both the sending and receiving station. The transmitting station sends a signal to say, in effect, 'I want to send a message – are you ready to receive?' If all is well, the receiving station replies, 'Yes, go ahead', and this exchange of signals is sometimes known as **handshaking**. Any equipment that uses the same communication protocol can be connected together.

If two computer systems with different protocols want to communicate, this can be done by a piece of equipment known as a **gateway**.

## Checkpoint

A **gateway** translates the protocols so that the two systems can communicate with each other.

## Baud rate

The speed at which data is transmitted is known as the baud rate, where 1 baud equals 1 bit per second (bps). This method usually transmits 10 bits for each character. The sending and receiving computer must both be set to the same baud rate, otherwise the data would not be received correctly, or possibly nothing will be received at all. The higher the baud rate, the faster the data can be transmitted.

## Flow control

When you take notes in class, if the teacher speaks faster than you can write, then you lose track of what is being said and the notes become jumbled. You can of course, politely ask your teacher to pause for you to catch up. Data transmission is much the same, and it is essential for the receiver to be able to say, in effect, 'Please wait a minute'. An example of this is when data is transferred from a PC to the printer. The PC can transmit data much faster than the printer can handle the data. Data is stored in the receiver's memory, known as the **buffer**, but there is a limit to the buffer's capacity. **Flow control** prevents the receiver being overloaded by the amount of data arriving.

Let's see how this works:

Sender $\rightarrow$ Data $\rightarrow$ Receiver

Receiver (cannot handle more data) $\rightarrow$ Sends message 'Receiver not ready'

Receiver (processes the data) $\rightarrow$ Sends message 'Now ready' to receive more data

Sender $\rightarrow$ Data $\rightarrow$ Receiver

There are several ways to send flow control characters within the protocol, and whichever method is used, this must be agreed between the sender and receiver.

## Checkpoint

**Flow control** controls data transmission.

# 10 How ICT systems are designed and implemented

This chapter describes the five stages required to implement an ICT system in an organisation.

## Overview: Information systems projects

Nowadays, most companies use computers in some way to support their business activities. For some this might be as little as one person using the word processor to produce letters while other companies rely on computers to handle the complete business operation. From time to time, the companies that do have computers need to upgrade their systems and companies that don't use computers realise their potential and decide to invest in a system. Whatever the reason, the companies are about to launch an information systems project. No matter how large or small the project, the stages that have to be followed in order to put a new system in place are very similar:

● **Investigation** – this looks at why the user needs to change the present system and, in general terms, what is required from a new system.
● **Analysis** – this looks in more detail at what a new system should provide and what hardware and software will be needed.
● **Design** – at this stage, a detailed breakdown of the required input, output and processing are considered together

with the user interface of the new system.
● **Implementation** – following detailed design, the new system is put in place and tested. User documentation is prepared and the people who will use the new system are trained to use it.
● **Monitoring, evaluation and maintenance** – once the system is in place and running satisfactorily, it must be regularly checked and maintained to ensure it continues to run smoothly. From time to time, adjustments might be necessary to ensure the system continues to meet the needs of the company.

The time from the launch of a project through to completion will vary depending on the complexity of the project. A large project for a multinational organisation or government department is likely to be complex and might require a team of IT professionals to be involved for many months, perhaps even years. A smaller project will involve fewer people and will take less time, but both will involve the processes described above.

## System design

### Investigation

What are the reasons that might bring about the need for a new system or an overhaul of an existing system?

Technology is under continual development

and, as you learned in Chapter 9, the power of the computer has increased in leaps and bounds over the past few years. Faster processors with increased memory; flat-screen monitors that take up less desk space; new software and improved peripheral devices such as laser printers force companies to re-examine their systems. Methods of communication are also changing rapidly. The use of e-mail means that more staff must have individual access to computers. Nowadays, more and more business is carried out over the Internet and the employment of teleworking, laptop computers and mobile telephones means 'the office' can be situated anywhere.

If an organisation wishes to remain competitive, it must keep its systems up-to-date and any one of the above reasons might force it to re-evaluate its existing systems. Whatever the reason, once a decision has been taken that a new system might be required, an investigation must be made to decide whether the new system is technically feasible and whether it is economically viable. The organisation needs to be sure that the costs of installing a new system or revamping an existing system will reduce overall operating costs and increase productivity or performance in the longer term.

This investigation is usually referred to as a **feasibility study**. This looks at the existing business practice and any problems associated with it. Its purpose is to consider in general terms what the new system should achieve and whether the current system could be modified (altered) to meet the new needs. If a new system were considered necessary, an estimate of the overall cost and a time scale for implementation would be given. The feasibility study will then be discussed in greater detail by the management of the company before a final decision is made on whether to proceed to the next stage.

## Checkpoint

A **feasibility study** is an investigation which looks at the current IT practices of a business with a view to recommending improvements to the current system.

Let's return to Jubilee 6th Form College and consider the following scenario.

When a student wishes to enrol on a course he or she is invited to visit the college to discuss the appropriate course with a college tutor. When a suitable course has been agreed, the student is sent to see an admissions officer who checks against a list of names to see if there is room for the new student to join the class. If so, the admissions officer helps the student to complete the enrolment form and, if appropriate, collects any necessary fee. The student's name is added to the class list and a receipt issued for any fee paid. The enrolment form is then filed away in a filing cabinet. This is referred to as a manual system – the list of names is maintained by hand, the receipt is produced by hand and the enrolment form is filed in a filing cabinet along with hundreds, perhaps thousands, of other forms.

What types of problems are likely to arise from using a system of this nature?

- Sometimes the admissions officer forgets to write the new student's name on the list and this can result in too many students in a class – quite a problem if each student needs access to specialised equipment such as a computer.
- Admissions staff do not always know if all the students on the list are attending the course. As a result, a course may appear full and new students are turned away, whereas there are still places available because some names on the list have not joined the course.
- The enrolment forms that record the student's address, telephone number, and so on, are occasionally filed in the wrong place or removed and not returned to the filing cabinet. This can lead to serious problems, for example when certificates need to be sent out.
- There is no method of identifying students on the college premises or differentiating one student from another.

In view of these problems, the college would like to set up a new system. It wants a reliable method of recording student details and numbers of students on each course. The college hopes that both student and course details will be entered directly into a computer system when the student enrols and it is hoped this will save time and produce accurate and up-to-date information on course enrolments. The college would also like each student to have an identity (ID) card which would carry the student's photograph and college registration number.

This is a simple example of a situation where the introduction of a new computerised system might be of great benefit to the college. In order to make a decision the college management and governors would first undertake a feasibility study to look into the current system and to consider the benefits a new system might bring to the college.

## Analysis

Once the feasibility study has been completed, a decision would be taken on whether to go ahead. If so, the next step would require a detailed analysis of the current system. This would be carried out by a systems analyst whose role would be to take the feasibility study one step further by carrying out a thorough examination of the individual components (parts) of the proposed system. This would include:

- investigation of hardware and software currently in use and proposals for replacing it
- observation of current work practices to see how jobs are done now and what improvement could be achieved
- interviews with staff at all levels to find out what they require from a new system, or a survey of existing staff by questionnaire
- study of existing business documentation such as forms, invoices, and so on.

Following the review of existing work practices, the systems analyst will be in a position to outline the objectives of a new system – the input, process and output. He or she will use a series of data flow diagrams to illustrate the way data flows within the current system and to show how it will flow in the new system. Diagrams would be made to illustrate input screens and the format for documents that will be output from the new system. The systems analyst will also update the original estimate for the overall cost of the system and the time scale for implementation. The analysis report

will eventually be passed to a team of system designers and therefore it must contain sufficient information for them to work on the detailed design of every aspect of the new system before its implementation.

## Charts and diagrams

System analysts use diagrams and **flowcharts** to provide a graphical way of describing computer systems. They provide an easy-to-understand overview of a system and different symbols are used to represent the following:

- the devices to be used
- the order of tasks to be carried out in the new system
- the media used for input, storage and output
- the files used by the system.

The symbols most frequently used are shown in Figure 10.1.

You can produce flowchart symbols similar to these by using **AutoShapes** on the Drawing toolbar in Microsoft® Word (see Figure 10.2).

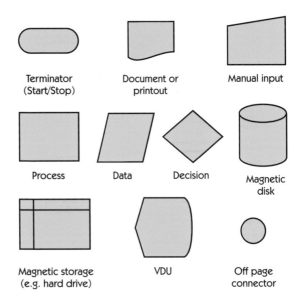

Figure 10.1 *Common symbols used in flowcharts*

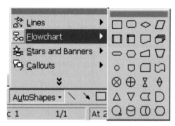

Figure 10.2 AutoShapes can be used to produce flowchart symbols

Let's return to the new enrolment process at Jubilee 6th Form College and then look at a flow diagram that might be used to represent the process.

When students come to Jubilee College to enrol on a course they are asked to complete an enrolment form similar to the one shown in Figure 10.3.

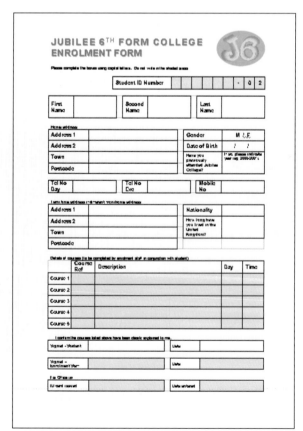

Figure 10.3 Jubilee College enrolment form

Students complete their personal details and together with the course tutor decide on the most appropriate course of study.

Once they have been offered a place on the course students take the form to the administration office where details are taken from the form and entered into the computer system. This data is saved and an ID card produced for the student confirming his or her place on the course.

A system flowchart to illustrate the process of entering the data into the system from the handwritten enrolment form, saving it on the hard drive and printing the ID card could be represented as a simple flow diagram as shown in Figure 10.4.

This is a very simple way of illustrating a computer system. However, the flowchart assumes all details have been completed by the

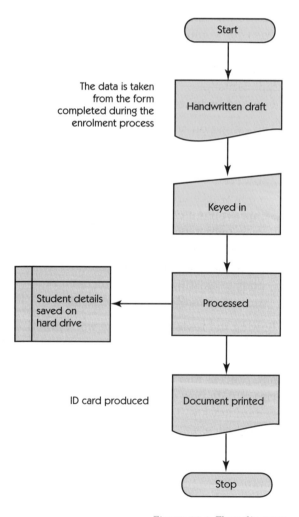

Figure 10.4 Flow diagram

student and that he or she is only enrolling on one course. In practice, it is quite common during a busy enrolment session for some details to be missed off the form or for a student to enrol on more than one course. For example, a student might be taking GCSE Maths together with an AVCE in ICT. In this case, the flowchart would be more complex and would require decisions or choices to be made during the process of entering the data. It would probably look similar to the one shown in Figure 10.5.

## Activity

The student association shop must make sure it is fully stocked before the start of the new college year. You have been asked to make a list of the items that need to be reordered and to help with this, you have been given a sheet showing what needs to be checked.

The list you have been given looks like this:

| Stock Reference No | Description | Reorder Level | No in Stock | Reorder? |
|---|---|---|---|---|
| AC 1353 | HB Pencils | 50 | | |
| HA 37612 | A4 Lined Notepad | 25 | | |
| AD 7843 | A4 Ring Binder – Black | 10 | | |

▷ Print the file: **SYS Worksheet 1** from the Chapter 10 folder on the CD-ROM and complete the flow diagram.

▷ Produce a simple flow chart recording the steps you will go through in order to produce your list. An example of the completed flow diagram is in the Chapter 10 folder on the CD-ROM in the file: **Activity 1 solution**.

## Design

It is only after detailed analysis that the design of the new system can begin and each stage will be thought about in great detail. A systems designer usually undertakes this stage of the

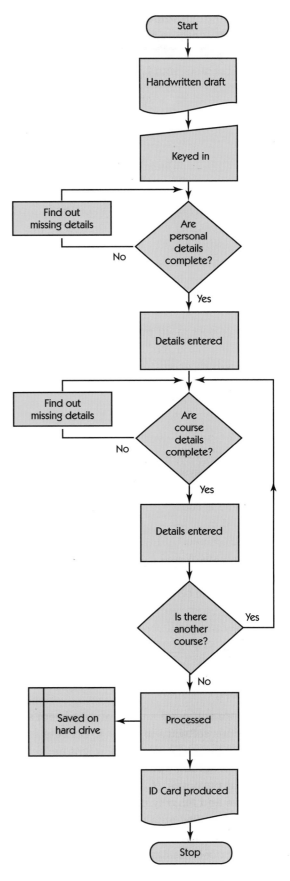

*Figure 10.5 More complex flow diagram*

project, although sometimes the systems analyst will continue his or her work. During this stage nothing will be set up on the computer. The design is still very much a manual process.

## Output

Strangely enough, the first stage in the design process involves considering the intended output from the new system. In other words, you need to think about what the new system must eventually be able to do in order to work out the processing capability needed by the system. Output might be to a visual display unit (VDU), printer or to a control device such as a heater or motor. In the case of visual or printed output, the systems designer will need to know what information should be displayed and, in the case of document production, how many documents will be required and how often. Designs will be produced to illustrate document layout, and so on.

## Input

Having decided on the output, the systems designer will think about what data needs to be input into the system and how that data will be obtained. For example, if manual input through a keyboard is required, will a form be completed in order to provide the data? If so, will the user need a data input screen on which the form is displayed in order to make interaction with the system user friendly? If data input is to be automatic, what type of sensor will be required? The design of both the form and data input screen will also have to be considered at some stage in the design process.

## Software

The system will need an operating system and applications software in order to process the data. Very large organisations might have software programs specially written for their individual purposes. However, this is a very expensive and lengthy process. Most companies will be able to use standard application software that has been written by software houses designed to meet the needs of a variety of users. The advantage of this is that

they can start to use it immediately and it is very much cheaper.

A designer might be looking at the design of spreadsheets and/or the creation of macros and templates that are going to be of benefit in spreadsheet or word processing applications.

Alternatively, if data is to be input into a database, a breakdown of data will be needed in order to establish both the data type and the volume of data to be handled so that an estimate can be made on the storage capacity required. The designer will specify the structure of the database and produce designs of data input screens and data output documents. Test data must also be designed to ensure the new system works as it is meant to.

The designer will produce detailed notes of any system configuration that might be necessary, for example the structure of files, folders and subfolders, and will also consider methods to ensure security of data.

## Hardware

The systems designer is also responsible for specifying the number and type of workstations to be provided together with printers and other peripheral devices. He or she will also decide whether a local or wide area network is necessary and will advise on security measures to protect the hardware.

When the designer has finished, he or she will provide the following documents:
- system flowcharts
- written descriptions
- specimens of data input and output documents
- data input screens
- diagrams representing directory/folder structure, and so on.

The completed design will provide sufficient detail to enable other members of the team to implement the new system in full.

### Checkpoint

During the **design** process a detailed breakdown of the required input, output and processing are considered together with the user interface of the new system.

## Activity

▷ Print the file: **SYS Worksheet 2** from the Chapter 10 folder on the CD-ROM. When a new system is designed much thought is given to the input, output, software and hardware of the new system. Use this exercise to put the activities under the correct headings.

▷ Think again about our scenario for Jubilee College. Produce a short report entitled "Design of new system for Jubilee College" and write a paragraph under the headings Output, Input, Software and Hardware listing the main considerations applying to the proposed new system. When you have completed your notes check them against our suggested list in the file: **Activity 2 solution** in the Chapter 10 folder on the CD-ROM.

## Implementation

As you have already seen, the design specification is very detailed, which means that implementation is simply a question of following the design instructions – a little bit like assembling a model or item of furniture piece by piece.

During this stage lots of things will be happening at the same time leading to the eventual creation of the new system:

- hardware and software are purchased
- networks are installed
- the file structure implemented
- new programs are written or existing software configured
- the system and/or software are tested using the test plan
- user documentation is written
- staff are trained to use the new system.

Installation of the hardware might seem straightforward, but in many cases there will be several other factors to take into consideration. For example, if a network is being installed, extensive cabling will be necessary. Even if the installation of a new system is merely an upgrade and fairly uncomplicated, terminals may still need to be repositioned and in some cases staff may have to move office.

If a complex program is being written, the program will be split into small parts and a separate team will work on each part, bringing the whole program together at the end. However, as you have seen, it is more likely that configuration of 'off the shelf' software will take place and the team will create the spreadsheets, databases, macros and templates recommended by the designers. The team will work together, each carrying out a small part of the overall program and producing the documents to go with it it. Documentation is essential to any new computer system, and is produced to help the user and the technical team.

## User documentation

User documentation is provided for the people who will be using the software to help them deal with everyday problems. It will include instructions to perform special functions within different software applications, such as using any macros or templates that have been designed, and illustrations to help users.

## Technical documentation

Technical documentation is written to explain the technical set-up of the system. In future years it is likely that modifications will be required and the team who originally set up the system might not be around to carry these out. The technical documentation will help ensure that any future modifications can be carried out with the minimum of disruption.

## Testing and training

When the hardware has been installed it will be tested to make sure it all works and that communication has been established between all the devices. Testing is always carried out under a range of conditions to see how the system reacts. For example, if you expect the output to be a figure less than 100, but an output of 1000 is accepted, you will know that there is something wrong with the system. Another example would be if a system has been designed to turn a light on when it becomes dark, but the light turns on in daylight, again you would know that there is a problem with the system. Testing data is also discussed on page 49. Similarly, any configuration to software will also be tested. New spreadsheet and database files must be checked to ensure they produce the results expected before they are put into use. Staff will also need to be trained to use the new software. Training is very important to ensure staff are confident in knowing how to use the new systems and overcome any potential problems. However, some companies spend little time and effort in training their staff and this can cause considerable problems when introducing the new systems as well as stress for the people using them.

New software systems are rarely implemented directly in case there are any serious errors that need to be put right. More often, they are run in parallel to the old system for a period of time or phased in slowly, section by section. No business can afford to be without its computer system nor can it afford to lose data so these measures are taken to ensure there is minimum disruption to the day-to-day operation of the organisation.

## Snapshot

### Hospital Trust implements speech recognition telephone system

*Problem:* Gloucestershire Hospitals NHS Trust was having difficulty managing the 500,000 external telephone calls it receives each month and couldn't attract and retain telephone operators.

*Solution:* It decided to invest in a speech recognition telephone system. External callers are met with a recorded greeting instructing them to say the name of the person they want and the system automatically puts them through. Telephone numbers of the area's 300 GP surgeries and other major UK hospitals are stored in a database and staff only have to say the surgery or hospital name to be connected. The system is so simple to use that the Trust did not need to train its staff to use it.

*Source: Computing*, 16 January 2003

## Monitoring, evaluation and maintenance

During the design and implementation stages, everything possible would be done to ensure a smooth change-over from the old system to the new, but it is only when the new system is in use that any minor errors may come to light. For example, there might be a coding error that has to be put right or changes may be needed to input screens or printed reports. Checks are carried out to ensure the system has met the original user requirements, is working properly and is easy to use.

The system is constantly being monitored and evaluated and this is an ongoing process because at any time the computer system may need slight modifications or additions. If the system has been well designed, any modifications will be quite straightforward, enabling it to meet the changing needs of the business/organisation for many years to come.

### Checkpoint

**Implementation** follows design and the new system is put in place and tested, user documentation is prepared and the people who will use the new system are trained to use it.

### Activity

▶ At Jubilee College we will assume that a local area network already exists and, as a result, the implementation of their new system will not be a highly complicated process. Make a list of everything you can think of that will need to be done to implement (or put in place) the new system. When you have finished compare your notes with our suggested list in the file: **Activity 3 solution** in the Chapter 10 folder on the CD-ROM.

### Checkpoint

Once the system is in place and running satisfactorily, it is continuously checked to ensure it runs smoothly and meets the needs of the organisation.

# ICT and society

This unit will help you to understand how far ICT systems affect everyday life. It explores how individuals as well as families, clubs and societies, work teams and community groups use ICT in their personal, social and professional lives. Some individuals and groups do not have access to ICT, yet ICT still affects their lives.

New ICT products and applications are constantly being developed and the pace of development is very fast. This unit explores how and why ICT can have negative as well as positive effects.

It considers how developments in technology have influenced and may continue to influence areas such as:

- business
- working styles and new employment opportunities
- legislation
- entertainment and leisure
- personal communications.

The unit builds on the contents of Units 1 and 2, and also your wider knowledge and experience of ICT.

### What you will learn

11 Available technologies
12 How ICT is used in business
13 Legislation
14 ICT in personal communications and community activities
15 ICT and people with special needs

# Chapter 11 Available technologies

This chapter introduces you to Internet technologies. You will learn about:

- the world wide web, e-mail, multimedia and encryption
- Internet connection, e.g. modems, ISDN, ASDL, broadband
- mobile telephone technologies e.g. SMS, WAP
- digital broadcasting
- personal digital assistants, (PDA) and organisers
- storage media, e.g. DVD, minidisk
- touch screen technologies

## What you will learn

Internet technologies
Connecting to the Internet
Mobile phones
Personal digital assistants – palmtop computers
Internet TVs and set-top boxes
Public Internet terminals
Multimedia
Digital broadcasting
Convergence of technologies
Security on the Internet
Storage media
Touch screen technologies

## Overview

In Unit 2 you learned how to use the Internet to find information and how to send e-mails. In order to do so, you had to use a wide range of technology. Technology plays an increasingly important part in our lives, whether it is in business, school or college or in our leisure activities. This chapter looks at the different technologies that are available to access and exchange information, and how these have developed.

## Internet technologies

The Internet is the world's largest wide area network and is often referred to as the network of networks.

### Fact file

The origins of the Internet go back to the 1960s when US universities and the Defence Department wanted to link their big main-frame computers. This original Internet was called ARPANET. Even as recently as 1995, many people would not have heard of the Internet, and certainly not have used it. Terms such as the world wide web, e-mail, **e-commerce**, chat rooms, bulletin boards and newsgroups would have drawn blank faces.

Nowadays, the Internet has opened up the world. Information can be passed between different countries across the globe at the press of a key. Via the Internet a company can advertise its services, give customer support, distribute software and take part in e-commerce.

### Checkpoint

**E-commerce** describes any business activity, such as placing an order, booking a holiday or even managing a bank account, that is undertaken online by electronic means.

## Intranets

Using the same technology as the Internet, intranets have been developed. An intranet is an internal communications system for a particular organisation or company and provides similar services to the Internet. An intranet can only be accessed by authorised users and allows secure e-mail communication and distribution of data. Many schools and colleges now have their own intranet.

## Extranets

Extranets are external networks linked to a company's computer system. They are of great benefit to companies as they are used to link with suppliers and other authorised people such as customers and can assist in such things as product ordering and product delivery. Whereas a company's Internet website can be accessed by anyone, its extranet can only be accessed by a limited number of authorised people.

## ●Snapshot

### Sainsbury's Information Direct

The superstore chain Sainsbury's does business with around 2000 suppliers. It is therefore essential that the organisation maintains good communications with them. IT plays a major role in the company's quest to improve services and reduce costs. Sainsbury's launched its extranet – Sainsbury's Information Direct (SID) – in 1998. Suppliers can access data on sales, availability, stock holding, and so on, as well as jointly managing promotions and events with the company via the extranet. Public information which suppliers find useful such as depot addresses as well as other specific online documents are available. Other areas of the extranet such as the business to business (b2b) toolkit are password protected and meet each supplier's individual needs. Suppliers have to register with Sainsbury's to gain access to these areas.

*Figure 11.1  Sainsbury's extranet – Sainsbury's Information Direct*

*Source:* Sainsbury's plc.

## World wide web

The world wide web, or web for short, is a part of the Internet where a set of multimedia documents (documents that can consist of words, sound, video, images or animation) are connected by way of **hyperlinks** so you can move from one document to another by clicking your mouse. Each document is called a web page and a set of web pages makes up a website. The web therefore is a huge collection of web pages stored on Internet servers throughout the world. In June 1993 there were only 130 websites, whereas now there are millions!

**Fact file**

According to the research company Jupiter MMXI, 18.5 million Britons accessed the web from home and work in January 2002. This is almost one-third of the total UK population. Over half of all those people accessed the MSN sites and just under 50 per cent went to the main Microsoft® site. You can visit these sites – go to www.heinemann.co.uk/hotlinks and click on MSN UK, or MSN or on Microsoft®.

In the early 1990s, the Internet existed only to people who were connected to it, and to be permanently connected the line would cost about £20,000. Cliff Stanford developed the very first Internet Service Provider (ISP) – Demon Internet – by buying a £20,000 line and sharing the cost between users. The date the very first user logged on was 1 June 1992.

**Activity**

> Print the file: **TEC Worksheet 1**
> from the Chapter 11 folder on the CD-ROM. This worksheet will help you to find out more about the development of the www by visiting the website of CERN.

## E-mail

As you learned in Unit 1, e-mail is one of the most popular uses of the Internet. To send an e-mail from a home computer, the PC will need to be connected to the Internet using the communications software supplied by an ISP (such as AOL or Freeserve), e-mail communications software (such as Outlook Express) and a modem.

The computer will be connected to its ISP by one of the following:

- an ADSL line – you will learn more about ADSL on page 179
- an ISDN line
- an ordinary telephone line – in this case, the computer will have a Dial-up Connection. This means that it is not linked permanently to the Internet, but the user will have to dial up to a special number provided by the ISP in order to connect.

In larger networks in business, another computer will probably be used to provide the link to the Internet. All the computers in the network will be linked to the Internet through that computer and it will not be necessary to 'dial up' to an ISP before sending an e-mail.

### Fact file

An increasing number of ISPs will allow you to log on to the same e-mail account that you usually use at home to check your e-mail using any computer with Internet access. BTopenworld is one example of an ISP with this service.

### Advantages of e-mail

- A message can be sent almost instantly to someone, and at a time when you choose.
- An e-mail can be sent to several people at once.
- E-mails can be forwarded onto someone else.
- It is a more reliable form of communication than using the telephone or post for placing an order, for example.
- You will usually be notified if the message fails to reach its destination.

- Some e-mail systems will notify you when an e-mail has been read by the recipient.
- The cost is much cheaper than using the post – the price of a local phone call – wherever in the world you are e-mailing.
- Files created in other software applications can be attached.
- Colour graphics can be attached.
- When you are connected to a local area network (LAN), you can use e-mail even if you are not near a phone.
- E-mail messages, and any attached files, can be saved and edited by the person receiving them, the recipient.
- E-mails can be sent from a variety of devices including many mobile phones.

### Disadvantages of e-mail

- There are still businesses and homes without the equipment to send e-mails, although the numbers are falling.
- Junk mail – often called **spam** – is a growing problem.
- There are security issues – viruses can be transmitted via an e-mail.
- Unless you have a new e-mail alert to tell you when you have new mail, you have to remember to check your mail box.
- People can suffer from e-mail overload. As it is so easy to communicate by e-mail, business people may become swamped with e-mails to deal with, all of which can be marked urgent.

### Checkpoint

**Spam** is the name given to junk mail (or direct mail) sent unsolicited to large groups of people via e-mail.

### Fact file

There are 37 million mobile phones in the UK, many of them with e-mail capabilities. In 2001, the media reported that a teenager was saved from a catamaran that was in difficulty in storm-lashed seas off Indonesia as a result of sending an SOS e-mail from her mobile phone to her boyfriend in England!

# Connecting to the Internet

In order to connect to the Internet you will usually need a computer, a telephone line, a modem, an ISP, web browser and e-mail software.

## Modems

A modem – **mo**dulator-**dem**odulator – is a device that converts the digital signals from a computer into analogue signals that can be sent down a telephone line. These analogue signals are then converted back to digital signals by a modem at the receiving end (see Figure 11.2). An analogue signal is a continuous signal, representing an output which can travel along a telephone line. Speech is a form of analogue transmission, whereas a digital signal sends information in the form of digital 'on' and 'off' pulses. The 'on' and 'off' pulses of digital transmission represent the binary digits (0s and 1s) that a computer can understand.

Modems can be internal or external. A home computer probably has an internal modem that slots into the motherboard. The most important aspect of a modem is the speed. The faster the modem, the quicker the information is received. This is an important if the user is paying for the telephone call while you are online. Some modems can reduce the cost of transmission by compressing the data before it is sent.

### Fact file

The speed with which the modem transfers data is measured in bits per second (bps). The very first modem for PCs in 1979 had a data transfer speed of 300 bps. Currently, the fastest modems transfer data at a maximum speed of 56 kbps (56 kilobits per second).

If your household can receive cable television, you may be able to connect to the Internet using a cable modem at far greater speeds than using a traditional modem. Also, if the computer or LAN is using an ISDN line, a traditional modem is not required. Instead, a special device called ISDN terminal adaptor will be needed.

## ADSL and broadband

As you saw in Unit 2, Chapter 10, ADSL – Asymmetric Digital Subscriber Line – allows very rapid data transmission along an ordinary telephone line.

The technology works by splitting the existing telephone line signal into two – one for voice and the other for data. This means that you can be on the Internet and still receive ordinary phone calls.

ADSL technology can work at up to 8 Mbit/s download, but UK services are currently up to around 2 Mbit/s, although in fact many ADSL providers limit users to around 500 kbit/s (about ten times faster than a standard modem). ADSL is known as **broadband** technology and available download speeds are increasing all the time.

An ADSL connection needs a special modem with a splitter. The splitter is only used if you are on the Internet. Its purpose is just to sit there looking for the high frequency messages that tell it that you are using the Internet.

### Checkpoint

The term **broadband** refers to telecommunication in which a wide band of frequencies is available to transmit information. Because a wide band of frequencies is available, more information can be transmitted at the same time (in the same way as more lanes on a motorway will allow more cars to travel on it at the same time).

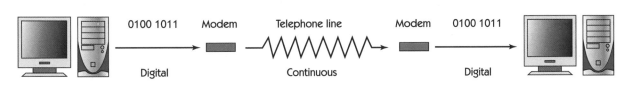

*Figure 11.2 Computers linked by modems and a telephone line*

Nowadays, most ISPs offer an ADSL service. However, it is only available to people who live within 5.5 kilometres of their local telephone exchange. It is also possible to subscribe to a broadband connection via cable television companies such as Telewest. The number of UK home users switching to broadband Internet access has been very slow. According to the Office for National Statistics, by the end of 2001, only 3 per cent of all UK Internet subscribers had a broadband connection. One reason for this has been the high cost of connection. However, in April 2002, BT reduced the cost of ADSL to both business and domestic customers. As a result, it is hoped that within four years one-quarter of all Internet connections will be through ADSL technology.

### Fact file

Go to www.heinemann.co.uk/hotlinks and click on ASDL to see a useful website and will give you up-to-date information about this technology and offers an up-to-date comparison between different providers.

### Activity

▶ Print the file: **TEC Worksheet 2**
▶ from the Chapter 11 folder on the CD-ROM. This worksheet will help you to find out if your home telephone number will support an ADSL connection and will enable you to investigate the different broadband connection options offered by BT.

## Internet Service Providers (ISP)

All home and business users need an ISP. Large organisations usually have a communications server permanently connected to the Internet and rent a high-speed connection (for example digital leased line) direct to their ISP.

Originally, all subscribers had to pay to be connected to an ISP, but nowadays many ISPs do not charge for this facility, although users will often be charged for the time spent on the Internet. This is the cost of a local telephone call. Increasingly, more ISPs are offering unlimited access online for a standard monthly charge. Examples of these are BT Internet or AOL. However, most of the ISPs offering this service penalise heavy users by cutting them off if they have been online for more than two hours. Users who reconnect repeatedly or spend too long online are considered to be abusing the system and barred from the service.

If you are lucky enough to have an ADSL connection at home, for a monthly fee you have continuous access, day or night without the worry of being cut off!

## Web browser

A web browser is special software that allows you to view web pages and to click on the hyperlinks. If you are using any version of Microsoft® Windows, you will probably use Microsoft® Internet Explorer. However, it is possible to download from the Internet a free copy of Netscape Navigator.

## Data transfer speeds

Have you ever sat at the computer waiting for a file to be downloaded from the Internet or for a website to open? Sometimes the waiting can seem endless. The time it takes the web server where the website is hosted to respond to a request to view a web page is known as the **response time.** The time it takes for a PC to load a web page once the request to view a web page has been responded to is known as the **download** time.

There are several factors that can affect the speed at which data is transferred:

● The speed of the modem, or the modem at the other end of the communications line. The faster the modem, the quicker data will be accessed.
● The type of telephone line – an ADSL line will offer far quicker access times, usually about ten times the rate of a standard telephone line with a modem.
● The size of the file being transferred –

graphics and sound, for example, take far longer than plain text.

- The site you are visiting may be very busy.
- The numbers of users online at the same time as yourself. If you are surfing during the evening or at the weekend, you will often suffer slower download and response times. Also the time of day will affect download time – America goes online at approximately 3 pm UK time.
- The amount of memory on the PC – browsers use up a great deal of memory storing details of the sites you visit.
- The amount of bandwidth available. Bandwidth describes the amount of data that can be transferred at one time via a communications line. The more bandwidth available, the faster the data will be transferred. Fibre optic cables have a higher bandwidth than traditional telephone lines.

## Mobile phones

Mobile phones are everywhere today. It seems like almost everyone has got one and although there are unanswered issues concerning danger from alleged radiation problems, it appears they are here to stay. Originally, mobile phones were large, expensive to buy and expensive to use. They were owned mainly by wealthy business people, but now they are small, relatively inexpensive and regarded as a must-have status symbol and a fashion accessory by many young people.

### Fact file

According to the United Nations, the number of mobile phones around the world will soon exceed fixed or land lines. It believes the billion-handset mark will soon be broken, with some countries such as Taiwan having more handsets than there are people.
(*Computer Active*, 21 February–6 March 2002).

## Short Message Service (SMS)

The services available to mobile phone users are constantly growing. One of the most useful is Short Message Service (SMS) – where, for a small charge, a text message of up to 150 characters can be sent to one or many people at the same time. As a result of this, a 'texting' language has developed as users have tried to minimise the amount of letters used to maximise what they can say in their message. Hundreds of thousands of these messages are sent every day. This facility has been developed further where, for example, football/cricket scores or racing results can be texted to a subscriber's phone immediately they happen.

### Fact file

Logica predicted that by the end of 2002 globally there will be 100 billion SMS messages sent each month! Go to www.heinemann.co.uk/hotlinks and click on Logica.

## Wireless Application Protocol (WAP)

Developing the potential of SMS further was the idea behind Wireless Application Protocol (WAP). This allows mobile phone users to access the Internet. It has not proved as successful as manufacturers and service providers had hoped, probably because current phones can only access text-only versions of websites and access times are far slower than accessing the Internet via a computer. However, this is likely to change with the development of WAP2 and more powerful phones with colour screens. This should see the full power of the web available to mobile phone users, for example it should be possible to watch a film downloaded from the web, on your mobile phone's screen in colour with stereo sound (via headphones).

## Multimedia Messaging Service (MMS)

Another recent development in mobile phones is Multimedia Messaging Service – MMS –

which is an advanced form of SMS. Instead of just sending a text message, the latest mobile phones will allow you to send a picture, text and voice all at the same time (see Figure 11.3). These phones are only a little heavier than the traditional mobile phone. When you go on holiday, instead of sending a postcard to your friends, you will be able to take a picture with a MMS phone and send it to your friends at home almost instantly!

*Figure 11.3 The Nokia 7650 – an MMS phone*

## Personal Digital Assistants – palmtop computers

Personal Digital Assistants (PDAs) have been around for some time, one of the better known being the Psion, which was brought out in the late 1980s. Current PDAs fall into two types using either the palm operating system (developed from the original Psion), or the more recent Windows Compact Edition (CE).

Modern PDAs are mini computers with fast processors and large memory capacities. They can be directly linked to desktop PCs and information exchanged. It is even possible to connect directly to the Internet to browse, download information, send e-mails, and so on.

Many of the popular desktop applications such as word processing, spreadsheets and databases have been modified to operate within the PDA environment. PDAs can also be used as voice recorders or personal music players; they can hold dozens of digital photos and most have the facility to recognise

handwriting so they can be used as notepads. One model even has an attachment to convert it directly into a digital camera! In time, most of these facilities will be combined with a mobile phone so only one piece of equipment need be carried around.

## Tablet PCs

Tablet PCs have been available for some time, but the latest models from companies such as Toshiba and Compaq combine the best of notepads and laptops (see Figure 11.4). The tablet PC can be used flat like a digital notepad so that you can take handwritten notes, or draw diagrams onto the notepad. These notes can be transformed into text documents. Some models even have speech recognition which allows you to dictate text or control applications by voice. Business people can then use tablet PCs in the office as they have a full-size keyboard and monitor, just like an ordinary laptop.

*Figure 11.4 Toshiba Portege 3500 tablet PC*

## Amstrad e-m@iler plus

This is a small device that plugs into a phone socket (see Figure 11.5). It can be used to make telephone calls and will act as a answerphone. It also allows the user to send and receive e-mails, send text messages to mobile phones, surf the Internet using its own web browser, send faxes and even download and play games. Because the e-m@iler plus uses an Internet browser which is specifically designed to display low graphic content sites, it only gives limited access to complex sites with lots of features.

Figure 11.5 Amstrad e-m@iler plus

## Internet TVs and set-top boxes

Another way of accessing the Internet is through an Internet TV or a set-top box, which converts an ordinary television into an Internet TV. These easy-to-use televisions can access the web or send e-mails – all while you are watching your favourite television programme. From this has come the term, t-commerce (e-commerce on television). Users can navigate the Internet using either an infra-red remote control or a keyboard. Keyboards are usually optional but are useful for writing e-mails. One benefit of using an Internet television or set-top box is that there is no need to buy expensive computer equipment (see Figure 11.6).

As with the Amstrad e-m@iler plus (see above), access to complex sites is restricted as Internet TV browsers do not currently support certain aspects of multimedia such as sound or moving pictures. In addition, Internet TVs generally do not have hard disks or any form of backing store, so it is not possible to store recently used web pages in the same way as a PC.

## Public Internet terminals

BT has installed 500 multi.phones in shopping centres, rail and tube stations, airports and motorway services areas throughout the UK. This is the largest network of public Internet terminals in the UK. From these phones you can make standard telephone calls, but they also allow users to access the Internet, send e-mail and text messages. BT has included 'hot buttons' on the touch screen to take users directly to entertainment, travel, recruitment, shopping and sports information sites. Alternatively, users can go straight to a website by typing the website address using a special keyboard.

Currently, the multimedia phones achieve more than one million hits a week. A new style of public Internet terminal has been designed and BT hopes to install 28,000 over the next five years (see Figure 11.7). The new terminal will support video images and be able to provide local information such as maps, directions and location-based services and retail

Figure 11.6 An Internet television

Figure 11.7 A public Internet terminal

opportunities. BT has included 'hot buttons' similar to the ones on the multi.phones to allow users quick access to specially selected sites.

## Fact file

If you just want to send a text message or an e-mail, there are currently 2,000 BT payphones which will allow you to do this.

## Activity

▷ Print the file: **TEC Worksheet 3**
▷ from the Chapter 11 folder on the CD-ROM. This worksheet requires you to undertake a survey of Internet access methods.

# Multimedia

In the early 1990s there were very few websites, and most of them were simply text-only sites. Nowadays, most sites include a large number of interactive features known as multimedia – the presentation of information by a computer system using graphics, animation, sound and text.

There are many examples of interesting sites which use multimedia – go to www.heinemann.co.uk/hotlinks and click on World Wide Internet TV (see Figure 11.8). This site provides links to online television and radio signals around the world. If you are learning French, log onto a French TV channel to practise your language skills.

*Figure 11.8 The wwitv.com home page*

## Plug-ins

It is necessary to have special multimedia software to enjoy some of the advanced features on a website. The software is called a 'plug-in' player and by installing it, you will be able to play an audio or video file in the same format as the plug-in. The software can usually be downloaded for free. Examples of popular plug-ins include Microsoft® Windows Media Player, Flash and Shockwave from Macromedia and RealPlayer from Real Networks. Therefore, if you have a Flash plug-in installed, you should be able to view websites using the Flash multimedia format.

One controversial plug-in is **MP3**.

## Checkpoint

**MP3** is a digital music format. Music files downloaded using MP3 format are of the same high quality as a traditional music CD.

When video tapes were first introduced and you could hire your favourite films on video, there were, and still are, many instances of pirate copies being produced and sold at a much cheaper price. In the same way, there are websites that will allow you to download copyrighted music files free of charge. A well-known example is Napster (go to www.heinemann.co.uk/hotlinks and click on Napster) which was prosecuted for distributing copyrighted music. Napster has been forced to try to negotiate copyright licences with major record labels so that it can relaunch its site legally.

On the other hand, one benefit of MP3 is that would-be musicians can distribute their music freely over the Internet in order to promote their music to a large audience – see Figure 11.9.

Using your own PC and commercial or free software, you can convert digital music from a CD into MP3 format. You can play MP3 files directly on your computer, you can record an MP3 file onto a CD or you can play MP3 files on a portable MP3 player. Portable MP3 players can play music for longer than a portable CD player, the length of play depending on its memory capacity.

Figure 11.9 The MP3.com homepage

Figure 11.10 The Pace digital TV adaptor

## Digital broadcasting

Originally, all radio and television broadcasts used analogue signals. However, there has been a digital revolution taking place over the past few years and you cannot have failed to have noticed that more and more digital radios and televisions are available. Television and radio signals are changed into computerised signals which have to be decoded at the receiving end so that you can watch your favourite television programme or listen to crystal clear music on your radio. It is also possible to listen to digital radio via the Internet.

### Receiving digital transmissions

Digital television (DTV) will allow you to receive digital transmissions from television stations. Television stations have installed digital transmitters and now record their programmes using equipment which can handle digital signals. DTV allows more channels to be transmitted using fewer frequencies. You can enjoy excellent quality widescreen pictures with exceptionally clear stereo sound. In order to watch digital television, it is necessary to buy either a digital TV adaptor for an existing television, such as the Pace digital TV adaptor shown in Figure 11.10 or a new integrated television set known as an iDTV.

There are different distribution systems – known as platforms – for receiving digital radio or TV signals. They include the following

- Digital audio broadcasting (DAB) – digital signals are sent from land-based radio transmitters to a radio set.
- Cable – cable companies such as Telewest and NTL send digital signals through cables in the ground to subscribers' televisions via a set-top box.
- Satellite – purchasing a satellite dish aerial allows subscribers to receive digital signals from companies such as Sky Digital. Originally, subscribers to Sky received analogue signals via satellite dishes, but transmissions in analogue have now ceased and subscribers had to change their equipment to receive digital signals.
- Terrestrial – it is possible to receive digital signals from ground-based transmitters to a television aerial as long as the viewer has the correct equipment. ITV Digital ceased broadcasting its pay service in early 2002 and the BBC together with Crown Castle were granted a licence to broadcast digital programmes in August 2002. As a result, a free digital broadcasting service called Freeview was launched. Freeview provides around 30 free digital TV and radio channels, including BB1, BB2, ITV, Channel 4 and Channel 5, and other channels such as Sky

News and UK History, plus a whole range of interactive services.

You will learn more about how DTV has affected personal communications in Chapter 14.

### Find out about

Go to www.heinemann.co.uk/hotlinks and log onto the Freeview and Independent Television Commission's (ITC) websites and find out more about the digital age.

## Convergence of technologies

The term convergence means the merging of media which in the past were separate. For example, the telephone, which was used only for speech, is merging with the Internet to include video. Sound technology is now used with video components and the Internet. For example, you can now view DVDs on a computer and surf the Internet on special Internet TVs. It may not be long before all entertainment and communication devices will be merged into one piece of digital equipment and all the content will be transmitted through one single information highway.

## Security on the Internet

In the Second World War many secret agents based in enemy countries used secret codes in order to send messages. The receiving agent in the UK would be able to translate the message by decoding the code words used.

Many people are concerned about security when shopping on the Internet. For example, is it safe to use a credit card? One answer is to shop only at secure websites. Such sites show a closed lock at the foot of the screen, and **data encryption** is used to encode the data before sending the information across the Internet.

### Checkpoint

**Data encryption** means encoding data in a special way so that the data is scrambled and meaningless to others. Every secure website has its own unique way of unscrambling the data – this is known as the decryption key. Keys of this type have been mathematically proven to be safe and secure.

A secure website will also require users to prove that they are who they say they are. This is often done by having to enter a user name and password or by entering a personal identification number (PIN) (see Figure 11.11, overleaf). Remember not to make a password easy or too obvious, such as your name, date of birth or friend's name. It is also a good idea to change passwords every so often. When using a site that requires a password, always log off properly and in the way the website recommends – reliable and security-conscious sites will always warn you if you fail to do so (see Figure 11.12, overleaf).

### Firewalls

Both business and home users who use the Internet to transfer or receive personal details, such as credit card numbers, also need to protect against hackers – people who try to gain access to your data without your agreement. A piece of software called a **firewall** is used to prevent this.

### Checkpoint

A **firewall** is software used to prevent unauthorised users gaining access to a computer system.

### Fact file

Home Internet users can download a firewall called Zone Alarm for free from Zonelabs in order to protect their machines, so long as it is being used for personal and non-profit use. Go to www.heinemann.co.uk/hotlinks and click on Zonelabs.

The correct details have to be given before the user can log on

The closed lock shows that the site is secure

*Figure 11.11  Smile banking log-on window*

Warning message that the correct logging off procedures have not been followed

*Figure 11.12  Logging off incorrectly from a secure website*

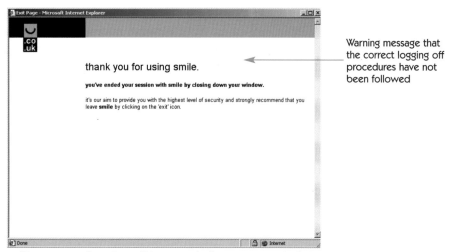

## Activity

▶ Print the file: **TEC Worksheet 4**
▶ from the Chapter 11 folder on the CD-ROM. This worksheet will help you to find out more about security on the Internet by visiting Scambusters.

# Storage media

## Floppy disks, ZIP disks, CD-ROMs and USB Storage Devices

Originally, data was stored on floppy disks, but as the demand for larger and larger hard disk sizes grew, together with the size of data files, the floppy disk's storage capacity of 1.4 MB was soon outgrown. Then ZIP drives became available which offer storage greater than 250 MB, but the real answer to storage problems was considered to lay in CDs. Originally designed for recorded music, the CD's capacity of up to 700 MB is ideally suited for data storage.

Most modern computers are fitted with CD-RW drives, which means they can record as well as play back CDs. Currently, there are two types of disk available:

- CD-R CD Record – this can only be recorded on once but played back many times
- CD-RW CD Rewritable – this can be both recorded on and played back many times.

## Pen drives/USB memory sticks/ Keychain drives

The latest method of data storage comes in the form of pen drives, sometimes referred to as USB memory sticks or Keychain drives. These are removable memory sticks with a USB connection. When you plug them into the USB port on your computer, it will automatically detect it as another removable drive without the need to reboot your computer. You can use them to read, store, move, copy or delete any files that you would normally have saved on a floppy disk drive, CD or hard drive. You can even run applications, view videos or play Mp3 files from the pen drive.

Pen drives are extremely small (around the size of a pack of chewing gum) and therefore very portable. They will allow you to transport data between different PC's and laptops as long as they have a USB port. Currently pen drives are available in different capacities up to a huge 2 GB of disk space depending on the manufacturer and it is inevitable that storage will grow. Data can have a life span of up to 10 years on a pen drive and the drive itself is extremely resilient to damage and loss of data as there are no moving parts.

*Figure 11.13  A pen drive*

## DVDs

A further development of CD-ROM technology has been the DVD or Digital Versatile Disk. Although this disk looks identical to a CD, it has a huge storage capacity, currently up to 9.4 GB of information!

The development of DVD has come about because of the need to find an alternative to video tapes for storing cinema films. It is now possible not only to have the whole film on one disk but also the facility to select different 'chapters' in the film, to have a variety of languages and subtitles, and even additional material such as 'the making of' documentary. The picture and sound quality on DVD is far better than tape.

Another area that uses increasing amounts of data are computer games. Here again, the large capacity of DVD offers the benefits of more detailed, realistic gaming.

DVD recorders are now being fitted to PCs, which not only allow very large amounts of data to be transferred or backed up to the DVD disk but also users will be able to watch films via their computer. DVD recorders will also make it possible for digital camera owners to create their own home movies on DVD.

In addition, separate DVD players are available in the same way as video recorders and these will allow viewers to watch their favourite film on the television. You can even record a television programme using the more expensive DVD recorders, while enjoying all the benefits of DVDs.

## MiniDisc

Another form of storage is the MiniDisc developed by Sony. A MiniDisc looks rather like a floppy disk, but is smaller, being 7 cm square. You can record and erase files on a MiniDisc in the same way as a floppy disk. However, a MiniDisc can hold around 100 times more data – about 140 megabits in data mode or 160 megabytes in audio mode.

MiniDiscs can be pre-recorded or blank and recordable. They can store about the same amount of music as a CD, but use a digital compression technique called ATRAC (Adaptive Transform Acoustic Coding) when storing music. This technique changes the music very slightly, although it is unlikely that most people would notice this.

The latest MiniDisc player from Sony, the MZN1, works just like a normal MiniDisc but has the benefit of allowing high speed data transfer of MP3 files from a personal computer (see Figure 11.14).

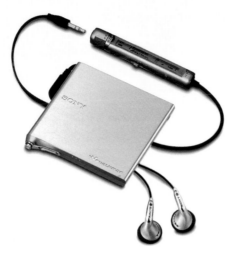

*Figure 11.14  The Sony MZN1*

## Touch screen technologies

As you learned in Chapter 9, a touch screen is a display screen covered with a touch-sensitive transparent panel. Touch screens are easy to use – they allow you to use a computer system by touching icons or links on the screen. You will often find touch screens in public places, for example BT's multi.phones, mentioned on page 183, use a touch screen. Uses of touch screens include the following:

- Public information systems often use touch screen technologies as they are generally user friendly. You will find them in museums, information kiosks and tourist offices, for example.
- Customer self-service touch screen terminals are often used at busy self-service restaurants or shops. Customers are able to place their own orders which saves time waiting to order.
- Restaurants and point of sale systems – have you ever noticed that when ordering a meal the waiter or waitress will often enter your order via a touch screen? This is much faster than entering text.
- Control/automation systems – touch screens are useful in systems in industrial process control. Operators can monitor and control difficult operations by simply touching the screen.
- Computer-based training – touch screens are more user friendly and can help to make learning fun and interactive.
- Assisting people with disabilities – touch screens can help some people who have difficulty using a mouse or keyboard to use a computer which they wouldn't be able to do otherwise.

### Activity

 Print the file: **TEC Worksheet 5** from the Chapter 11 folder on the CD-ROM. In this worksheet you will investigate examples of touch screen technology in your local shopping centre.

# Chapter 12 How ICT is used in business

This chapter looks at how ICT is used in business and how it has affected work styles. You will study:

- where people work and how business practice has changed
- how the use of e-mail, mobile phones and laptops has affected people's work patterns
- the ICT training and skills employees require
- how ICT affects the way people interact at work – e.g. using e-mail instead of speaking directly to each other
- the types of jobs available as a result of ICT as well as those lost.

### What you will learn

The information revolution
How ICT has affected the office
How ICT has affected the retail industry
How ICT has affected banking
How ICT has affected design and manufacturing
How ICT is likely to affect you

### Overview

ICT has had a major effect on how business is carried out. If you worked in an office 30 years ago, the main method of communication between businesses would have been by post or telephone. If an urgent letter needed to be sent, it would be delivered 'by hand', that is, someone would actually go to the recipient to deliver it.

Over the last 20 years or so, technology has played an increasingly important part in the way we communicate and carry out business. It is now common to see business people travelling on a train working on a laptop computer. They may receive phone calls on their mobile phone – often to the annoyance of other passengers! They will be able to connect to the Internet and send e-mails. In other words, they are in a 'mobile office' and are able to carry out their business on the move. The urgent letter that used to be sent 'by hand' can now be faxed or e-mailed. As a result, the speed at which people work has increased.

## The information revolution

Until 20–30 years ago there very few computers. Then in the 1980s and 1990s there was an explosion of information technology. The arrival of this new technology has brought us into the information age and has led to major changes in the workplace.

In order to fully appreciate the effect that the 'information revolution' has had on the business world and our economy, you need to find out about life in the workplace before the impact of ICT. The easiest way of doing this is to ask the people who experienced these changes for themselves.

### Activity

▶ Print the file: **BUS Worksheet 1** from the Chapter 12 folder on the CD-ROM. This worksheet will help you to find out about the impact of the information revolution on the workplace.

## How ICT has affected the office

The role of the office has not changed very much over the last 20–30 years. Its purpose has always been to provide administrative support to a business. However, the processes by which this support is provided today are very different from 20–30 years ago.

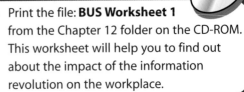

### Computerised office systems

The introduction of computerised office systems such as word processing and desktop publishing, database and accounting software alongside other automated office equipment, for example e-mail and computer-controlled telephone systems, has led to huge changes.

With the introduction of the new technology came fears about mass unemployment, but over time these proved to be groundless and, while some jobs did disappear, many became much easier and more interesting.

Your investigation into business activities in the office of 20 or 30 years ago probably revealed that the main method of communication was by post or telephone. Letters and other documents were produced on typewriters. The typist usually produced one original document with extra copies made at the same time by layering carbon paper between sheets of paper. If the typist made a mistake (or the author of the document changed his or her mind), it was quite usual for the document to be retyped in full.

Computers removed much of the monotony from the typist's work and many typists retrained as word processor operators and acquired new skills that enabled them to edit and manipulate text, automate routine tasks, use mail merge and desktop publishing skills. As a result, their jobs became far more interesting and they were able to complete more work in the same amount of time.

Twenty or 30 years ago the accounts clerk had to complete ledgers by hand and had to repeat complicated calculations time and time again. Nowadays, data processing operators enter the data into the computer and the software performs calculations automatically, resulting in business systems that provide a far more efficient means of data analysis.

We hear about the 'paperless office' and indeed in some businesses the traditional paper-based filing systems for payroll, stock, sales and orders, and so on, have become redundant along with the filing clerks who were employed to maintain them. However, for most businesses the computer seems to generate more paper than ever!

The installation of local and wide area networks has paved the way for the office as we know it today. The communication links that a network provides enable data to be held on one central computer system, which can be accessed by all departments, regardless of whether they are in the same building, in different towns or even different countries.

Much of this data will be stored in databases and there are literally millions of databases in use in the workplace.

*Figure 12.1  Computers have made typists' work easier and more interesting*

The data held in a company database is very valuable and companies go to great lengths to ensure data security and reliability. Loss of data could mean the loss of hundreds of thousands of pounds' worth of lost business and, for this reason, specialist staff are employed to manage the systems. The job of the database manager is to ensure the system is set up so that staff have access only to data they are authorised to see. Similarly, he or she must make sure that only certain staff are able to change data. The database manager must also ensure the database is regularly backed up and that the back-up copies are stored in a secure environment.

## New ways of working

Many new ways of working stemmed from the arrival of the network, the database and the Internet.

### E-mail

E-mail is fast becoming the principal method of communication *within* companies and is increasingly used for informal communications *between* companies. This means that many business people who once had secretaries to produce their correspondence now have to use the computer and do it for themselves.

While e-mail is seen by many as a more convenient way to communicate, others feel it makes business dealings rather impersonal. Without the opportunity for spoken communication, there are less chances to build up business relationships.

The use of e-mail might have reduced the amount of time spent on the telephone and made the exchange of information very much faster but, as a result, it is not uncommon for an employee to find him or herself spending an increasing amount of time dealing with countless e-mails (many unsolicited and irrelevant) and therefore unable to get on with the real job in hand.

## Call centres

Call centres handle many day-to-day routine tasks that were once undertaken by an army of clerical staff. Nowadays, instead of writing letters to place orders, arrange insurance, and so on, a person only has to pick up the telephone, speak to an operator and within a few minutes the business is completed. The operator is able to call up the individual's details directly from the database stored on the company's computer system. As a result, the operator has all the relevant information on the screen in front of him or her and is usually able to give an immediate answer to the enquiry (see Figure 12.2). For example, if a business wishes to order items from a catalogue, the operator can confirm availability and agree a delivery date; a query can be answered very simply over the telephone whereas a few years ago this would have involved writing a letter. Look at Figure 12.3 to see just how much time can be saved.

*Figure 12.2 A call centre*

Large companies have call centres throughout the UK – and indeed some companies are considering relocating their call centres outside the UK to countries such as India where labour costs are very much cheaper. One disadvantage of call centres from the customer's point of view is that they seldom manage to speak to the same person twice since telephone calls are automatically routed to whichever centre can deal with the enquiry first. One day you might be talking to Huddersfield and the next it may be Glasgow. As a result, many people feel that they do not get a 'personal service' and are no longer treated as valued customers. On the other hand, call centres are usually open until late in the evening and over the weekend, which benefits people who work in jobs where it is difficult to make telephone calls during the day.

## Teleworking

Teleworking has brought about a major change to the working patterns of many people. Instead of sitting at a desk in an office, an employee can work from home with a PC or laptop that interacts with the company's computer system via a modem and the telephone network. The employee can communicate via e-mail and has instant access to the company's computer database and files.

From the employee's point of view, the advantage of teleworking is that it can offer a better quality of life. Time is not wasted travelling to and from work and cheaper living accommodation can often be found out of town. In addition, the flexibility in working hours is ideal for people who need to fit their work schedule around children and school times or for disabled workers who find it difficult, or even impossible, to commute. There is also a benefit to the environment because fewer commuters mean fewer cars on the road leading to a fall in petrol consumption and pollution.

However, home working can have its disadvantages too. The employee may feel isolated and miss the support of colleagues and there is always the temptation to put work off in favour of something more appealing!

From the employer's point of view, the company does not need to rent so much office space, resulting in lower rents, heating and lighting costs. In addition, staff can be recruited from a wider area because they do not need to live within commuting distance of the office. A disadvantage to the employer could be the difficulty in controlling staff and promoting teamwork.

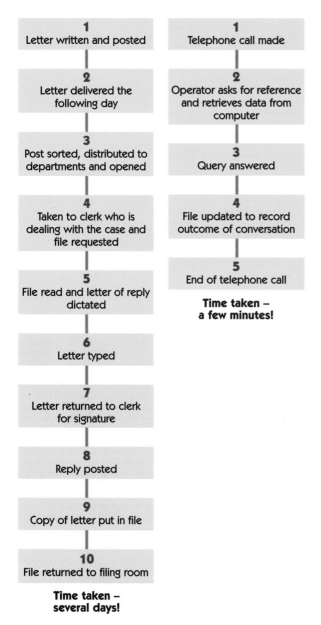

Figure 12.3 Call centres can save time

## Video conferencing

Video conferencing (or teleconferencing) is a system where video links enable people in different locations to see and speak to each other via their computers (see Figure 12.4). A small camera is fixed to the top of each computer VDU and the image is displayed on the computer screens. This means that it is not always necessary for employees to leave their offices and spend time travelling to meetings. Meetings can be arranged at short notice, although discussions may not always be as productive as if the participants were all sitting round the same table. Of course, if the meeting required documents to be shared or signed, then video conferencing would not be suitable.

*Figure 12.4  Video conferencing allows people in different locations to hold a meeting without leaving their desk*

## Mobile phones and laptop computers

The increased use of both the mobile phone and laptop computer have also affected the way people do their jobs. The mobile phone ensures employees are never out of contact with the office. With the aid of a laptop computer, they can have detailed information about clients or products readily available and can produce extremely professional presentations when trying to earn new business for the company. Paperwork can be cut to a minimum as new sales can be processed quickly via a modem. The disadvantage for some employees is that the office never closes, and many people seem to spend increasingly large chunks of their leisure time working, either at home or while travelling.

## Environmental issues

Large office buildings use computer control systems to manage environmental conditions such as heat and light and thereby reduce energy consumption and costs. For example, sensors are used to measure light levels and detect movement or temperature. The data from the sensor readings is processed by the computer control system from where instructions are generated that switch on lights or adjust the heat.

## How ICT has affected the retail industry

The introduction of computers into the retail industry has revolutionised the way we shop – both in-store and online. Apart from some small businesses, most supermarkets, shops and stores use electronic point of sale (EPOS) terminals. These are computerised sales checkouts that link the sales desk to the store's stock database and bank.

At most sales desks an assistant will use a bar code reader to scan the bar code (see Figure 12.5). The computer recognises the bar code and generates the price of the item at the

*Figure 12.5  A sales assistant uses a bar code reader*

till and at the same time alters the stock level in the stock database. The computer also recognises special 'multi-save' offers and makes the correct reduction on the bill. This is how shops can so readily offer promotions such as 'three items for the price of two' or '20 per cent discount for one day only'. If the customer wishes to pay by card rather than cash, his or her debit or credit card is 'swiped' and the money is automatically transferred from the customer's bank account to that of the store. In fact some supermarkets even offer their own banking services.

The use of bar codes and EPOS terminals means there is no need to price items individually – no need to employ assistants to stick labels on every product on the shelves. If a price changes, only the database needs updating and the new price is shown at the till when the item is scanned.

The use of a database to record stock levels means store managers know instantly how much stock they have, which items are running low and which are selling well. Some computer systems are programmed to automatically raise a new order with the supplier when stock falls below a certain level. However, although it might appear intelligent, a computer database can only provide information based on the data fed into the system. This means that wastage and theft are not recorded, so an annual stock-take is still necessary in order to reconcile (check) actual numbers on the shelf with the computer records.

The use of computers provides management with instant and up-to-date information about daily sales figures. This, in turn, means decisions are made based on accurate information which makes it much easier and more reliable to predict market trends.

The Internet has added new terms to our vocabulary – cyber shopping, e-shopping, e-commerce – and has opened up a totally new shopping experience both for the customer and the retailer. Today, most well-known stores offer the opportunity to shop online as they realise the potential of the international market place presented by the Internet.

This offers consumers a wider choice of goods 24 hours a day and the opportunity to shop around for the best buys from the comfort of their own home. It saves time, fares and parking charges and gives the housebound the same opportunities as the able bodied. However, at the same time it poses a threat to town centres as they continue to struggle to compete with large out-of-town shopping centres.

## ● Snapshot

### Smart tag technology

The superstore chain Tesco is reported to be the first retailer in Europe to start an in-store trial of new smart tag technology that could revolutionise the way products are manufactured and sold.

In partnership with Gillette, the razor blade manufacturer, the supermarket is about to begin the trial of radio frequency identification (RFID) chips. The smart chips, which could replace bar codes, can be read wirelessly by a scanner, allowing products to be monitored throughout the supply chain. The tiny tags are being attached to packs of razor blades. Staff will be able to check stock levels, sell-by dates and whether a product has been purchased. The tags could also help beat shoplifters – scanners can detect if a product has been paid for when it leaves the shop.

The possibilities with RFID are endless. If the three-month trial proves successful, the tags could feature on a wider range of Tesco's products. For example, using RFID chips on food products will help the store to know when products are nearing their sell-by dates and will make it easier to identify products.

*Source: Computing, 16 January 2003.*

## Marketing

It is only in the last couple of years that online shopping has produced significant sales figures. Until recently, consumers have usually shopped in two ways – either by visiting a shop in person or phoning up and ordering something they have seen in a catalogue or advertisement. The long-established mail order industry has always relied on large glossy catalogues to attract customers. Mail-order companies usually print two catalogues a year – one for spring/summer and another for autumn/winter. These catalogues are a very expensive outlay that most high street stores have not been willing to consider. However, today, many businesses have their own websites and many of them offer the opportunity to shop online.

Retailers such as Marks & Spencer, Next and John Lewis have online catalogues, a much cheaper alternative to glossy mail-order brochures. Unlike paper-based catalogues, which are produced several months in advance, online catalogues can be kept up-to-date. New items can be added daily and goods that are no longer available can be removed. Customers can be given more information about items and can often zoom in to see fine details enlarged.

Supermarkets have identified new marketing methods too. It is not uncommon to see their vans out on home delivery runs. The opportunity to order weekly groceries and household items online for delivery the same day is a bonus for those who are housebound or tied up with busy work commitments.

Many supermarkets offer loyalty cards to their shoppers and in exchange for shopping regularly with the store, the customer receives money off-vouchers and special offers. The advantage to the store is that it can very easily record customer details in a huge database providing easy and instant access to valuable data on shopping and spending habits. They use this information to target likely markets for new products and services.

## Advertising

In order to attract new customers, businesses have traditionally promoted their products or services by advertising in newspapers and brochures and on the radio, TV and billboards. Today, there is an enormous market open to them through the Internet. By registering its website on a search engine's database, a business is able to ensure its products are brought to the attention of potential customers

searching for similar products. For example, if you were looking to buy a particular digital camera or hi-fi system, you are likely to use a search engine to look for possible suppliers. The companies that are suggested to you have all registered with that search engine – it is not just luck that brings their names to your screens! Have you also noticed that many companies have advertisements that seem to pop up from nowhere when you are using the Internet? 'Banner advertisements' also often appear at the top of websites.

The ease of recording client details on a database and using mail merge for mail shots offers a quick and inexpensive way of reaching another huge potential market. There are companies that concentrate on producing specialised mailing lists that are sold on to businesses. Look closely at any form you fill in and somewhere on it you are likely to see a small box that you must tick if you do not want your personal details passed on to other organisations.

You will find that banks, building societies and insurance companies also use customer details to send out information about a wide range of other products and services they offer.

## Online or electronic auctions

These are a means of cutting costs and simplifying the buying process. Companies sell their products to the buyer bidding the highest price. Some companies offer specific goods such as digital cameras, printers, and so on, while others offer airline seats or hotel accommodation. However, you will usually always find that there is a get-out clause which states that not all offers may be accepted.

Some companies are now using online auctions to obtain goods or services by inviting suppliers to bid for a contract. In this case, the best or lowest priced offer wins. Consignia (the Post Office) is considering adopting online auctions for purchasing supplies, and the Forestry Commission is considering replacing its traditional method of selling with online auctions as it believes it will offer a far greater efficiency in sales.

# How ICT has affected banking

The days of the typical high street bank with a branch on every corner are now history. More people use remote systems for their day-to-day banking transactions and choose telephone or online banking rather than visiting the bank in person. In fact, some banks only offer Internet banking. These new systems give access to bank accounts 24 hours a day, 365 days a year and enable customers to check balances, pay bills and transfer money without leaving home. Bank staff employed in call centres are able to give instant decisions on requests for loans and the money can be made available very quickly. Customers can also use the Internet to compare the products of various banks to make sure they get the best deal.

We are fast becoming a cashless society that prefers to use credit and debit cards when shopping rather than cheques or cash. Customers no longer need to visit the bank during opening hours to withdraw money. Instead, automated teller machines (ATMs) or cash point machines enable customers to withdraw money 24 hours a day anywhere in the world. Some customers have switched their bank accounts to supermarkets who nowadays offer their own banking services. Employees' salaries are paid directly into their bank accounts by Bankers Automated Clearing System (BACS) and bills are automatically settled by direct debit.

The outcome of these changes has resulted in branches closing or merging and as a result, there are fewer jobs in banking. For example, new computer systems clear the much smaller number of cheques in circulation far more quickly and banks need less staff to process them.

Rural communities, in particular, have been seriously affected by the closure of smaller branches, causing great inconvenience to customers. The elderly often find it difficult to get into town if they no longer drive and they cannot rely on public transport because bus services in country neighbourhoods are often rather infrequent.

Nowadays, such a large proportion of the population uses debit and credit cards that credit card fraud, which was unheard of 20 or 30 years ago, is now a major problem. Some banks have tried issuing cards with embedded photos as a further proof of identity. However, by 2005 we should all be using signature-less credit cards. Banks are investing millions of pounds updating the present system to enable customers to key in a four-digit pin number instead of signing credit transaction slips. The Post Office is shortly to introduce a similar system which is designed to eliminate much of the current credit card fraud estimated to cost almost £1 million per day.

# How ICT has affected design and manufacturing

## CAD/CAM

The use of computerised technologies such as computer-aided design and computer-aided manufacture (CAD/CAM) systems enable designers and engineers to develop and test new products before companies invest in expensive new machinery. For example, a new car design can be tested to see how it is likely to behave in a road crash long before the first prototype is built. If necessary, the design can be altered to overcome potential problems. Once the design is finalised, the CAD/CAM system will automatically produce the blueprints for the dies that are made before mass production begins. The whole CAD/CAM process from design through the manufacturing process results in better quality, more reliable products.

Architects have transferred their design skills to CAD software and can produce clear, detailed drawings quickly and accurately. Changes to the designs are easily made without the need to produce completely new drawings. 3D-CAD software will turn a 2D drawing into virtual reality enabling the client to tour a new building – a powerful marketing tool. Large projects, such as the development of new shopping centres or office buildings, are designed within a fixed budget and computers support the management of such projects, comparing actual costs with projected costs.

This provides project managers with accurate information that enables them to keep projects within budget and within the timescale.

CAD software is also used in the design of sports equipment such as racing cars, yachts, skis, football boots and specialist hi-tech sports wear. With the aid of the computer, calculations can be made which will determine the maximum speed or durability of new designs and new materials.

## Robots

If you ask most people to name something that links computers and industry, they are likely to suggest the robot and indeed the robot has had an enormous impact on traditional manufacturing industries such as the car industry. In the 1980s countless factory workers lost their jobs as robots were introduced to the production line and took over repetitive tasks such as welding, assembly work and paint spraying. Although the initial outlay to automate production and install robots is expensive, in the long term production methods are more accurate and the quality of output is consistent. Unlike humans, robots can work 24 hours a day in all environments – cold, dark or hazardous. They don't have bad days, go sick or strike and they don't need tea breaks or holidays. In the long term, savings will be made on fuel bills and labour costs and production rates will improve. However, it is important to remember that if one robot

*Figure 12.6 Robots form part of the production line*

breaks down, it can bring the whole production line to a total standstill (see Figure 12.6).

Robots contain three basic components, or parts:

- a sensor to detect environmental conditions
- a microprocessor to process the information detected by the sensor
- an actuator to respond to the detected condition, for example produce a movement or switch on something like a paint spray.

## Newspaper printing

Newspaper printing has also changed a lot in recent years. Traditionally, the pages of a newspaper would be assembled letter by letter into blocks that would fit together to form the finished page. This was a highly skilled job carried out by compositors who were employed to set the newspaper up ready for printing. If a late story broke, it was not unusual for the compositors to reset the whole page.

Nowadays, journalists word process their own stories and e-mail the copy to the editor from a PC or laptop anywhere in the world. Special desktop publishing software is used to produce the final layout, import the pictures and arrange the columns. It is very easy to manipulate the design of a page if a late story has to be included and as a result, the compositor's role has disappeared from newspaper production. This is an example of 'de-skilling', where a job requiring a high level of skill has been replaced by a computerised operation.

In Unit 1, Chapter 6 case study 1 explains how you can find out how computer technology played such an important part in the production of this book.

Throughout this chapter we have looked at the effect the introduction of ICT systems has had on our daily and working lives and, although the impact has been massive, it has not been as great as was originally predicted. It had been believed that millions of workers would be out of work as ICT 'took over' in the workplace, but in fact many new jobs have been created and, for many workers, their new jobs are far more interesting.

## How ICT is likely to affect you

Naturally, it takes time for these new and exciting innovations to become available to all of us, but this section looks at what life might like be in the not-too-distant future.

First of all, let's see how you might be affected when you go to work.

In order to find a job you must aim to be multi-skilled, adaptable and computer literate. The higher your qualifications, the greater your chances of an interesting job that will pay a good salary. If you choose to go to work rather than continue in further or higher education, most employers will be looking for good GCSEs and ideally a qualification in ICT to demonstrate your ability to use the standard software applications such as word processing and spreadsheets. If you continue into further or higher education you will be using the standard software applications regularly to support your studies. If you look in computer journals, you will see vacancies in all areas of ICT.

---

**WANTED**

**High calibre staff**

*for*

Project Management

Data Protection

Business Systems Development

Service Management

Software Testing

Information Security

Java/Oracle/VB/C++ Development

Software Engineering

Defence Systems Engineering

Strategic Architecture

Web Design

Application and Network Support

---

*Figure 12.7 ICT vacancies*

The variety of jobs in systems development and support is wide ranging. Alternatively, you might be seeking a job where you are using software for graphic design, product design, architecture, fashion, media, publishing, administration, finance – the list is endless. Whatever your eventual career path, there are exciting opportunities for young people who are skilled ICT technicians.

If you find employment in an office, you will probably find yourself working in a large, open-plan area. Since your employer will rely almost totally on computer systems to run the business, security will be very important and you will be issued with a security card of some description in order to gain access to the building. Many employers run training departments and in recent years much of their work has been involved in enabling older members of staff gain basic computer skills. Remember many of their staff started work before computers were invented and, unlike you, did not have the opportunity to use them at school. In addition, staff need to be trained to use the specialist software applications that many organisations use. You can expect to have access to a workstation that is part of a networked system and you will need a password to access the data stored on it. Your working environment (the heating, air conditioning, and so on) will probably be controlled by a computer system.

Much of your day-to-day communication will be via e-mail. Your job might require you to produce documents (letters, reports, brochures, price lists, and so on) and the use of special features within the software such as templates and mail merge will help to ensure you produce accurate work that reflects the house style of your company.

If you are working in a call centre, you will probably be expected to vary your working pattern to enable you to work some evenings and weekends. You will speak to customers on the telephone and access their details on the computer while dealing with their enquiries. It is possible that some of your colleagues will work from home. However, your job may not be safe in the longer term – at any time your employer might consider relocation overseas where labour costs are cheaper.

Instead of travelling to meetings, you may use video conferencing facilities so that you can conduct your business with people in different parts of the world via webcams and computers.

If you are employed in the retail industry, you will soon find yourself asking customers to enter their PIN number at the checkout to verify (check) authenticity of their debit or credit cards. You will be able to tell straight away which goods are available in the warehouse and will not have to worry about reordering stock because the computer will automatically generate a new order to the supplier when stock levels are low.

As a manager in a large store, you might use computer weather predictions to gauge the amount of seasonal stock to order. For example, are you going to have enough ice cream and sunscreen for a long, hot summer? Like most retailers, your employer will be encouraging people to buy online. Your company will have a website on which its goods are advertised and the amount of trade carried out online will increase year by year.

> ### Fact file
>
> In November 2002 we spent over £1 billion online – twice the amount spent in November 2001.

If you are working on the design of new products, you will use CAD software to produce the drawings and dies for your products. You will be able to test the durability and safety of your new designs with the aid of the computer before they are manufactured. When the manufacturing process begins it will probably be automated, producing goods 24 hours a day, seven days a week if consumer demand requires this. Computer-controlled robots will do many jobs, particularly dangerous or very dirty work. The factory will not employ a large number of manual staff and those that are employed will probably be trained in any one of several roles so that their skills can be used to the full. You will be able to check the progress of every individual order throughout the manufacturing process as the whole production line will be computer controlled.

## How might you be affected after you have finished work?

Before you get home from work your personal computer control system will have switched the lights on, closed the curtains and turned the oven on ready for your supper. When you arrive home, you might run your finger over a small scanning device in order to open the front door – you will not need a key. Biometric technology will match your fingerprint against its memory store. You will use your leisure time to help you to relax after a stressful working week and will make arrangements to meet your friends by e-mail or mobile phone. You will use the Internet to shop, manage your bank account, look for a new job, listen to music, study, make travel arrangements, find a recipe and book your holidays, concert tickets, and so on.

> ### Fact file
>
> By 2006 you could hold an ID card encoded with personal details such as an iris scan or fingerprints. The UK Passport Service wants to introduce a smart identity card to improve security and prevent fraud. It will, however, need government approval in order to put the plan in place. A biometric-based passport would most likely be based on fingerprints, iris scans or facial recognition – or a combination – as not all methods are effective with all people. The digital image would be compared with a database containing 60 million images and would confirm the individual's identity. This would help in the war against benefit fraud, organised crime and terrorism. It is thought the public will be much more likely to accept the idea following the terrorist attack on New York on 11 September 2001. (*Computing*, 21 February 2002)

This chapter looks at the legislation (laws) which relate to ICT:

- Data Protection Act (1998)
- Computer Misuse Act (1990)
- Copyright, Designs and Patents Act (1989)
- Health and Safety at Work Act (1974)
- Health and Safety Regulations (1992)
- Regulation of Investigatory Powers Act (2000)
- The EU regulations on the use of computers
- The Internet Code of practice

In addition to the benefits of ICT you should also be aware of the drawbacks such as:

- international fraud
- the misuse of personal information
- intrusion such as "spam", chat rooms, viruses

## What you will learn

Laws and regulations relating to ICT

Misuse of ICT

Health and Safety

## Overview

The rapid advancement in technology over recent years has been matched by a rise in criminal activity. Laws, Acts and regulations are put in place by Government to protect people from the harmful effects of ICT. This chapter gives an overview of these laws and regulations that are being used to fight computer and Internet crime, and also considers how ICT is being misused. With the growth in computer usage, the chapter looks at the health and safety regulations designed to protect people from risk of injury.

The increased use of computers in recent years, and the new crimes that have arisen as a result, have shown that existing laws are unable to deal with the offences. Some laws contained too many loopholes; or the maximum sentences that could be imposed did not reflect the seriousness of the crime. New laws have been passed and existing laws have been amended to tackle the situation.

While you do not need to know the full details of these laws it is important that you are aware of their existence. You should have an understanding of them because they deal with issues that influence the way we work and behave. This section looks at the current relevant legislation.

## Laws and regulations relating to ICT

Theft and fraud have had their place in criminal law for hundreds of years, but the nature of the crimes has changed with the passing of time. For example, theft has traditionally related to the removal of 'tangible' (physical) items without the owner's consent. Nowadays, theft of data is a problem. Knowing that loss of data could jeopardise an organisation's ability to trade can prove to be too much of a temptation for some unscrupulous people. Similarly, loss of sensitive data on product or medical development for example, could enable a competitor to launch a new product first and establish itself as the market leader.

Consumers have little protection from rogue Internet traders who open websites offering goods for sale. Unsuspecting customers think they are dealing with legitimate businesses and place orders over the Internet, passing on their credit card details to guarantee payment. The money is then withdrawn from their bank accounts, but the goods are never delivered. Later, customers try to contact the company but find the website closed and, without a telephone number or trader's address, there is little they can do to recover their money. On the other hand, genuine businesses also find themselves victims of crime. It is not uncommon to find a dishonest consumer using a stolen credit card in order to obtain goods fraudulently.

Some of the most difficult crimes to fight against are those involving the global network of the Internet. The laws of any one country do not govern the Internet and successful crime detection relies on the cooperation of police forces worldwide. There is little control over material that is posted on the Internet and it is virtually impossible to prevent illegal material from being published.

We are all aware of the existence of computer hackers and their efforts to gain unauthorised access to computers and the files stored on them. Although some hackers might be considered harmless, others aim to do damage.

## The Computer Misuse Act (1990)

This Act was set up to deal with misuse of computer systems when existing laws were found to be inadequate. Its primary purpose is to act as a deterrent to would-be hackers and it is designed to offer protection from:

- unauthorised access to computer programs or data
- unauthorised access with further criminal intent – e.g. fraud or the deliberate planting of computer viruses
- unauthorised modification (changing) of computer material.

### Checkpoint

The **Computer Misuse Act** is in place to discourage unauthorised access to computer systems.

### Fact file

The Home Office has revealed that in 2001 there were 25 prosecutions under the Computer Misuse Act, with 21 people found guilty and eight sent to prison. The Act formed a part of a further 58 criminal cases.

The low number of prosecutions under the Act is thought to be due to two factors: companies are not keen to report breaches in their systems so as to avoid poor publicity; and the police have insufficient manpower to deal with computer crime.

(*Computing*, 16 January 2003)

## The Copyright Designs and Patents Act (1988)

This Act was originally set up to protect the work of authors, artists and composers from being reproduced or copied without permission. Current European copyright law extends for 70 years after the death of the author/creator and during this period the work (book, work of art, software, photograph, music score, and so on) may not be reproduced without permission.

This original Copyright Designs and Patents Act was in existence long before computers were invented and it has since been widened to include computer software in order to prohibit the making of illegal copies.

When you buy computer software it comes with a licence that allows you to install, use, access, display or run just one copy of the software on one computer and one notebook. Your school or college will have purchased a network licence in order to be granted permission to run the software on all the machines in use.

Imagine a small business starting with just one computer. The owner will have bought the software for that computer and will have the necessary licence. As the business expands, the owner might decide to install a network and use the same software on the network, forgetting to buy a new licence. The owner has, in fact, broken the law, even though it was not intentional.

This law affects everyone who owns a computer. You must not let anyone else borrow your software to install on his or her computer and, similarly, you should not borrow software from a friend and install it on your computer. The software houses have, after all, invested a great deal of time and money in order to develop the software and they treat this very seriously. In order to help protect software copyright, the Federation Against Software Theft (FAST) was set up in 1984 to investigate software piracy and it prosecutes when instances of illegal copying of software come to its attention.

If you look in the Help menu of Microsoft® Word software, you will see the option 'About Microsoft Word'. Here you will find details of the licence holder and a product registration number. It also carries a strong warning: 'This computer program is protected by copyright law and international treaties. Unauthorised reproduction or distribution of this program, or any portion of it, may result in severe civil and criminal penalties and will be prosecuted to the maximum extent possible under the law'.

## Checkpoint

The **Copyright Designs and Patents Act** protects software copyright.

## Fact file

Software manufacturers are working on the development of software that must be registered within 30 days or it will stop working. Additionally, it cannot be copied on to more than one PC and one notebook.
(*Computer Active*, 15 November 2001)

## The Data Protection Act (1998)

This Act extended and reinforced the original Data Protection Act of 1984. This was introduced to deal with the increasing amount of personal data being held on computers and the potential misuse of that personal information. Think of the many different organisations that hold computerised records containing details of our personal lives, employment history, financial and medical records, and so on. Under the Data Protection Act, these organisations must ensure that the data remains confidential and, in Chapter 9, we looked at some of the measures taken to ensure the security of computer systems.

The responsibility for ensuring this information remains confidential does not only rest with the organisations themselves. Staff working within these organisations also have a responsibility under the Act to ensure personal information is not disclosed, however innocently. Staff must be aware of straightforward things they can do to protect the confidentiality of the data. For example:

- Passwords should be kept secret. A note stuck to the side of the computer is not a sensible way to remember it!
- Personal information should not be passed on to third parties at any time. Imagine a situation where an employee had access to personal information. Think of the consequences if a list of addresses and details of valuable house contents fell into the wrong hands. Similarly, staff working with confidential data must be very careful not to disclose personal information during a conversation, however innocently.
- Computer screens in public places such as the doctor's surgery should not be visible to the general public. It could be very unfortunate if somebody waiting at the reception desk read personal and confidential information on screen about another patient.

## Find out ...

Find out more about laws relating to ICT by visiting relevant web sites such as the Data Protection Commissioner and the Health Safety Executive. Use the skills that you learnt in chapter 5 to find these web sites.

*Figure 13.1 Never disclose personal information in public*

Companies wishing to hold data must first register with the Data Protection Information Commissioner who has the power to limit the data they can hold and also the authority to inspect a company's computer system to make sure it is not breaking any rules. Companies are not authorised to use the data for direct marketing. The person the data is about, your parent or guardian for example, has a right to see any data held and to have it corrected if it is inaccurate. We are also entitled to ask who is processing data about us and why.

**Fact file**

Any organisation holding and using data is referred to as the 'data user' and the subject of the data (that is, who the data is about) is referred to as the 'data subject'.

## Regulation of Investigatory Powers Act (2000)

This Act resulted from the rapid technological changes in recent years such as the growth of the Internet and the vast amount of material conveyed over it. It gives the government the power to access websites and monitor the use of the Internet and other electronic communication systems. The rising criminal use of encryption (coding) techniques when sending information over the Internet does create situations that could become threatening. For example, consider the possibility of a terrorist attack. This would require a tremendous amount of planning and any organisation setting up such an attack would need to communicate with its members all over the world. The easiest way to do this would be to send coded (or encrypted) messages via the Internet.

This Act effectively gives the government unrestricted access to a person's electronic communications – both e-mail and telephone – without that person's knowledge. In addition, any access granted does not have to be disclosed – ever. Under the Act the government can demand that an Internet Service Provider (ISP):

- provides access to a customer's communications in secret
- fits surveillance equipment to enable the government to carry out a mass surveillance of communications
- provides decryption facilities for encrypted (or coded) messages.

The government can force an ISP to intercept any one of it customer's communications for a variety of reasons:

- if it feels there is a threat to national security
- in the process of preventing or detecting serious crime
- to safe-guard the economic well-being of the UK.

The introduction of this Act has led to serious debate. Some people are very disturbed that the government now has unrestricted access to electronic communications in a way that would not be acceptable in the case of postal communications. They feel that the exact reasons for intercepting electronic communications are too vague.

**Checkpoint**

The **Regulation of Investigatory Powers Act** gives the government authority to intercept electronic communications.

## The Health and Safety at Work Act (1974)

This Act was introduced in order to make sure that the time you spend at school, college or at work is spent in a safe environment that will ensure your well-being while there. For example:

- You can expect to find safe entrances, exits and fire escapes. Fire extinguishers must be provided and should be checked regularly.
- The computer and electrical equipment you use must be checked regularly to make sure it is safe and not likely to develop electrical faults.
- Hazardous substances must be stored in

safe storage areas with warning signs showing their location.

- All places of work (and study) must have a written statement detailing the health and safety policy together with accident investigation procedures.
- Staff (and students) must receive training to ensure they are aware of their rights, obligations and fire procedures. Fire drills are held to ensure everyone knows what to do in an emergency. Your obligations while at school or college are to behave in such a way that does not harm yourself or your friends.

At work employees have a duty to undertake safe working practices by:

- dealing with or reporting any hazards, such as trailing wires or obstructions
- ensuring they know the fire drill and that routes to fire exits are kept clear
- not lifting heavy equipment.

> **Checkpoint**
>
> The **Health and Safety at Work Act** ensures that the environments in which we work and study are safe places.

## The Display Screen Regulations (1992)

These are European regulations relating to the use of display screen equipment (that is, computers and VDUs (visual display units)) and lay down certain standards that must be adopted. The Display Screen Regulations are provided in order to make sure employees using computer equipment are working in a safe environment.

The computer, together with the desk it sits on, the computer operator's chair and the immediate surrounding area are known as a workstation. Under the 1992 regulations, the employer is required to carry out a regular check or analysis of workstations to ensure they comply with the regulations. The employee, in turn, should use the workstation correctly and inform the employer of any problems so that they can be corrected.

Your teacher will almost certainly show you a video on health and safety to make sure you understand how to work safely in an IT environment. Many of the things you learn from the video will stem from this legislation. Alternatively, you might like to check out the Microsoft® website that provides useful information. Go to www.heinemann.co.uk/hotlinks and click on Microsoft® health and safety.

> **Checkpoint**
>
> The **Display Screen Regulations** ensure that the health of those working with computer equipment is not put at risk.

The most common health-related problems that can result from using computers in the workplace are outlined below.

### Backache

There is an old saying 'Prevention is better than cure!' and there is certainly much you can do to prevent the risk of recurring backache. Your immediate working environment offers several ways to try and prevent health problems.

Desks should have a non-reflective surface and be at the correct height, with sufficient space for a computer, mouse mat, telephone and supporting documents. There should be enough space around the desk for you to change positions and vary your movements.

Bad posture is the main cause of backache and if an employee is working *continuously* at a VDU, he or she should be able to take a short break (say 5–10 minutes) away from the screen after an hour's *uninterrupted* screen or keyboard work. Ideally, the employee's job will involve a variety of tasks so that this situation should not arise in the first place.

The ideal working position is to sit with your eyes level with the top of the screen and your feet flat on the floor. Since we all come in different shapes and sizes, it is important to use a chair that can be adjusted to suit each of us. A suitable computer chair will probably have five feet with castors to increase stability and to allow freedom of movement. You will be able to adjust the height of the seat to suit your own height and also the position and tilt of the backrest in order to support your back. People who are short in height and whose feet don't reach the floor should ask for a footrest to be provided to support their feet.

Some form of exercise during lunch breaks (such as a walk or game of football) is a good way to help prevent or relieve backache.

## Eyestrain

Sitting in front of a VDU all day long can cause eyestrain or headaches and to avoid potential problems, an employer should offer free and regular eye tests to VDU operators. However, by following some simple guidelines yourself, you can do a lot to help look after your eyesight.

The first thing is to adjust your working position. The screen should tilt and swivel and be positioned approximately an arm's length away. Remember your eyes should be level with the top of the screen. The ideal position for the computer is at right angles to a window. In order to keep sun off the screen and help reduce glare, blinds should be provided at the windows. If glare is a problem, then an anti-glare shield can be fitted. The office should be well lit and the lighting should offer a contrast between the screen and surrounding area. If the light is too dim, documents will be hard to read.

The image on the screen should be stable and not flicker. In addition, the brightness and contrast on the screen should be adjustable. A copyholder at screen level will make it easier for you to move your eyes from the copy to the screen. Changes in activity will enable you to take your eyes off the screen and adjust the focus.

## Repetitive strain injury (RSI)

Repetitive strain injury (RSI) is the name given to disorders resulting from repeated movements. It is not a new disease and has affected workers performing repetitive movements for many years. Symptoms can affect the neck, shoulders and upper limbs, causing numbness and tingling in the arms and hands and in severe cases some sufferers cannot even lift a kettle or pour a cup of tea without experiencing unbearable pain.

To reduce the risk of RSI, keyboards should be separate from the VDU and should be designed to tilt. Look under your keyboard now. Does it have two small feet at the back that can be positioned up or down? The keyboard should have a matt surface and the symbols on the keys must be contrasted and legible. A wrist rest can be used to support the wrists. Alternatively, you could try an ergonomic keyboard which has been designed to place the hands at a more natural angle than the standard keyboard.

## Stress

For many people, the introduction of IT systems can be very worrying, especially if they have not been trained to use the equipment or reassured about the security of their jobs. Some workers fear their productivity will be monitored, putting their jobs at risk if they under-perform. To help reduce these problems it is important that the software provided should enable employees to complete their work efficiently without presenting unnecessary problems or obstacles.

## Radiation

From time to time, there have been concerns about the effects of radiation emitted from VDUs. In particular, it has been suggested that pregnant women are at risk of miscarriage as a result of exposure to this radiation. However, there is no conclusive medical evidence to support this and research suggests that the radiation from a VDU is actually less than that found in natural sources.

What you have just read is a brief summary of health and safety issues resulting from continuous use of IT equipment. However, the chance of any of these things happening to you is very slim providing you remember to adopt good working practices from the outset.

### Checkpoint

Get into the habit of checking your working position by adjusting your chair and screen before you start work at the computer.

## The Internet Code Of Practice

The Internet Code of Practice (ICOP) is a standard of practice designed to protect all Internet users – those who post information on the Internet and those who view it. It covers a wide range of topics and the following points give an outline of the content. (The full ICOP can be viewed through www.heinemann.co.uk/hotlinks – click on ICOP).

- **Audience** – information must be suitable for viewing by its target audience and should not cause offence. Pages aimed at children must not contain indecent material.
- **Advertising** – advertisements should show the corporate identity of the advertiser and the full postal address. Prices should clearly show additional charges such as postage and packing. Advertisements must be legal, honest and truthful and must not be misleading.
- **Copyright and information ownership** – permission must be obtained before links to other pages are provided and these links should be checked regularly to ensure they are still accessible. Publishers must ensure they have international permission to use copyright material they do not own, and information provided by people other than the publisher must be identified and credited to the original owner.
- **Information** – private data such as e-mail, network and postal addresses, telephone numbers, payment card details, and so on, must not be disclosed to third parties. Information must not deliberately mislead and publishers must disclose the use to which information collected by websites will be put. The download time for images must be kept to a minimum.

ISPs must ensure that their subscribers are aware of the codes of practice and they must investigate sites that do not conform, discontinuing service if serious breaches are discovered.

## Misuse of ICT

The Internet and the web have led to many benefits which even ten years ago would have been unheard of. For example, people can now communicate with ease with businesses and friends wherever they are in the world, they can shop online and buy goods from abroad, often at greatly reduced prices.

Unfortunately, these benefits have also led to an increase in fraud as new technology is not only speeding up transactions, but also making them increasingly anonymous.

**Fact file**

The British Chamber of Commerce, an association for small and medium-sized businesses in the UK, has warned that viruses, hacking and credit card fraud are costing companies millions a year.

There have always been 'get rich quick' schemes advertised in the press and now websites, e-mail, newsgroups and bulletin boards can also be used to carry out fraud. New, supposedly wonderful, business opportunities which require you to pay in advance for the tools to run the business, such as making jewellery, models or packing envelopes, are now advertised on the Internet and rarely fulfil their promises. It is perhaps worth remembering that if an opportunity sounds too good to be true, it probably is!

Most auction sites do their best to ensure that people putting items up for sale do not cheat the buyers. However, according to a report produced in 2002 by the Internet Fraud Complaint Centre in the USA, nearly half of all Internet fraud involves online auctions. Nearly 25 per cent of the complaints involved either non-delivery of goods or non-payment. In one well-publicised case of fraud, a British couple paid £4,700 at an Internet auction to an 18-year-old American student in Seattle for a Rolex watch, only to receive a photo of the watch instead!

Although the majority of companies offering people the opportunity to buy goods online are genuine, unfortunately there are some that are not, and some goods ordered online fail to arrive. It is therefore important to check that the company you are dealing with has a phone number and postal address. If possible, use only sites which have been recommended to you as reliable.

Businesses themselves can also be victims of fraud. People using stolen credit cards, false names and addresses and anonymous e-mail accounts can cost companies large sums of money.

## Bulletin boards and chat rooms

While the majority of messages posted on **bulletin boards** and in **chat rooms** are genuine, many are not.

There have been cases in the USA of people using bulletin boards and chat rooms to 'talk up' companies in which they hold shares, hoping that this will increase the share price. These people then sell their shares in order to make a quick profit, after which they stop talking up the shares and the share price often falls. This is known in financial circles as 'pumping and dumping'. 'Trashing and cashing' is the opposite. Here false or misleading messages are posted on bulletin boards and in chat rooms which hint that a company is running into financial problems. As a result of these rumours, the share price can drop, allowing the person who started the rumour to buy the shares cheaply and then benefit when the share price recovers once the rumours are found to be untrue.

A **chatroom** is a place on the world wide web where you can hold a typed conversation with someone anywhere in the world in real time.

## Unsolicited e-mails – spam

According to the National Consumers League, the main consumer lobby in the USA, 94 per cent of people responding to a survey said that they had received e-mails offering financial services or advertising money-making schemes such as the one shown in Figure 12.2.

Just as direct mail – sometimes called junk mail – is sent to many people to encourage them to sign up for new goods and services, e-mails are increasingly being used in this way. In some cases, bulk e-mailing is being used by unscrupulous people to get customers.

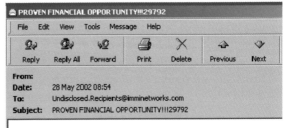

Figure 12.2 *Example of an unsolicited e-mail*

Junk e-mails are known as spam. A spam e-mail is an unsolicited mailing, usually to many people.

One example of e-mail fraud is the unlucky UK businessman who travelled to India to meet a non-existent client due to an e-mail hoax.

In 2002 the European Parliament passed the Electronic Communications Privacy Directive which has ruled that companies cannot send marketing e-mails unless the customer has agreed to receive them. However, 90 per cent of spam, like the one in Figure 12.3, comes from outside Europe, so spam is unlikely to stop in the foreseeable future.

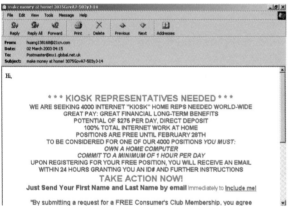

*Figure 12.3 Example of a spam e-mail*

## Spam do's and don'ts

- Never answer a spam e-mail. Even one hit among thousands of e-mail mailings is a reward and will encourage the creators of spam to continue.
- Never respond to instructions on a spam e-mail which indicate that you will be able to remove your e-mail address from the address list. This is normally just a trick and alerts the e-mail sender that your e-mail address is active. Your address will then be placed on more lists and you will receive more spam.
- Websites that promise to remove your address from spam lists are often spam address collectors – ignore them.
- Use the block facility of your e-mail software, or buy software to filter spam.

## Computer viruses

A computer system can become infected from **computer viruses**:

- through downloading software from the Internet
- from an attachment to an e-mail
- through transfer from one computer to another via a floppy disk
- through using pirate software which is infected.

### Checkpoint

A **computer virus** is a program written specifically to attack computer software and data. Viruses can spread, or multiply, very quickly.

There are currently more than 53,000 known computer viruses. One of the dangers the Internet has introduced is the speed with which damaging programs or viruses can be spread via e-mail. You usually don't know that your system has a virus until things start to go wrong.

Most organisations treat the risks of infection very seriously, controlling e-mails being sent and received over the Internet and not allowing staff to take disks between work and home and vice versa. Anti-virus software is therefore essential.

## Anti-virus software

Anti-virus software works by scanning files to detect (spot) and remove viruses from hard and floppy disks. The process of removing a virus is known as disinfecting. It is very important that the anti-virus software is up-to-date. New viruses are continually being written and they could miss detection by out-of-date anti-virus software. Virus writers are locked in an endless battle to try to beat the anti-virus and security companies. As soon as a new virus appears, anti-virus companies work to produce a 'pattern' file that tells their software how to spot and stop the virus. Often a successful virus will lead to other people producing copycat viruses that differ only slightly from the original.

### Fact file

The 'I Love You' virus caused more than £7 million damage worldwide by infecting about 45 million computers!

## Misuse of personal information

The increasing use of ICT in our daily lives has also led to an increased misuse of personal information. One of the main aims of the Data Protection Act 1998 is to prevent misuse of personal information, but nevertheless such misuse still occurs. According to the Information Commissioner for the Data Protection Act, nearly three-quarters of all adults in the UK are worried about the amount of personal details being stored electronically by companies and organisations and in 2000–1 8,875 people complained about alleged breaches of data protection.

Think of the times you have completed an application form and have given your personal details. It could be to join a club or place an order for a product. Nowadays, most of this information will be stored on a computer on huge databases. Once collected, the data can be transferred very easily to other computers. Although in the majority of cases the data are used correctly and within the terms of the Data Protection Act, this is not always the case. Mistakes can also happen and one person's details can be muddled with those of someone else. There are even companies that will sell or rent the information held on their databases to third parties.

The Information Commissioner has recently undertaken a study of how information is collected on websites and has found that many did not act in line with the Data Protection Act. It is not only small companies that do not comply with legislation put in place to protect the consumer. At the time of writing, the European Commission was investigating Microsoft® because some people were concerned that the way Microsoft® collected personal information might break privacy laws.

### Activity

▷ Print the file: **LEG Worksheet 1** from the Chapter 13 folder on the CD-ROM. This worksheet requires you to investigate the privacy policy for a number of websites.

# Chapter 14

# ICT in personal communications and community activities

This chapter looks at how ICT has affected daily life, for example:

- the Internet
- mobile phones
- entertainment and leisure
- education and lifelong learning.

It also looks at the way ICT is used in community activities, for example:

- cyber cafés
- public libraries
- on-line discussion forums
- information services
- travel information
- satellite positioning systems.

## What you will learn

ICT and personal communications

ICT in community activities

## Overview

Throughout this unit, you have been looking at ICT and the Internet and how it has affected working lives and businesses. As a result of the changes in technologies, how people go about their daily lives has greatly changed. We are now able to do things that would have been unheard of even 10 years ago. This chapter looks at how ICT has affected personal communications and how ICT is used in community activities.

## ICT and personal communications

### Interactive digital TV

You learned in Chapter 11 about how digital TV is the way forward in broadcasting and is having a major impact on the way we

communicate. The BBC offers, for example, a range of interactive services called BBCi. During the 2002 Commonwealth Games, if you were lucky enough to have access to BBCi, you could choose which sport to watch and have access to constantly updated news.

**Digital broadcasting** has allowed the cable company Telewest to be involved in a number of projects to test a new concept called iSeeTV (see Figure 14.1). iSeeTV allows customers to speak to and see company representatives without leaving their home. The software enables customers to see call centre staff on their television while they talk to them on the phone. During the pilot, Iceland, the frozen food retailer, joined up with Telewest allowing customers in Birmingham to talk to an onscreen 'personal shopper' who was able to answer queries, talk about payment options and tell the customer of special offers and available products.

Similarly, the financial services company, AMP Pearl, took part in the trial with Telewest using iSeeTV, to offer financial advice to Birmingham customers in the comfort of their home. This is a more economic way of reaching customers than the traditional home visit by a representative. An advantage of using iSeeTV is that the customer can end a session simply by pressing the off button on his or her remote control.

*Figure 14.1  The iSeeTV website*

Debenhams was the third retailer to participate in the pilot, reaching customers in an area where they did not have a store. The advantage for customers is that they feel that they are speaking to a real person – which they are – and they can see product demonstrations, watch video clips about products and record the session for viewing later.

Not only can Telewest customers in the Birmingham area buy goods, they can also talk to NHS Direct nurses to obtain advice on health matters. During the nine-month pilot, this service had up to 150 requests for live consultations each week and was reported to be growing in popularity. The advantage to patients is that they can receive personal advice out of normal doctor's surgery hours.

## Checkpoint

**Digital broadcasting** refers to television and radio signals which are changed into computerised signals and which are decoded at the receiving end.

## The Internet

The Internet has opened up the world. When you shop on the Internet, the location of the shop does not matter. Often shopping online can mean that you have access to 'Internet-only' special offers. Amazon Books is an example of a major success story for online shopping. Amazon began in the USA with only a website and a warehouse. It now has a website in the UK where you will find just about any book you can think of! To see it, go to www.heinemann.co.uk/hotlinks and click on Amazon. Because Amazon has fewer running costs than a high street book shop, such as premises, heating, sales staff, it is able to offer books at a lower price.

## Fact file

In 2000, online purchases accounted for only 0.66 per cent of retail sales. They are estimated to increase to 5 per cent by 2005.

When shopping online you can purchase goods from anywhere in the world. CDs, for example, are often much cheaper in the USA. Be warned though, although goods can be cheaper abroad, you will have to pay for import duty and VAT if you spend more than £18, including post and packaging. International packages must have a standard label giving the value and type of goods so that Customs and Excise know how much import duty and VAT to charge. This is collected by the Post Office when it delivers the goods, the Post Office adding its own fee for doing this. You therefore have to be very careful to calculate that these extra costs do not wipe out any savings you may have made by buying the goods abroad rather than in the UK.

Although many people still worry about fraud when shopping over the Internet, in practice, it rarely happens. So long as you are careful and only make purchases from secure sites, buying over the Internet is as safe as using credit or debit cards in a shop or over the phone.

## Tips for shopping online

- Compare prices on a number of sites, bearing in mind any additional costs such as postage or import duties.
- Only buy from companies you have heard of. If you haven't heard of the company, ask if any of your friends know of it, search the Internet for more references to the company, or even ask about it in a relevant newsgroup.
- Keep careful records of confirmation messages, adverts and e-mails by printing them out.
- Always ask for the delivery time and if you do not receive a confirmation of your order, e-mail and ask for one.
- Make sure that you know the telephone number and postal address of the organisation. It is easier to protect your rights if you are using a UK site, but remember that a website with .uk in its domain name does not necessarily mean it is a company based in the UK.
- Credit cards give extra protection for purchases over £100.

## Disadvantages of online shopping

- It is not possible to try on clothing that you may be buying, unlike in a shop where you can check to make sure that it fits properly and you are happy with the appearance.
- It is still necessary to make arrangements for the delivery of items. For people out at work all day, this can be inconvenient as goods are often only delivered during weekdays, 9.00 am – 5.00 pm.
- When buying groceries, many people still like to choose their own to make sure that the vegetables, for example, are fresh and firm or that the goods are not damaged.
- It is not possible to pay with cash or by cheque, so the buyer must have either a credit or debit card.
- Some people are concerned about security.

## Online auctions

Buying and selling goods through online auctions has become increasingly popular, the largest and best known auction site being eBay. To see it, go to www.heinemann.co.uk/hotlinks and click on eBay. You learned about the misuse of ICT in Chapter 13, so bear in mind that if you are tempted to bid for an item, read the description carefully to ensure that what you are bidding for is actually what you want when making a bid.

### Mobile phones

Mobile phones have been of great benefit to anyone 'on the move' such as lorry drivers, sales representatives, managers, and so on. They can be lifesavers in emergency situations or just give people confidence that if they breakdown in their car, help is only as far away as the touch of a few buttons.

Of course, some people see mobile phones as a nuisance, especially when they are used in public places such as restaurants or ring in places like the cinema. It is quite common when travelling home from work, school or college to hear someone holding a long conversation on his or her mobile phone. This can be irritating, and it is now possible when going on a long train journey to book seats in 'mobile free' carriages. In these carriages mobile phone owners must switch off their phones so that they do not disturb their fellow passengers.

**SMS** technology (text messaging) has allowed people to keep in contact with each other very easily and is also being used in business to improve communications. For example, a theme park queue management system has been developed using SMS and Alton Towers uses this service to help visitors make the most of their day by organising personal ride times. Visitors buy a voucher and then send an SMS message with the code on the voucher to the system. They then receive their schedule for popular rides within a few minutes.

**WAP** and WAP2 technology will allow the user to access the Internet 'on the move'.

Despite the many advantages of mobile phones, there are disadvantages:

- Mobile phones can be a nuisance if used in public places.
- The cost of the phone calls is high compared with phone calls made on a land line. It is also expensive to use a mobile phone to ring home while abroad.
- There is some concern that there may be possible health risks, both from using a mobile phone or from living close to a mobile phone mast.

## Entertainment and leisure

CD-ROM drives are the norm when buying a PC, and CD-ROM disks offer a wide choice of multimedia software designed for leisure interests. Most computer games are now supplied on CD-ROMs rather than on a floppy disk, and you may well have a selection of CD-ROMs to help you with your GCSEs. Special multimedia software, for example the plug-in **MP3**, has resulted in people being able to enjoy music over the Internet. You might already have your own portable MP3 player or have a MiniDisc player on which you play your favourite sounds.

Whereas a few years ago it would have been unheard of to watch a film using a DVD player, or through a PC, today this is becoming increasingly popular.

As technology develops, so our demands on the technology increase. When computer games were first available, a special tape drive was needed and games would take a long time to load. The graphics used with the games were very simple, for example Pacman. Nowadays, games have become very realistic, using 3D graphics, and they only take a few seconds to load. It is possible to play games with people from all over the world over the Internet, and some of these games require players to pay a monthly subscription for access to the servers to allow them to take part. People form groups and will play together either among themselves or against other groups.

DVDs are still mainly used for films. However, it is possible to buy games and other software using this format which offers more storage space and removes the need for several CD-ROMs. Games and other software on DVD format are currently not widespread, but within a few years this is likely to change.

It is increasingly common for young people to spend many hours at their computers, either playing games, e-mailing their friends or surfing the Internet. There has been some controversy over this as many of the games played contain violence that does not represent normal social behaviour. As a result, some young people are losing important interactive social skills and are at risk of becoming locked in an isolated cyber world. More children are becoming obese through lack of exercise and experiencing health problems at an earlier age than would normally be expected.

## Education and lifelong learning

Computers in education have been around since the 1980s – although the computers of today aren't much like the first computers used in schools and colleges. In fact, the rapid changes in technology and the cost of upgrading hardware and software mean that some schools and colleges find it hard to keep up-to-date. Even so, there are growing numbers of computers in schools and colleges. This is because the government has set a target – to be achieved by 2004 – of at least one computer per eight pupils in each primary school and one computer per five students in each secondary school. In 1994 there was only one computer per 23 primary school pupils and one computer per ten secondary school students.

Teachers are now able to access resources on the government's initiative, Curriculum Online, a concept which will be extended to colleges via College Online in the near future. Go to www.heinemann.co.uk/hotlinks and click on Curriculum online. In 2003 it was announced that the government had approved the development of the BBC Digital Curriculum to complement Curriculum Online so that teachers can access free as well as priced digital learning materials to help deliver their courses.

## Computer skills

Computer skills are essential both for your school or college and future business life. Word processing, graphics, desktop publishing and spreadsheet software are widely used in the preparation of school projects and coursework. CD-ROM resources, such as multimedia encyclopaedias containing textual information, pictures, video and sound clips, help students to research school projects.

## E-learning

Computer-aided learning packages mean that students can learn at their own pace and can repeat lessons/exercises as often as is necessary. They also offer students the opportunity to study additional subjects when a specialist teacher is not available. However, learning without the aid of a teacher by sitting at a computer screen can be boring. On the other hand, you might find yourself turning to an online teacher to help you with homework or revision for your examinations.

Before the Internet, if people wanted to study, they either went to school, college or evening classes, or enrolled on correspondence courses where they could study in their own homes. Correspondence courses could make the student feel very isolated and did not give immediate feedback. Now, the Internet has built a global community, so through the Internet you can join a community of students studying from London to Los Angeles to exchange ideas, tips and anything to support your studies.

The Internet is increasingly being used in education. Latest statistics from the government show that whereas only 17 per cent of primary schools, 83 per cent of secondary schools and 31 per cent of special schools in the UK were connected to the Internet in 1997, by 2002 over 99 per cent of *all* schools were online (see Figure 14.2).

The BBC's website provides useful materials to help you with your studies – this is an example of online learning. Go to www.heinemann.co.uk/hotlinks and click on BBC. A new term has been coined to describe online learning and learning from computer-aided packages – **e-learning** – the 'e' standing for electronic.

An example of online learning is the government's initiative, Learndirect (see Figure 14.3). Students of all ages can register and take courses from home, at a Learndirect centre or wherever they can access the Internet. The

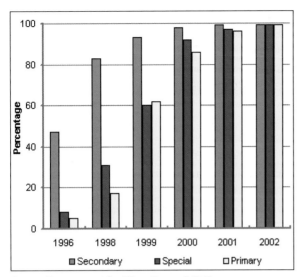

*Source:* Department for Education and Skills

*Figure 14.2  Percentage of schools connected to the Internet*

## Checkpoint

**E-learning** refers to learning through electronic sources. Examples of ways of e-learning are via the Internet, an intranet or an extranet, computer-based learning using a CD-ROM or software package, learning via satellite broadcasting or interactive TV.

## Researching on the Internet

The Internet is also a valuable source of up-to-date information for students when researching projects, but it must be used with caution. You learned in Unit 1 how to search the Internet – sometimes a search can bring up thousands of possible links and it can be quite hard to narrow it down. Follow the tips given in Unit 1 to help you to get the most from the Internet. It means that you do not have to visit the library; you can do a large part of your research on the Internet, but don't forget the issue of copyright.

## What will the classroom of the future look like?

The National Grid for Learning was launched by the government in 1998 with the aim of improving ICT provision in schools. It involves the development of a wide range of digital resources for teaching and learning. As a result of this project, many initiatives have been developed – your school or college is very likely to be taking part.

An example of one such project is the London Grid for Learning, and there are many more throughout the UK. The London Grid for Learning (NGfL) consists of 33 London boroughs that have got together to form an intranet for all London schools at very fast broadband connections – see Figure 14.4. It provides students with the opportunity to develop skills in using the Internet and e-mail while controlling the material available to them and preventing access to unsuitable sites.

Through the NGfL, students can access material from every subject at every level. They

advantage of online learning is that you do not have to attend a college or school, but can study in the comfort of your own home. Learndirect courses are broken down into small bite-sized chunks so that if you are busy, you can still fit a little time to do some online learning – some Learndirect courses take just 15 minutes!

The Continuing Education & Training Services has more than 800 students studying on Learndirect courses – see Unit 1, Chapter 6 (page 85).

*Figure 14.3  The **learndirect** home page is shown with the permission of Ufi Ltd. **learndirect** is a trade mark of Ufi Ltd.*

*Figure 14.4 London Grid for Learning home page*

the classroom of the future. Thirty schools are to be involved in the project where every teacher will be given his or her own notebook PC, Internet access, lesson planning software and other high-tech teaching aids. The schools involved will also develop other new classroom practices using new technologies such as using interactive boards.

Many schools are now moving to wireless networks so that students can use laptop computers in any classroom and not be restricted to certain computer rooms. So you can see ICT is having a major effect on how your lessons are taught and when and where you can take part in learning.

can use the NGfL anywhere they can access the Internet – at school, in the public library, at home, through the TV, even on holiday if they want! Every student has his or her own e-mail address on the London Grid and has a computer work folder, personal to them. Teachers are able to put work into students' folders with a couple of clicks. Teachers are also able to set up online discussions groups and be able to monitor them. It will soon also be possible to download video clips and take part in **video conferencing**. This means that if a student has to go into hospital for a long period, they can still take part in lessons through video conferencing and the worry of falling behind with their school work is avoided.

At the beginning of 2002, the government announced a new 12-month project to develop

## Checkpoint

**Video conferencing** – sometimes called teleconferencing – is a means of holding meetings and discussions between people in distant locations by way of video links made through computer systems.

## Find out …

Is your school or college linking in with other schools or colleges in a 'Grid for Learning'?

## ● Snapshot

### A day in the life of …

… a pupil in a secondary school that is effectively integrating e-learning with traditional learning techniques.

Uzman arrives in school at 8.30 and goes straight to the open learning area. He logs on to retrieve some marked homework ready for today's English lesson. Last night he completed two homework assignments on his home computer and stored these in his user

area on the school system. His friend Jenny had also done the same, but had borrowed one of the school's laptops as she has no computer at home. As they look at their marked homework they discuss what they did for last night's assignments.

After assembly, first period is GNVQ Science, in which digital learning materials on the school's intranet feature prominently. Currently pupils are working through these in a three-week block. Uzman works independently on the unit on physical forces and regularly discusses his experiences with other pupils doing this topic through a virtual learning community of which he is a member. However, he knows that he can e-mail his science teacher to seek help with any assessment tasks he has not understood. He also knows that, for this lesson, the teacher has prioritised direct support for another group of pupils who are having rather more difficulty with some of the ideas than he is.

Second lesson is Geography – a straightforward traditional lesson on volcanoes with no ICT except that the teacher uses the digital projector to show digitised news footage of a volcano that had erupted the previous day in Hawaii and provides the class with three websites for the pupils to explore either at home or in the open resource centre after school. The pupils have to identify the gaps in the information provided on these sites and then identify further sites and later on give a presentation in groups, using the interactive whiteboard.

Fourth period and it's off to the D&T workshop where Uzman's group is currently working on a CAD/CAM project using a sophisticated design package. Uzman gets into a discussion with the teacher and three other pupils about the design of the photograph frames they are working on. The teacher tries to get the group to develop their designs so that they are more adventurous and unusual. As a result of this, Uzman goes to one of the available machines and tries out various changes to his design. He stores these in his user area and decides to look at them later, working from home.

Uzman is following a GCSE short course in ICT and this comes next. The class is currently working on the validity and bias of data. The lesson takes place in an ordinary classroom where the teacher has access to a fixed computer on the network and the Internet. Using digital projection facilities, the teacher visits a site for an environmental lobby group and compares this with a government site on global warming. A lively discussion ensues and the class works in small groups to identify what clues to look for in a website address and in the content available on entry to the site.

The school operates a Seventh Period session in which pupils can voluntarily follow the activity of their choice. This includes a range of clubs and other extra-curricular activities. Uzman goes to the 'ICT for all' club where he is working with three other pupils on the development of parts of the school's website. They are creating pages about the school's sports teams and are including digital video clips that they have filmed and edited.

*Source:* From 'Transforming the Way We Learn', Department for Education and Skills, 2002.

## ICT in community activities

### Cyber cafés

For people who do not have an Internet connection at home, it is still possible to access the Internet, using a public Internet terminal such as BT's new multi.phone which allows the user to connect to the Internet in the same way as you would go to a pay phone to make a telephone call.

Another way to access the Internet is at a cyber café, where for a charge, you can use a computer to surf the Internet, check e-mail or chat with someone in a chat room.

**Fact file**

If you are going on holiday and you want to keep in touch with your friends through a cyber café, there is a Cybercafe search engine to help you find the nearest one – see Figure 14.5. Go to www.heinemann.co.uk/hotlinks and click on Cybercaf to see a list of over 6100 cyber cafés throughout the world. It will even give you advice on how to set one up! You can also find details of public Internet access points and kiosks in over 160 countries.

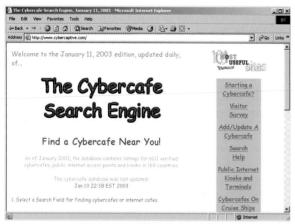

*Figure 14.5 The Cybercafe search engine*

**Find out …**

Use the Internet to find out the nearest cyber café to your school or college. Investigate how much it costs and what facilities are available.

**Fact file**

Students in the Philippines used computers at a cyber café to create the 'I Love You' virus. Technology was used to track down the source of the original e-mail.

## Chat rooms

A chat room allows you to hold typed conversations with people throughout the world in real time. Unlike e-mail, where you have to wait for a person to log on, check the mail box and then send a reply, chat rooms are where several people meet online to discuss a common interest. Websites often provide lists of chat rooms available, and also provide the opportunity to create a new chat room and invite other like-minded people to join.

There has been a great deal of concern about chat rooms. In March 2001, the Internet Crime Forum recommended the creation of a kite marking programme for chat rooms in an attempt to prevent them being used by dishonest people. However, if used sensibly, they offer an ideal way of chatting to people throughout the world. Many businesses with representatives in different locations sometimes use chat rooms to hold meetings. Some universities and colleges put teachers in chat rooms, where they are available to support students with their studies online.

## Watch out!

- Remember, if you are using chat rooms that people may not be who they say they are. Users of chat rooms usually use a nickname, rather than their own name.
- Never give out personal details such as your address or telephone number to people using a chat room.
- NEVER arrange to meet someone you have 'met' through the Internet. There have been several cases of older people posing as teenagers in chat rooms.

If you take the above precautions, then chat rooms can be a useful source of information and fun.

## Newsgroups

These are similar to chat rooms, but whereas chat rooms are 'real time', newsgroups are discussion areas on the Internet, where you can post a message and read replies from other people. Some colleges have created newsgroups for students studying on a particular course, where students can post a message and obtain support from other students. Newsgroups are ideal places to share common interests, debate issues, or help you solve a particular technical problem. Newsgroups are accessed through your ISP.

Some newsgroups have people responsible for checking incoming messages and deciding whether or not they are suitable for posting on the newsgroup. These newsgroups are called **moderated** newsgroups and have the advantage that discussions tend to be relevant to the topic. **Unmoderated** groups sometimes offer irrelevant and misleading information.

Newsgroups are particularly useful if you want to solve a particular problem, for example finding out where you can buy a discontinued product, asking advice on a medical problem, solving computer-related problems. There is almost certainly going to be a newsgroup to suit your purpose.

## Discussion boards

A discussion board is the name given to any on-line bulletin board or forum where you can leave messages and expect to see responses. Responses to messages are often sent direct to members' own e-mail addresses. Like Newsgroups, these are ideal places to share common interests and ask like-minded people for their views on topical issues.

Newsgroups, chat rooms and discussion forums can be used to generate support for topical issues. A message can be posted to encourage members of groups to e-mail their MP to lobby his/her support for current debate. An example of this in recent years was the fuel crisis in 2000 when technology helped lorry drivers to co-ordinate their protest.

## ICQ (I Seek You)

ICQ software will enable you to take part in instant messaging without having to go to a chat room. The software will let you know if any of your friends are online and you can then have a real time chat. ICQ software can be downloaded for free – go to www.heinemann.co.uk/hotlinks and click on ICQ. When you first install the program you will be given your own unique ICQ number. You will be able to use the searchable directory so you can search for people to chat to who might have similar interests.

## Information services

Even before you started your ICT GCSE course, you were probably aware of the huge potential for finding information using ICT. You may have heard of UK Online, but what is it? UK Online (Figure 14.6) is an initiative that aims to ensure that all government services are available electronically by 2005. It works to

meet the Prime Minister's target for internet access for all who want it and supports work across the government to develop the UK as a world leader for electronic business. To see it, go to www.heinemann.co.uk/hotlinks and click on UK Online. Using this site, you can link to over 900 different government websites to find the information you are looking for. For example, in the future you may wish to research for a suitable course to study at university. You will find that there is a link on the UK Online government website to make your search easier and quicker.

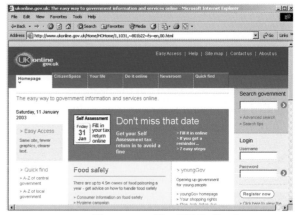

*Figure 14.6  The UK Online home page*

At the beginning of 2003 there were 6000 UK Online centres where anyone can access the Internet. The centres can be in a public library, in a college, in a community centre, a village hall, in an Internet café and some may even be mobile centres.

Libraries have a wide range of CD-ROMs such as encyclopedias available – these are very useful when undertaking research for your studies.

## ● Snapshot

### The Internet Bus

In Peterborough a specially equipped 'Internet Bus' started its rounds in January 2003 taking ICT directly to the more disadvantaged areas of the town. It is a purpose-built UK Online Internet mobile centre which will give people in the local community the opportunity to take part in introductory sessions using the Internet in a very informal setting.

Linked to this government initiative is another called 'The People's Network'. This initiative is to ensure that there is an ICT learning centre in every UK public library and that local libraries have the latest state-of-the-art computer technology to make the Internet accessible to everyone in the community. By the beginning of 2003, 71 per cent of all public libraries were online.

## Activity

▶ Print the file: **PC Worksheet 1** from the Chapter 14 folder on the CD-ROM. This worksheet will help you to find out more about ICT facilities available at your local library.

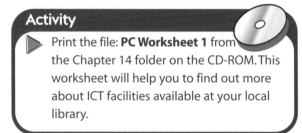

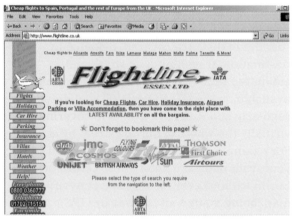

*Figure 14.7 Flightline is a specialist website offering travellers flights, car hire, accommodation, and so on*

## Public transport and travel information

In the days before the world wide web, if you needed to book a train ticket or plan your train journey, you would probably have either gone to the local railway station or rung a special telephone number for train times. The Internet has simplified this process – not only can you check train times easily via the Internet, you can book your ticket via websites, for example The Trainline. Go to www.heinemann.co.uk/hotlinks and click on The Trainline.

It is now possible to plan almost any journey from the comfort of your own home. As a result, more and more people are arranging 'do-it-yourself' holidays abroad, rather than going to a travel agent. There are specialist websites such as Flightline (go to www.heinemann.co.uk/hotlinks and click on Flightline) to book flights, car hire, accommodation and any other services required to enjoy a holiday abroad.

It is also possible to surf the Internet looking for privately owned holiday accommodation on sites such as Costablanca holidays and book direct with the owners. (For an example, go to www.heinemann.co.uk/hotlinks and click on Costa Blanca holidays.)

A growing number of small travel agents have been forced to close as the increase in

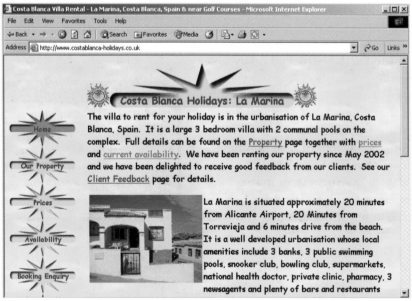

*Figure 14.8 A website offering privately owned holiday accommodation for rent*

people making their own travel arrangements has affected the travel agency industry. However, some people may worry that the accommodation booked may not exist and so will prefer to use the services of a travel agent.

## Activity

▷ Print the file: **PC Worksheet 2**
▷ from the Chapter 14 folder on the CD-ROM. This worksheet asks you to investigate the cost of holidays via the Internet and via travel agents.

## Satellite navigation

In 1995 the US government launched into orbit the last of 24 positioning satellites. A **Global Positioning System (GPS)** receiver can 'see' at least several satellites in the sky at any one time from *any* point on Earth. This means that the GPS receiver can usually pinpoint a user's position to within a metre or so in seconds. This technology has been invaluable in outdoor pursuits such as sailing where accurate navigation is crucial.

Finding your way around by car has traditionally been done by reading maps. Now, thanks to GPS technology, there is a much easier way. Today, most car manufacturers offer a model in their range that is fitted with satellite navigation. This consists of a small TV screen mounted on the dashboard that displays an electronic map and is linked to a computer and a tiny satellite receiver. Signals from satellites circling the Earth are picked up by the receiver, the information is converted via a computer into data which plots exactly where the vehicle is on the ground. This data is then translated to show the position on the electronic map on the dashboard. The mapping technology is based on a CD-ROM or DVD which contains details of every street in the country, so to get from A to B all the driver needs to do is type in his or her starting and finishing points, the computer will work out the route and guide the driver with clear voice commands to the destination. This will be backed up by the electronic map clearly showing the vehicle's position all the time.

Other added benefits are that the CD contains a massive database of other information such as railway stations, airports, hotels, restaurants, petrol stations and car parks. For example, if the vehicle was running low on fuel, the driver could request the system to locate the nearest petrol station and guide the driver there.

A recent enhancement to the system is Traffic Management Control – TMC. With TMC, the computer constantly monitors traffic information and if the computer detects a delay ahead, it will offer the driver the choice of an alternative route to get around the problem. The screen also gives a very accurate readout of distance covered, distance to destination, travelling time so far and estimated time of arrival. The information available on the CD-ROM/DVD is updated regularly and disks are available covering virtually the whole of Europe street by street. For example, it is possible to be directed from your front door to a hotel in the centre of Berlin without ever looking at a conventional map, being guided all the way by GPS!

In Unit 1, Chapter 6 you can find out how Computer Cab, a London-based taxi company, uses satellite navigation to run its business (page 92). You can also learn about the advantages of using satellite navigation when travelling on holiday (page 90).

## Checkpoint

**GPS (Global Positioning System)** makes it possible for people with ground receivers to pinpoint their geographic location. The system is owned and operated by the US Department of Defence but is available for use around the world.

# Chapter 15

# ICT and people with special needs

This chapter looks at ICT and people with special needs. You will learn how ICT technology and specially-adapted hardware can improve communication for those with:

- sensory impairment
- limited mobility
- physical or multiple disabilities
- learning or language difficulties.

## What you will learn

Environmental control systems
Visual impairment
Hearing impairment
Physical and mobility disabilities
Other special needs

## Overview

Did you know that there are 2 million people in the UK who are either blind or have very limited vision and that one in seven people in the UK has some form of hearing loss? Many people with special needs, for example the disabled or the visually impaired, are now able to enjoy an improved quality of life due to huge advances in the use of ICT. This chapter looks at how ICT can help people with special needs.

## Environmental control systems

Environmental control systems refer to special equipment that enables people with disabilities or special needs to control their environment where they find it difficult to use standard methods of control. For example, some people find day-to-day tasks such as turning lights on

and off, opening windows, using a television or CD remote control impossible.

With the help of switches, a simple action made by a person can make something happen. Figure 15.1 shows one type of switch which can be used to turn on such things as a lamp or radio. Some switches need to be pressed down, others need only to be touched and others simply need a person to move close to them to activate them. Switches may be used by people who have one or several disabilities.

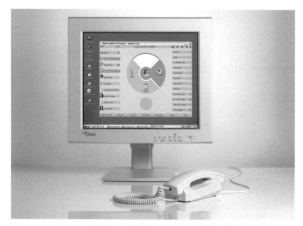

*Figure 15.1 A voice activated computer*

There are even very specialised switches that can be operated by puffs or sips of air or electrical activity within muscles.

Special devices such as the Sicare Pilot can be used to control and operate a wide range of appliances by using voice recognition or even a wink of the eye. A disabled person can program the device in order to do such things as answer and dial the phone, turn lights on and off and open curtains and windows.

Special door systems can be installed in the home of someone with physical disabilities which enable them to open and shut doors by using a voice command, winking or touching a remote control switch.

These environmental control systems allow a person with disabilities or special needs to carry out day-to-day tasks and lead as normal a life as possible.

## Visual impairment

Shut your eyes for a moment – can you imagine how you would undertake all the normal tasks that you take for granted? How can ICT help the blind or visually impaired? In many cases hardware or software can be adapted in order to make it useable by someone with partial or no sight. For example, common word processing applications and computer operating systems such as Windows 2000 and Office 2000 include options that enable the user to customise how the screen looks, make text larger, alter the resolution and reverse the contrast, change the colour, and so on, to make the screen easier to read.

In addition, specialist equipment is available which has been designed for use by people with visual impairment, for example the Siemens/ALVA mobile phone organiser. This equipment is known as **access technology**.

*Figure 15.2 Siemens/ALVA mobile phone organiser*

### Braille translation software

Blind people and people with very poor sight may use **Braille** to communicate.

Braille translation software can be used to translate words and figures which are input in Braille into a text version, or translate text into Braille. An electronic Braille display is a device which can be placed under a normal computer keyboard and allows the user to read the contents of the computer screen by touch in Braille. Braille embossers connect to a computer in the same way as a printer and will print Braille output from a computer by punching dots onto paper (see Figure 15.3). **Optical character recognition (OCR)** software can be used to scan text into a computer and then either converted to Braille, enlarged on screen or 'read' aloud by a speech synthesiser attached to the computer.

*Figure 15.3 A Braille embosser*

### Screen magnification software

For the partially sighted, screen magnification software can by used to magnify the output on the monitor up to 32 times. As this increases the size of the image on the screen, a large monitor is usually used as well as the screen magnification software.

## Speech output and voice recognition software

Speech output software is a special program which enables text displayed on a screen to be spoken by a speech synthesiser. A screen reader is a very sophisticated tool which allows the contents of a screen (menus, dialogue boxes, tool tips, and so on) to be read out and will enable a visually impaired person to have access to a computer.

Whereas speech output software talks to the user, voice recognition software enables users to speak to their computer and produce a correctly spelt document.

## Video magnifiers

Closed-circuit televisions (CCTVs) or video magnifiers can be used as a magnifying aid for people with some vision. Printer material and objects are placed under a camera and the magnified image is displayed on a computer monitor or television screen (see Figure 15.4).

*Figure 15.4 A video magnifier*

## Accessing the web

Using access technology, visually impaired people with limited or no sight can use the Internet to access the web. However, it is important that websites are designed properly and that a text alternative exists for every non-text element, for example graphics, on the web page. The Web Accessibility Initiative (WAI), part of the World Wide Web Consortium (W3C), publishes web content accessibility guidelines which, if followed, will ensure that a website has a good standard of accessibility to all users, including those with special needs.

### Fact file

The supermarket chain Tesco has a special website, which allows customers who are visually impaired, or who use access technologies such as a voice screen reader, or who wish to override the default font sizes and page colours so it is clearer to their eyes, to easily access online shopping. Go to www.heinemann.co.uk/ hotlinks and click on Tesco.

### ●Snapshot

**Bill, student**

Bill is partially sighted and finds reading large amounts of print difficult. He is studying for a diploma in Aromatherapy and Alternative Therapies. Bill uses a video magnifier to read printed material and look at diagrams. The video magnifier was the first piece of equipment Bill acquired, and because he needed little training he was making use of it within minutes of it being delivered.

'Getting to grips with the computer was a longer process, as I had never used one before my sight deteriorated. Now I use a combination of screen magnification and speech output for word processing and the Internet.'

Using his computer on the Internet Bill is able to research the therapy products available through specialist suppliers, and uses the information in his studies.

'I have also joined discussion groups using the e-mail system, and have learned a lot just reading the messages that people send in.'

*Source:* RNIB website, 'Accessing Technology': Go to www.heinemann.co.uk/hotlinks and click on RNIB.

Steve is a Customer Services Adviser at the RAC Call Centre. Before he joined the RAC in 1997 he had not used computers or access technology at all.

'The absence of this equipment limited the range of computer-based tasks that I could do and so, I was, to a point reliant on my colleagues' help. The application of access technology has completely revolutionised that way in which I work. Jaws for Windows enables me to navigate the various screens, whilst I discuss everything from an enrolment to a breakdown with a member.'

Steve was worried at first that using speech output whilst working would make him less efficient than his sighted colleagues.

'Before I started this job I did have some reservations about my ability to meet the high standards of performance set out by my employer. But I have no difficulty in listening to the speech output whilst holding a telephone conversation and my overall performance is amongst the highest in the call centre. The technology I use allows me to operate on the same basis as my sighted colleagues. I am extremely pleased that I am able to do a job of this nature, especially as just a few short years ago the absence of this technology would have prevented me from working in this and many other areas.'

*Source:* RNIB website, 'Accessing Technology': Go to www.heinemann.co.uk/hotlinks and click on RNIB.

## Fact file

A blind man is suing South West and American airlines because their websites are incompatible with the software he uses to convert website content into speech.

## Activity

▷ Print the file: **SN Worksheet 1**
▷ from the Chapter 15 folder on the CD-ROM. This worksheet requires you to investigate the special devices available to help a partially sighted person.

## Hearing impairment

Imagine living in a world with little or no sound. How would you know if the telephone is ringing, or if an alarm is sounding? ICT plays an important role in assisting people with a hearing impairment in their day-to-day lives.

The use of e-mail and text messages (SMS) on mobile phones has opened up a new world of communication to the hard of hearing. In schools and colleges, ICT can be used so that students are not dependent on the spoken word. For example, interactive whiteboards are an ideal demonstration tool because students can see what is happening without the need to listen and interpret instructions.

A whole range of technology has been developed to assist the hard of hearing. Special devices are available that can be used around the home to alert the hard of hearing to such sounds as the doorbell, telephone, smoke detector, burglar alarm or even a crying baby. Most of these devices will use extra loud audible alarms, flashing lights or vibration to alert the person. Transmitters are placed close to whichever sounds the person wishes to monitor such as a telephone, a baby sleeping in a cot, the door bell, and so on. When a transmitter picks up a sound it will activate one of a series of small lights or a vibrating alert on a pager that the person is carrying around with him or her (see Figure 15.5).

Telephones can be purchased which can amplify incoming or outgoing speech, adjust the pitch and volume of the ringer, and often have an indicator which shows when there is an incoming call.

BT has recently launched videophones which will allow deaf people to communicate using sign language. The phones can even be connected to a TV to enable large screen viewing. This feature will be of particular help to deaf people who also have a visual impairment.

*Figure 15.5 A videophone*

## Audio frequency induction loops and induction systems

Many people with hearing difficulties find it hard to hear in places such as classrooms, conference halls, meeting rooms, and so on. This is due to the blurring effects of poor room acoustics. Induction loops – see Figure 15.7 – and infrared systems can be used to overcome hearing difficulties in larger places. Infrared systems and induction loops work by replacing the sound path between the source of the sound and the listener with either an inductive (magnetic) or infrared signal, which is not affected by acoustics or other sounds. With loop systems the listener's own

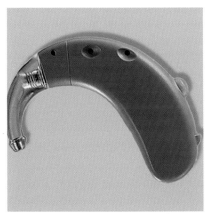

*Figure 15.6 A hearing loop*

hearing aid is used as a receiver to convert the signal back to sound. Infrared systems use special receivers to convert the signal back to sound.

## Physical and mobility disabilities

Computers and ICT can improve the lifestyle of people with physical disabilities, offering them independence and opportunities for employment. **Teleworking**, for example, means that people who find it difficult to commute can work from their own homes and video conferencing enables them to hold meetings and exchange information without leaving their home or place of work.

Video conferencing can also allow children in hospital to be included in lessons at their school. Online shopping enables people with physical and mobility difficulties to purchase all their daily requirements – nowadays, there is very little that cannot be bought over the Internet. Home banking allows them to pay bills and manage their finances. ICT has truly opened up the world for this group of people.

Computer equipment can be adapted for use by those with a physical disability. The response of the keys pressed on a keyboard can be adapted to ignore tremors and long slow presses. Special software can be used to predict words being typed which can speed up writing. Mouth sticks and head pointers are pointing devices worn on the head for people who only have movement of the head and can be used to press the keys of a keyboard. An infrared head pointer is available which allows simple head movements to control the screen cursor via an infra-red link (see Figure 15.8).

### Checkpoint

**Teleworking** allows an employee to work from home with a PC which interacts with the employer's computer system via the telephone network and a modem.

*Figure 15.7. Steven Hawking's wheelchair has been adapted to enable him to use ICT operated devices*

People who have difficulty using a mouse, can use devices such as a rollerball or a joystick as an alternative, or the keyboard to control the pointer on the screen.

Some people find it difficult to use a standard keyboard. Miniature keyboards and compact keyboards are available which help people with a muscular weakness and require less effort and reach. Expanded keyboards such as a Maltron have larger keys that can be more easily hit.

*Figure 15.8 A keyboard adapted for a disabled user*

Touch sensitive screens and touch monitors enable the physically impaired to interact with a computer. Touch screens are very useful in helping disabled people develop visual skills and hand-eye coordination.

### Checkpoint

A **touch sensitive screen** is a display screen covered with a touch-sensitive transparent panel. Data is input into the computer when the screen is touched.

Robotic wheelchairs and robotic limbs can help physically disabled people regain mobility and improve the quality of their lives.

### Fact file

Researchers at Northampton University are developing software to help wheelchair users in unfamiliar locations. Known as the Wheelyroute navigation system, it automatically identifies problem areas in a town centre so that obstacles such as hills, steps or cobbled streets can be avoided.
(*Computer Active*, 7–20 March 2002)

## Other special needs

So far you have learned how ICT can help improve the lives of people with visual or hearing impairments or physical disabilities. Very often, people can have a combination of these disabilities. For example, a visually impaired person may also be deaf and therefore would benefit from using a telephone which will not only amplify sounds, but has larger than normal buttons to make the numbers easier to read.

### Learning difficulties

People with learning difficulties find it harder to learn – these difficulties can range from being mild or moderate to very severe and there are estimated to be nearly 2 million people in the UK who have some form of learning difficulty. Again ICT can provide a range of resources to help these people. For example, **speech recognition** systems will mean that the user can create text or control the computer by his or her voice. Touch screens are easier to use than a keyboard, and overlay keyboards with symbols or on-screen grids are alternatives to a normal keyboard.

Special assessment software is available for teachers to help them to assess the abilities of students with learning difficulties. Drill and practice software will help these students learn new concepts. Special software is designed specifically to meet the differing needs of these students. Multimedia which has a combination of moving images, graphics, text and sound can assist and encourage learning.

ICT can help dyslexic people with their reading, spelling and writing. Assessment software will help identify people with dyslexia, and other software is available to help them improve their reading. Changing the background and text colours on screen also helps many dyslexic people as research has shown that black print on white paper is difficult to focus on for long periods and can be difficult to read. Word processors make writing simpler as it is easier to alter a piece of text until it is right and the special software which predicts words being typed is helpful.

## Checkpoint

**Speech recognition** (voice recognition) is the ability of a machine or program to recognise and carry out voice commands, or to convert the spoken word into text.

## Speech and language difficulties

Many people, for example someone with autism, can find it difficult to communicate. ICT can play an important role in helping these people either by providing equipment and software to encourage speech or, where someone cannot speak at all, by providing communication aids. A sound-activated switch can be used to send a message to a computer in order to help someone speak. There are devices where keys are pressed to send out a message to help someone who cannot communicate at all by speaking. Again, technology such as touch sensitive screens and overlay keyboards help people with speech and language difficulties to communicate.

## Fact file

The US company Xybernaut has developed a computer called XyberKids which is worn in a backpack and enables children with special needs to communicate. It consists of a backpack, powerful speakers, flat panel display and small processing unit. Using the equipment, children can communicate by pressing buttons. It has proved helpful to autistic children, as well as children with cerebral palsy or physical disabilities. (Go to www.heinemann.co.uk/ hotlinks and click on Xybernaut.)

# Assessment

## How will I be assessed?

Unit 1 is assessed through a 2½ hour, computer based, examination set and marked by Edexcel, while Units 2 and 3 are internally assessed through a portfolio of evidence. Your results for each unit will be a mark from 0–100 which can be related to an equivalent grade. Remember that this qualification is equivalent to two GCSEs.

| | A*A* | AA | BB | CC | DD | EE | FF | GG |
|---|---|---|---|---|---|---|---|---|
| Uniform marks (Maximum 100) | 90 –100 | 80 –89 | 70 –79 | 60 –69 | 50 –59 | 40 –49 | 30 –39 | 20 –29 |

For Units 2 and 3 you have to provide evidence that proves you have met all the assessment requirements for each unit, and you keep this in a portfolio of evidence.

## What exactly is a portfolio of evidence?

This is the file in which you store your completed assessments, and should be kept separate from your everyday file where you keep notes and any current work. It is essential that the file is well organised. Portfolios which are well organised, clearly referenced and neatly filed, generally do contain the work the index says they contain.

Your teacher will mark your assessments and the marks awarded will affect your final overall grade for the qualification. An external moderator from Edexcel will look at your portfolio of evidence to ensure that the evidence exists for the mark that has been given. On opening a well organised file the external moderator will naturally be impressed. On the other hand a disorganised, messy portfolio may well contain all the necessary evidence, but if the external moderator cannot find it, he or she cannot confirm that the evidence actually exists.

Naturally as a student of the Applied GCSE in ICT, you will be expected to make full use of ICT in the production of your portfolio of evidence for each unit. Be warned – work that is entirely hand-written will not gain any marks.

Look at the section on 'Tips for a successful portfolio of evidence' on page 239.

## What will my portfolio of evidence contain?

Each unit will require you to undertake different tasks to generate the evidence for your portfolio. A full description of the requirements is given on page 233.

Prior to the examination Edexcel will issue pre-release material and questions will relate to this material. Do make the most of the activities in the pre-release material as completing them properly will ensure that you are fully prepared for the actual tasks set in the examination. You will be allowed to re-sit the examination once.

## What does the pre-release material consist of?

The pre-release material will be based on a case study and you will receive an Activity Booklet, which consists of a scenario and a set of five practical hands-on activities related to it. These five activities will allow you to practice your skills in five different areas:

- communication, searching and selection of information: retrieving information from the Internet
- presentation of information: using word processing/publications software
- organisation and analysis of numerical information: using spreadsheet software
- organisation and analysis of structured information: using database software
- organisation and presentation of information using multimedia software: using presentation software such as PowerPoint®.

You will, of course, be expected to practise the effective file management and standard ways of working which you learned about in the preparatory unit of this book. Always save your work regularly. Edexcel state that all printouts should consist of only **one A4 sheet** wherever possible.

### Activity 1: Using the Internet
Refer back to Chapter 5 where you learned how to search the World Wide Web (www) and to navigate round a website. You will be given the URL of the company in the case study and the tasks in Activity 1 will enable you to practice these skills. Much of the information obtained from the website will be needed in later activities, so don't forget to bookmark the URL for later use. Also remember the rules about copyright you learned in Chapter 13.

### Activity 2: Using Word Processing/Publications Software
Firstly you will be asked to design a new company logo, and then produce business documents required by the company using relevant information from the web site. The documents may include an advertising flyer, a letterhead, and invoice or a business card. Refer back to Chapter 7 to remind yourself how to ensure the documents are suitable for their purpose.

### Activity 3: Using Database Software
The tasks in this activity will take you through step-by-step many of the concepts and skills which you learned in Chapter 3, that may be assessed in the examination. You will need to be able to plan the design of a relational database, implement the design and produce reports.

### Activity 4: Using Spreadsheet Software
In order to undertake the tasks in this activity refer back to Chapter 2. You will need to design a spreadsheet laid out in a suitable format using a variety of formulae.

### Activity 5: Using Multimedia Software
You will be required to plan and prepare a presentation, which you will then pilot making changes as a result of feedback. Chapter 7 provides tips on making a good presentation.

## What about the examination?

The examination you will take is computer-based, but not online, and will last 2 hours and 30 minutes. All the activities in the examination will relate to the case study and will build on the work you undertook for the pre-release material. The examination itself is un-tiered and you can achieve grades ranging from A* –G.

Each activity in the exam is progressive and there is no choice of questions. You will be required to undertake activities that test your skills using the following types of software:

- word processing/publication
- database
- spreadsheet
- multimedia.

Unlike the activities for the pre-release material, the exam will not require you to access the Internet. You will not be able to bring textbooks or any other material into the examination.

Do make the most of the activities in the pre-release material as completing them properly will ensure that you are fully prepared for the actual examination. Edexcel will only allow students to re-sit the examination once.

# Unit 2 — ICT in organisations – Guide to unit assessment

For Unit 2, you will be assessed on your portfolio of evidence. The assessment evidence for Unit 2 falls into two parts:

- The first part is based on an investigation into a named organisation or a department within an organisation. You will need to include a report on:
  a) the different purposes for which the organisation/department uses ICT
  b) the ICT system used in the organisation/department and how it meets the needs identified in (a).

- The second part of the assessment evidence requires you to design and implement an ICT system. You will need to include:

  c) a design specification for the system including information sources, input, process and output requirements, and the types of application software needed

  d) evidence that you successfully implemented, tested and evaluated the system, together with guidance for the user.

## Investigating the business/department

Your teacher will give you guidance on what will be a suitable organisation or department to investigate. Be careful not to choose a very small organisation which has a very limited use or potential use of ICT. On the other hand, trying to understand the workings of a large organisation such as Tesco, which has a very diverse use of ICT, would be unmanageable.

The following are possibilities of organisations you could investigate:

- the company where your mum, dad or another family member works
- where a family friend works
- where your teacher has a contact
- where you have had work experience
- where you have a part-time job

Alternatively, you could, with the guidance of your tutor choose a local organisation where you arrange to meet someone in the business to ask specific questions to find the information you require.

## Designing and implementing an ICT system

This part of the assessment evidence does not have to be based on the same organisation you investigated for (a). Read Chapter 10 carefully, before you start your assessment. You will learn everything you need to know on how to successfully approach this assessment. Discuss your choice with your teacher – it is important that you do not attempt to design an ICT system for too large an organisation which will be unmanageable. It is better to design a system for a small local organisation as not only is it a more manageable task, but the organisation might be able to implement it fully.

## How can I achieve the best marks?

The following chart shows the information you need to obtain for this unit and how marks are awarded.

| What you need to do | Possible marks | Hints |
|---|---|---|
| (a) Investigate the different purposes for which an organisation or department uses ICT | If you produce a report into the chosen organisation/department that identifies some purposes for which it uses ICT you can achieve **up to 4 marks.**<br><br>If the report details a range of purposes for which it uses ICT you can achieve **up to a further 3 marks.**<br><br>If you write *full* details of a *wide* range of purposes for which it uses ICT you can achieve **up to a further 3 marks.**<br><br>**Total possible marks = 10.** | In order to achieve the maximum marks you will need to ensure that you give a clear description of the work of the organisation/department which covers its main functions, together with other relevant information, for example the number of people working there or the amount of stock it keeps on the premises.<br><br>Make sure you include all the main purposes for which the organisation or department uses ICT and describe them fully with a well-stated reason for its use. For example, a DIY store may use ICT to keep stock records up-to-date so that items can be automatically ordered when the stock falls below a certain level. As a result items should never be out of stock and customer satisfaction will be high. |
| (b) Describe the ICT system used in the organisation or department, and how it meets the needs identified in (a) | If your report describes the main hardware components used, together with some of the main applications software, giving an indication of their purpose you can achieve **up to 6 marks.**<br><br>If your report *clearly* describes the main hardware components used, together with the main application software and you have linked each application software to a specific purpose, you can achieve **up to a further 4 marks.**<br><br>If you write a report which *fully* describes the main hardware components used, together with the necessary applications software AND you give an evaluation of how the system as a whole satisfies the purposes identified in (a) you can achieve **up to a further 4 marks.**<br><br>**Total possible marks = 14.** | To achieve the maximum marks you will need to demonstrate that you have a clear understanding of how the components all work together as a system and how the system supports the needs of the organisation or department.<br><br>You will need to include descriptive comments about the system as a whole, as well as about the various components. There should be explicit links between the components and the purposes for which ICT is used in the organisation or department. Finally you should include evaluative comments about the extent to which the system meets these purposes. For example, the sales department receives up to 5,000 orders a day, and the capacity of the system is only just great enough to cope with this. |

| What you need to do | Possible marks | Hints |
|---|---|---|
| (c) Produce a design specification for a system including information sources, input, process and output requirements, and the types of application software needed. | If you work with support and guidance from your teacher to produce a basic design specification showing a *basic* understanding of some of the input, process and output requirements and you provide details of hardware and software needed, you can achieve **up to 7 marks.**<br><br>If you work with *limited* guidance from your teacher to produce a design specification with some detail showing a *clear* understanding of the main input, process and output requirements and you provide details of hardware and software needed, you can achieve **up to a further 5 marks.**<br><br>If you work independently to produce a *detailed* design specification which shows a creative and comprehensive understanding of input, process and output requirements and provides details of hardware and software needed, you can achieve **up to a further 5 marks.**<br><br>**Total possible marks = 17.** | In order to achieve maximum marks for this unit, you will need to work independently. This means that your teacher can support you initially in your choice of system and then can give you *occasional* help when you request it.<br><br>The scope of the project must be *clearly* defined to include information about what is required, for example the video shop database should state exactly what information about customers is needed, and whether there should be restricted access to any of the data.<br><br>Your initial designs must be accurate enough for the user to judge their suitability.<br><br>Final designs should be broken down into manageable sub-tasks. You should give enough details so that a third party could implement them effectively.<br><br>Finally, you should include a test plan that will effectively test the whole system. |
| (d) Implementation, testing and evaluation of system, together with user documentation | If you work with support and guidance from your teacher to produce evidence of successful implementation, including results of some basic testing and evaluation, and user documentation for the system, you can achieve **up to 7 marks.**<br><br>If you work with *limited* guidance from your teacher to produce evidence of successful implementation, including results of *effective* testing and evaluation, and *clear* user documentation for the system, you can achieve **up to a further 5 marks.**<br><br>If you work *independently* to produce evidence of successful implementation, and include results of *detailed* testing and evaluation, and *detailed* user documentation for the system, you can achieve **up to a further 5 marks.**<br><br>**Total possible marks = 17.** | In order to achieve maximum marks you should have worked independently (see hints for (c) above).<br><br>You will need to give evidence that the system has been successfully implemented. This can be through annotated hard copy or witness statements provided by your teacher or customer.<br><br>The implemented system should fulfil all the objectives, and conform to the design in (c). Evidence should be shown that the intended tests have been carried out and constructive use of the results has been made where appropriate.<br><br>You should evaluate the proposed system as a whole – this can be a short comment to confirm that a particular part of the system meets its requirements fully. You should also concentrate on the areas which could be improved, including a *clear* indication of how this part of the system falls short of requirements. You can, if you wish, include suggestions for improvements.<br><br>Your user documentation should be clear and detailed enough for someone who is familiar with ICT, but who has not used the system before. |

For Unit 3, you will be assessed on your portfolio of evidence. For the unit you will need to produce an investigation of how ICT systems affect everyday life. You will need to compile a portfolio with reports on the impact of ICT on:

a)   the way you do things at home and at school/college

b)   an adult in employment, including the way it has had an effect on his/her working style

c)   a person with special/particular needs

d)   your local community.

When you are investigating each of these different aspects of ICT use, you will need to consider:

e)   the legislation that protects individuals and groups from the misuse of ICT.

Your evidence for this unit can be in the form of leaflets, reports, posters or presentations.

## Undertaking the investigations

Your teacher will give you guidance on appropriate investigations, but you will find it useful to take into account the following:

a)   You will need to consider the impact of ICT on your home and school/college life and describe a wide range of technologies that you use including an evaluation of the extent to which they meet your needs. You will find Chapters 11 and 14 particularly useful for this section.

b)   When investigating an adult in employment, you will need to consider the range of ways that the adult uses ICT in his/her daily life, and not restrict the investigation to the use of ICT in the workplace. You could choose to investigate how ICT has affected your Mum or Dad, or another family member in their working life. Alternatively it could be an acquaintance, such as a neighbour, a family friend or if you have a part-time job, someone you work with. Chapter 12 covers the topics you will find useful for your investigation for this section.

c)   When you investigate technology that will aid people with special and particular needs, you will need to consider how technology such as touch screens and voice activation has improved the quality of life and helped these people communicate effectively. You will find the Internet has a

wealth of information to help you with your research. Websites, such as that of the Royal National Institute of the Blind (Go to www.heinemann.co.uk/hotlinks and click on RNIB) will prove very useful for your investigations. You should read Chapter 15 before you start your investigation into this topic.

d)   You may, if you wish, consider in detail the impact of ICT on one community activity, or alternatively you could look at the way various community activities use ICT differently. You could choose to investigate the use of ICT within a local youth club, sports group or a fund-raising group, for example. Consider the ways the groups operated before using ICT, the impact the new technology has on current operations and the likely impact future technology would make. Before commencing your assessment for this section, make sure you have read Chapter 14, which looks at how ICT has affected personal communications.

e)   While you are carrying out the investigations for parts a–d of this unit, you should be considering how legislation affects the use of ICT by different people. You should bear in mind issues such as software licensing, copyright and file exchange. In addition, you will need to investigate the impact of legislation on organisations use of ICT in different areas, for example administration and operation of networks, e-mail and health and safety issues. Chapter 13 will be extremely useful for you for this section of your assessment.

You can include the most relevant legislation relating to your investigations for parts a–d in the evidence for these sections. Alternatively, you may, if you wish, include a separate section in your portfolio of evidence which covers aspects of legislation relating to ICT.

## How can I achieve the best marks?

The following chart shows the information you need to obtain for this unit and how marks are awarded.

| What you need to do | Possible marks | Hints |
|---|---|---|
| (a) Investigate the way you do things at home and at school/college | If you produce a report that describes some of the technologies you use at home and at school/college and give some indication of how these meet your needs, you can achieve **up to 5 marks.**<br><br>If the report describes a *range* of technologies you use at home and at school/college, with an explanation of how these meet your needs, you can achieve **up to a further 3 marks.**<br><br>If the report describes a *wide* range of technologies you use at home and at school/college, with an evaluation of the extent to which these meet your needs, you can achieve **up to a further 3 marks.**<br><br>**Total possible marks = 11.** | In order to achieve maximum marks the range of ICT you discuss should be representative of all the main uses of ICT you have in your personal, social, home and school/college life.<br><br>You must include an evaluation of the extent to which the technologies meet your needs. To achieve full marks, you must write at least one evaluative comment about each personal, social, home and school/college use.<br><br>Don't just make comments such as 'I use the Internet'. Include the reasons for using the Internet, and expand your evaluation to include times when it is more appropriate to ask questions directly to people. For example, if you are researching about life in an office 30 years ago, you would probably want to speak to someone directly to find out about their personal experiences and ask them specific questions relating to their working life. |
| (b) Investigate the impact on of ICT on an adult in employment, including the way it has had an effect on his/her working style. | If you describe *some* of the technologies used by an adult in employment and identify some ways in which these meet their needs and have affected working styles, you can achieve **up to 6 marks.**<br><br>If you describe a *range* of technologies used by an adult in employment with an explanation of how these meet their needs and have affected working styles, you can achieve **up to a further 4 marks.**<br><br>If you describe a *wide* range of technologies used by an adult in employment and evaluate the extent to which these meet their needs and have affected working styles, you can achieve **up to a further 4 marks.**<br><br>**Total possible marks = 14.** | To achieve maximum marks you should ensure that the range of technologies discussed represents all the main uses the adult has for ICT in their professional/personal, social, home and work life.<br><br>Include an evaluation about the extent to which the technologies meet the adult's needs. An example of a good evaluation would be 'I use the Internet to bank because I am able to carry out transactions 24 hours a day from work or at home and can print a bank statement whenever I wish without having to telephone the bank to request one'. This would achieve more marks than a statement saying 'I use the Internet to bank because it is quicker'. |

| What you need to do | Possible marks | Hints |
|---|---|---|
| (c) Investigate the impact of ICT on a person with special/particular needs. | If you describe *some* of the technologies used by a person with special or particular needs, with some identification of how these meet their need, you can achieve **up to 5 marks.**<br><br>If you describe a *range* of technologies used by a person with special or particular needs, with an explanation of how these meet their needs, you can achieve **up to a further 3 marks.**<br><br>If you describe a *wide range* of technologies used by a person with special or particular needs, with an evaluation of the extent to which these meet their needs, you can achieve **up to a further 3 marks.**<br><br>**Total possible marks = 11.** | If you describe fully all the main uses a person has for ICT in their personal, social and professional life (if appropriate) you will achieve high marks. An evaluative statement of the extent to which the technologies meet the person's needs would go beyond saying 'The Braille characters on the keyboard mean I can feel what they are, even if I can't see them', but also may include negative aspects and go on to say 'however it takes a longer time to type, and therefore I am thinking of getting voice recognition software instead.'<br><br>To achieve top marks, you will need to include at least *three* evaluative comments covering personal, social and possible professional uses (if appropriate). |
| (d) Investigate the impact of ICT on your local community. | If you describe *some* of the technologies used in the local community, with *some* identification of how these meet local needs, you can achieve **up to 5 marks.**<br><br>If you describe a *range* of technologies used in the local community, with an explanation of how these meet local needs, you can achieve **up to a further 3 marks.**<br><br>If you describe a *wide range* of technologies used in the local community, with an evaluation of the extent to which these meet local needs, you can achieve **up to a further 3 marks.**<br><br>**Total possible marks = 11.** | You will need to ensure that you describe a range of uses, which are representative of several main uses the local community makes of ICT to achieve high marks. Your evaluative statements should include the extent the technologies meet community needs. For example an evaluation such as 'classes are held at the public library on how to use the Internet, however as they are for unemployed people only, not everyone has access to them' will achieve high marks.<br><br>For full marks you should include at least *three* evaluative comments. |
| (e) The legislation that protects individuals and groups from the misuse of ICT. | If you indicate *some* of the relevant legislation and how it protects people and groups from the misuse of ICT, you can achieve **up to 5 marks.**<br><br>If you describe the *most relevant* legislation, why it was introduced and how it protects people and groups from the misuse of ICT, you can achieve **up to a further 3 marks.**<br><br>If you describe *all relevant* legislation and why it was introduced, and include an evaluation of the extent to which it protects people and groups from the misuse of ICT, you can achieve **up to a further 3 marks.**<br><br>**Total possible marks = 11.** | Include a description of a comprehensive range of legislation to achieve high marks together with an evaluation of the extent to which the legislation is effective or appropriate.<br><br>You should link each person or group you investigated in a–d to the legislation which is most relevant to them. To achieve full marks you should give at least *three* evaluative comments as to whether the legislation is effective and appropriate. |

## Tips for a successful portfolio of evidence

- Ensure that you make the appropriate choices for your investigations:

- **For Unit 2:**
  - ✓ Discuss your choice of organisation to investigate with your teacher.
  - ✓ Discuss your proposed system with your teacher before commencing work.

- **For Unit 3:**
  - ✓ Discuss your choices of areas in society to investigate with your teacher and discuss legislation relevant to these choices.
- Arrange to meet your teacher regularly to discuss your progress.
- Your teacher will set you deadlines by which you should submit work – keep to them.
- Write an action plan which includes when and how you intend to undertake each part of the assessments.
- Be organised – if you rush your work you will not have time to look at it critically before you hand it in. You should always look at your work and evaluate how it could be improved before submitting it. The following suggestions may help:
  - ✓ Did you gather enough information/evidence?
  - ✓ Are you satisfied with the report and its presentation?
  - ✓ Are there any improvements that could be made – e.g. a long paragraph of text could be listed in bullet points, as in this section, or perhaps a diagram could be included to make the text easier to follow.
  - ✓ Have you proof-read your work thoroughly to avoid silly spelling or grammatical errors which spoil the overall effect?
  - ✓ Have you done all the work required for the assessment?
- Aim to finish your work at least one week before the deadline set by your teacher. When you have completed the work required for each unit, ask yourself whether you can honestly say you have met the requirements for full marks. If you haven't, you will have time to remedy this.

# Index